ELGIN CATHEDRAL

And the Diocese of Moray

HISTORIC SCOTLAND
ALBA AOSMHOR

ELGIN CATHEDRAL

And the Diocese of Moray

Richard Fawcett and Richard Oram

HISTORIC SCOTLAND
ALBA AOSMHOR

First published by Historic Scotland 2001

This revised edition published by Historic Scotland 2014

ISBN: 978-1-84917-173-1

Cover images

Main picture: View towards the west front of Elgin Cathedral

Top left: Detail of a stone carving of a man's face holding a ring in his mouth, carved on part of
a shield on a tomb slab

CONTENTS

LIST OF ILLUSTRATIONS

Section 2 opening page: The east front of Elgin Cathedral with the River Lossie in the foreground (Historic Scotland © Crown Copyright)

10.1   David's Tower at Spynie Palace, named after Bishop David Stewart (Historic Scotland © Crown Copyright)

10.2   The ruins of Holyrood Abbey from the north-east. Bishop George Douglas was buried in the church at Holyrood. (Historic Scotland © Crown Copyright)

10.3   The old church of St Giles, Elgin, which served as the cathedral of Bishop Alexander Douglas. Douglas was buried in the south aisle of the church

10.4   Detail from John Slezer's 'Prospect of the Town of Elgin' (1693) showing the cathedral and chanonry

11.1   Elgin Cathedral, the south elevation (Historic Scotland © Crown Copyright)

11.2   The north flank of Elgin Cathedral in 1693 (John Slezer, *Theatrum Scotiae*)

11.3   The south flank of Elgin Cathedral in the late seventeenth century by John Slezer (The Bodleian Libraries, University of Oxford, Gough Maps 38, fol 24r, drawing top left)

11.4   The south flank of Elgin Cathedral in 1747 by John Campbell (Historic Scotland © Crown Copyright)

11.5   View of Elgin Cathedral from the south-east in 1769 (Thomas Pennant, *A Tour in Scotland*)

11.6   View of Elgin Cathedral from the south-east in 1791 (Francis Grose, *The Antiquities in Scotland*)

11.7   Map of the area around Elgin Cathedral in 1828 by John Wood (Historic Scotland © Crown Copyright)

11.8   The interior of Elgin Cathedral from the west in 1826 (W Clark, *A Series of Views of the Ruins of Elgin Cathedral*)

11.9   View of Elgin Cathedral from the south-east in 1826 (W Clark, *A Series of Views of the Ruins of Elgin Cathedral*)

11.10   The late-thirteenth-century effigy of a bishop excavated at Elgin Cathedral in 1936 (Historic Scotland © Crown Copyright)

11.11   The fragments of a rose window from Elgin Cathedral (© Mike Pendery)

PREFACE

The cathedral at Elgin which is the principal subject of this study was the central component in a much larger entity, the diocese of Moray. In many ways, the history of the cathedral is the history of the diocese, for the development and fate of the one were inextricably linked with those of the other. This book is a greatly expanded version of a publication on the cathedral that was first published in 2001, with new sections on the history of the bishops and diocese by Richard Oram, and modified sections on the architecture of the cathedral by Richard Fawcett.

The first section considers the medieval cathedral, starting with the history of the diocese from its earliest recorded origins in the twelfth century until the Protestant Reformation in mid-sixteenth-century Scotland. There follows a description of the surviving buildings and an analysis of the main phases of their development from the early thirteenth-century origins of the cathedral. There is next an account of the arrangements that were made for the funding of the cathedral and its associated college of canons, vicars, chaplains and choristers, together with an exploration of the provision for the bishops and their household. This section also includes a brief examination of the economic resources of the province of Moray which provided bishops and canons with their income. Its final part offers a short discussion of the other ecclesiastical establishments that were associated with the cathedral and its surrounding 'college' or chanonry, principally the almshouse known as the Maison Dieu, the leper hospital, and the cathedral school.

The second section looks at the cathedral after the Reformation, considering its history, the bishops of Moray, and what has been done to the building in recent centuries.

ACKNOWLEDGEMENTS

In preparing this study we have gratefully received the assistance of a number of individuals and bodies. Amongst these have been Professor Geoffrey Barrow, Derry Gilmour, John Knight, Mike Pendery and Dr Alasdair Ross, all of whom have either read through parts of the text and offered valued comments, or provided important information. Stuart Harrison gave his views on the *ex situ* rose window, while Ashley Bartlam and Ewan Hyslop discussed the building stones. We offer warm thanks to the Mackichan Trust who provided funds to visit a number of sites with foliage sculpture related to that at Elgin, and to the University of St Andrews for giving permission to quote from the late Professor Donald Watt's edition of *Scotichronicon*.

Elgin Cathedral, doorway from the presbytery into the north choir aisle, looking towards the chapter house
(Historic Scotland © Crown Copyright)

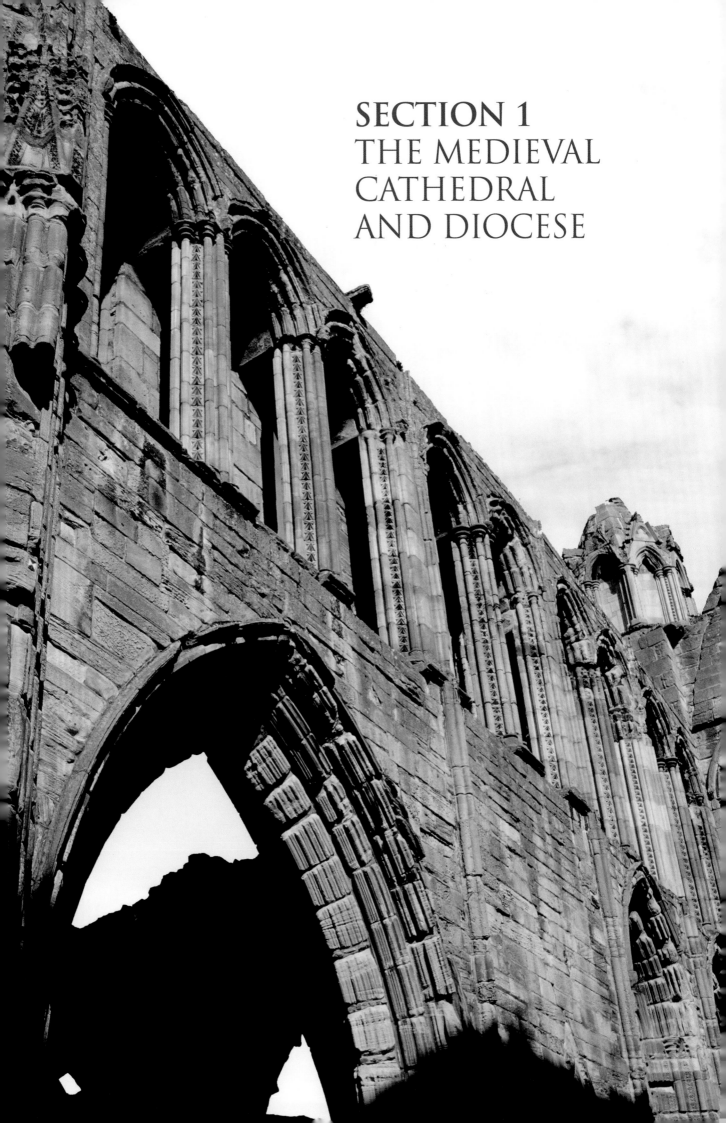

SECTION 1
THE MEDIEVAL
CATHEDRAL
AND DIOCESE

1.1   The south tower and chapel of Elgin Cathedral with the graveyard in the foreground (Historic Scotland © Crown Copyright)

1 HISTORY

While the basic building-block of the medieval church in western Europe was the parish, the territory which received its main spiritual services – baptism, marriage and burial – from a designated church and whose population contributed a tenth (teind in Scotland, tithe in England) of their produce for the support of it and its priest, the principal component of Church organisation was the diocese. Based on a unit of civil administration into which the provinces of the late Roman Empire had been divided, each with a city at its heart, the diocese had acquired a more specifically ecclesiastical character as the structures of civil government had decayed and leadership locally had fallen increasingly into the hands of the bishops who oversaw Christian life in the city-territory. Across those parts of Europe where there was a Roman civil tradition, including large parts of southern Britain, there was a long history of urban-based bishops whose authority extended across the rural hinterlands dominated by the city in which they were based. North of the Humber, the only major Roman urban centres had been York and Carlisle and only at the former had anything like a continuous urban tradition survived the centuries of upheaval and inward migration of pagan Angles to become the seat of a bishopric following their conversion to Christianity in the seventh century.

In the territory that became Scotland there had been no Roman urban tradition. Here, however, whilst Christianity had foundered in the centres of the old Roman provinces in most of what is now England, in some of the tribal kingdoms north of the former imperial frontier, Christianity remained and began to spread from the fifth century. By the seventh century, the pagan Picts of north-eastern mainland Scotland had accepted Christianity and the first bishops serving the country north of the River Forth begin to emerge hazily into the historical record. While some of these clerics were evidently based in important ecclesiastical centres, such as Kingarth on Bute, it is difficult to establish what territories they served. As the power of the Anglian kingdom of Northumbria spread northwards in the seventh and early eighth centuries, ecclesiastical structures followed in the wake of political conquest and colonisation. Much of the area we now know as Lothian fell under the jurisdiction of a bishopric based on the island of Lindisfarne off the Northumberland coast, whilst what is now Galloway was served from an already ancient church site at Whithorn. Another bishopric may have been established in the lower valley of the River Clyde, possibly at Govan, but later at Glasgow. For the north-east, the Northumbrians established a diocese with its bishop's seat at Abercorn on the southern shore of the Firth of Forth, between modern South Queensferry and Blackness. Intended to provide spiritual oversight for the Church in Pictish territory, as Northumbrian influence north of the Forth retreated in the late seventh century and then collapsed in the mid-eighth century, that bishopric apparently ceased to function.

How the country north of the Forth, parts of which were probably thoroughly Christian by the end of the seventh century, received the services which only bishops could provide is not known. There seems to have been an important bishopric based at Rosemarkie in Easter Ross, possibly serving the northern Pictish kingdom of Fortriu which may have stretched from there along the south coast of the Moray Firth, but there is no clear evidence that it continued to function through the long era of Scandinavian raiding and colonisation in the late eighth and ninth centuries.[1] Indeed, there is no evidence for the continuation of religious activity at most of the known sites of major churches along the coastlands of the north and east of mainland Scotland north of St Andrews.

Within Moray proper there is no indication of how the Church was organised or functioned. Although many claims have been made in the past for the existence of early monasteries in the coastal districts of Moray, there is no recorded evidence for any. Absence of evidence, as has often been said, is not evidence of absence, and fragmentary sculptural evidence from several sites suggest that they were the location of important religious centres by the eighth or early ninth century. The most important of these appears to have been Kinneddar, at the south-western edge of modern Lossiemouth, where a very local cult of St Gerardine appears to mark the location of an early missionary centre

1.2   Part of a cross-slab from a Pictish stone, Kinneddar church
       (© Crown Copyright: RCAHMS. Licensor www.rcahms.gov.uk)

or monastery.[2] The broken fragments of many Christian monuments – upright slabs carved with crosses and two stone box shrines which contained the remains of holy men who were venerated as saints, perhaps including Gerardine – have been unearthed over the centuries during grave-digging in the kirkyard of the later medieval church and in its wider neighbourhood (Illus 1.2).[3] The imagery used on one of the two shrines is rich with royal symbolism and may speak for the patronage of the community here by a kingly benefactor in the eighth century. It is likely that such rich sculpture stood within the enclosure of a monastery, but without excavation that suggestion must remain only conjecture. Antiquarian digging in the nineteenth century and geophysical surveys in the 1990s at the site appear to have identified the sites of the medieval episcopal palace and cathedral/parish church which succeeded the earlier centre, overlying an older long-cist cemetery and what may be an earlier earthwork enclosure, but the stone sculpture remains at present our only tangible evidence for the existence of a major religious community at Kinneddar before the twelfth century.[4]

Although there was clearly an important monastery at Kinneddar, and carved stones of Pictish sculptural form from Birnie suggest that there may have been another early religious site there, there is nothing to suggest that either was the seat of an early bishop. What evidence there is for early episcopal centres in northern Scotland points towards a possible diocesan seat at Mortlach in Glen Fiddich, now subsumed into Dufftown, and a second one at Rosemarkie in the Black Isle, seat of the medieval bishopric of Ross. Mortlach formed a peculiar salient projecting north from the deanery of Mar in the later medieval diocese of Aberdeen, almost separating Moray's Strathbogie deanery from the main part of the diocese of Moray to its west. Although it appears to be a mere appendage stuck on to the remote western end of Aberdeen diocese, the church at Mortlach was of tremendous importance in the diocese; not only was it one of the wealthiest churches in the region by a factor of ten, it was also the location of a major residence of the later medieval bishops of Aberdeen. This importance seems to stem from its status at least in the mid-eleventh century as the seat of a bishopric. Although there is much debate over the authenticity of the records which identify Mortlach as an episcopal see, there is general acceptance of the view that its successor at Aberdeen only became the seat of the north-eastern Scottish bishopric in the 1130s.[5]

What drove this possible move east from the hills of Glen Fiddich to the new site at the mouth of the River Don? The answer may lie in the political upheavals of the period, during which King David I of Scotland (1124–1153) (Illus 1.3) undertook the thorough-going conquest of Moray and began its integration into his kingdom.[6] Since the 1040s the line of Scottish kings represented by David had been locked in a contest for the kingship of the Scots with a rival lineage based in Moray. Following the defeat and death of Macbethad (Shakespeare's Macbeth) in 1057 and that of his stepson and successor Lulaig in 1058, the tide in that struggle had shifted almost decisively in favour of David's family.[7] Twenty years later, David's father King Malcolm III conducted a punitive expedition into Moray which took much booty and hostages and brought a long period of stability and peace which apparently lasted down to the early 1100s.[8] There are shadowy hints and whispers in the few surviving chronicle sources, twisted and expanded into elaborate and lengthy narratives by later medieval writers, which suggest that the peace was breaking down in the early 1110s, but there is no hard evidence for any real challenge mounted to Malcolm III's heirs from any member of the Moray lineage before the 1120s.[9] That challenge erupted into life in 1130 when Óengus or Angus of Moray, grandson of King Lulaig, mounted a bid to topple David I from his throne. Beyond the most basic of details nothing is recorded of the campaign led into Moray by David's commanders that followed the defeat and death of Óengus at Stracathro. There is a hint of stubborn resistance which inflicted heavy casualties on the Scottish king's army, but David's superior resources ground down all opposition to what was nothing less than a full-blown invasion and conquest.[10]

Following Stracathro and the subjugation of Moray, David started a long process of colonisation designed to bring about the full incorporation of the conquered territory into his realm. As part of that process, David may have begun to overhaul radically the ecclesiastical structures of the northern part of Scotland, for he intended to use the

ALCOLOHVS dei
falutem. Nouci
quandam abt
pro falute dm
S; poftqm dii
uenerabit men
locuf ille non er

1.3   David I, depicted on the Kelso Charter. David (left) is represented as Solomon, the perfect Biblical king, with his long hair and beard conveying the image of a patriarch. The figure on the right is his grandson Malcolm IV. (Reproduced by kind permission of the Trustees of the National Library of Scotland/Image courtesy of Roxburghe Estates)

bishoprics as instruments to tighten his control. It is possibly as part of this process that the seat of the north-eastern bishopric was moved from Mortlach to Aberdeen.[11] This brought the bishop's seat closer to David's centres of power, but the legacy of Mortlach's earlier status ensured that it remained attached to Aberdeen as the king began to mark out the diocese of Moray beyond it, rather than the church being detached from the new Aberdeen diocese and added to the newly defined Moray diocese.

At this point our evidence for how exactly a see of Moray came into existence fades out and we move into the realms of conjecture. As is discussed in Chapter 2, a man holding the title of bishop of Moray appears to have been in office in the second half of the reign of King Alexander I (1107–1124), but we have no evidence for where he had his cathedral, or whether he was a recent appointment to a newly created see or the successor to a long-established bishopric. We have a possible incumbent, but we have no known episcopal seat from which he operated; suggestions that it was Birnie represent a modern gloss put on thirteenth-century references to earlier bishops having moved their see at will between the churches of Birnie, Kinneddar and Spynie. Perhaps the most obvious suggestion is that his see was Mortlach, which is located more logically as an episcopal centre for a diocese that extended round the north-eastern rim of the Cairngorms from the western parts of Mar into the Moray plain and valley of the Spey. As later disputes settled only in the 1220s over the boundary between the dioceses of Moray and Ross in the west suggest, the bishops based

on Rosemarkie may have had a sphere that once stretched south and east of the Beauly Firth, of which the Ross-held parish of Ardersier was just a relic.[12] A single territorial diocese stretching from the east coast at Aberdeen to the district around Beauly in the west made little sense as a mechanism which could aid Scottish kings in their efforts to tighten their political control over the north; a divided diocese, with one centre in the far east serving the emerging earldoms of Buchan and Mar in the north-east proper and a second stretching from Strathbogie to the Aird with a base in the centre of the Laich of Moray, has a greater logic to it. The evidence for a line of Aberdeen bishops based at Mortlach before the move of their seat eastwards is exceptionally late and fantastical, and may be a fiction devised to give them greater antiquity.[13] That no bishop of Aberdeen/Mortlach can be identified with certainty before c 1140 does offer some slender support to the notion that the earlier bishopric had served a quite different diocese and that the incumbent at the time of the reconfiguration may have gone to the portion carved off from his see rather than relocating to Aberdeen. This decision may have been driven as much by the king's need to have a man with pre-existing local ties and knowledge in oversight of the territory from where the military and political challenge to his kingship had come. Royal power may not have been much more firmly entrenched in the region that became Aberdeen diocese, but there it does not seem to have faced the hostility that it met in Moray west of Strathbogie and the Spey. All of this, however, is conjecture built on a handful of fragmentary

2.1   The stone figure of a bishop that once stood high up on the central tower at Elgin Cathedral (Historic Scotland © Crown Copyright)

2 THE PRE-REFORMATION BISHOPS OF MORAY

In this chapter the careers of the men who occupied the bishopric from the early twelfth to later sixteenth centuries are explored. Some have left rich records of their acts and details of their conduct of the business of their bishopric which allow us to see them as more than just names in the parchment accounts. There is disappointingly little information for the activities of some of the earliest bishops, especially those who held office before the beginnings of the effective organisation of the structures of diocesan government under Bishops Richard and Brice. For the thirteenth- and fourteenth-century incumbents we have much more detail, especially for that most ambitious of clerics, Bishop Alexander Bur, but for several of the early-fifteenth-century bishops we have little evidence for their presence in and running of their diocese. From the mid-fourteenth century we can also see a change in the character of the men who held the bishopric, from individuals who may have held high office or great influence in the political life of the kingdom but who remained primarily active diocesans involved in the daily religious life of their see, to career civil servants for whom the office of bishop offered mainly financial rewards for their service to the king. Several of such men were still high-minded and deeply pious individuals who took great pains to ensure that their diocese generally, and the spiritual needs of their flock especially, were adequately provided for. Others, however, fit all too easily into that grossly stereotyped image of the corrupt and worldly pre-Reformation prelate.

Gregory

Contrary to claims made that King Alexander I (1107–1124) founded the bishopric of Moray in the first year of his reign,[14] evidence for an established diocese functioning in the region before David I's conquest of Moray is ambiguous. There was, however, a man with the title 'bishop of Moray' active and on record in Alexander I's reign: Gregory or Giric, to give his name in Gaelic form as he was probably known, who occurs as a witness to royal charters. Sometime around 1114/5 he witnessed a charter of the king to the new Augustinian priory which had been founded at Scone.[15] Again as Gregory,

bishop of Moray, he witnessed David I's great charter to Dunfermline Abbey, which was issued probably in 1128.[16] Beyond these two brief notices of him, however, we have no record of his career or his actions as bishop. There is no evidence to provide any indication of his background and certainly nothing to support suggestions that he was a monk in a pre-existing 'Pictish Church of the Culdees' and was promoted by the Scottish king as a means of subverting that native institution from within and gradually turning it over to the incoming Continental Roman traditions in the church.[17] It has been suggested that he may be the same man who occurs as bishop of Dunkeld from the late 1140s, possibly having been translated to that more prestigious see by King David I. In the time of Bishop Brice de Douglas (1203–1222) we learn that his predecessors as bishop had had no fixed cathedral but moved around as they deemed appropriate between one of three locations: the churches of Birnie, Kinneddar and Spynie.[18] On no grounds other than its obviously twelfth-century architecture, Birnie has been assumed to have served as Gregory's cathedral.[19]

William, 1152–1162

It was probably in 1152 that David appointed his chaplain, William, to the see of Moray.[20] He had been in the service of David and his son, Earl Henry, from possibly as early as 1136, appearing on occasion as a witness to their acts in Huntingdon, St Andrews and Edinburgh.[21] Following his consecration, he appears as a witness to two charters of David I, issued in Stirling and St Andrews.[22] Evidence for his activity in the reign of Malcolm IV suggests that like his contemporary Bishop Andrew of Caithness, he was rarely in his titular see. He first appears as a witness to one of Malcolm IV's charters datable only to some point between May 1153 and April 1156, issued at Jedburgh.[23] He appears subsequently at Dunfermline, Roxburgh, Selkirk, possibly Berwick, Edinburgh, Perth, and Peebles, but even where the business of the documents concerned subjects in his own diocese the transaction took place no closer to Moray than Perth.[24] Given the evidence of his charter attestations, therefore, it looks like William was very much a curialist, a man who spent the majority of his time in the royal household rather than in his diocese.

Although the administrative structure of his own see was still very undeveloped, in 1159 it was Bishop William and the king's chamberlain Nicholas who led a delegation to Rome to meet with Pope Alexander III to seek the elevation of the see of St Andrews into a metropolitan archbishopric for all of Scotland.[25] It is likely that he accompanied King Malcolm IV and his brother William on their journey to France to participate in King Henry II of England's military campaign against the city of Toulouse and, whilst Nicholas went directly to Rome, William seems to have first gone with the king to Aquitaine.[26] William himself arrived in Rome after the death of Pope Hadrian IV on 1 September and found himself in the middle of a contested papal election and schism created by the emergence of rival popes, Alexander III and Victor IV.[27] Early in 1160, having declared Scottish support for Alexander III and been appointed by him in return as papal legate, but with the request concerning St Andrews' metropolitan status refused, William returned to Scotland. The letters which he brought from the pope had suggested that William should be translated from Moray to St Andrews, where his legatine powers would offer some compensation for the failure to secure the elevation of the see to an archbishopric, but this suggestion was not followed. On 13 November 1160, Arnold, abbot of Kelso, was instead elected to the bishopric, and the following Sunday he was consecrated at St Andrews by Bishop William.[28] It may have been age or ill health which had led to William being passed over for the bishopric of St Andrews, for just over a year later in January 1162 he died.[29]

Whatever the qualities that had secured him election to Moray and eventual commission as a papal legate, Bishop William left behind him a see which was still on a very insecure footing. Despite both the pressing spiritual and political need to install a successor into a diocese where the bishop was actively constructing the basic framework of Church government and serving also as a local agent of the Crown, it was only the see of Ross which was provided with a new pastor in 1161.[30] An obscure reference in the Chronicle of Holyrood for 1163, that King Malcolm IV 'transported the men of Moray' ('transtulit Moravienses'), was for long taken to mean that there was some major disturbance in the region and that this had led to the prolonging of the vacancy in the bishopric. By the late thirteenth century when a chronicle account which survives in the fourteenth-century compilation known as Gesta Annalia was written, the two words of the Holyrood account had been expanded into a complex tale of the king of Scots directing the wholesale transplantation of the people of Moray because of their faithlessness and violence.[31] This seems an implausible

interpretation of the original account's meaning and it has been suggested instead that what was being referred to was a relocation of the see of Moray.[32] If that is the case, then it appears that the king's efforts did not end the hiatus, for in 1164 the bishopric was still reported to be vacant.

Felix, 1166–1171

Felix has left few traces of his activity as bishop; indeed even the dates of his election and death are unknown. The closest he can be dated is on the internal evidence of a charter that he witnessed at a gathering of the king's court at Elgin some time between 1166 and 1171, which is the known date of the election of his successor Simon de Toeni.[33] No act attributable to him survives amongst the early records of the see of Moray and, as a list of bishops compiled during the episcopate of Bishop John Winchester (1436–60) reveals, he and his early predecessors had been effectively expunged from the corporate memory of the diocese.[34]

Simon de Toeni, 1171–1184

The vacancy in Moray was filled in 1171 when the Cistercian monk Simon de Toeni, formerly abbot of Coggeshall in Essex and a cousin of King William, was elected.[35] In January 1172 he was consecrated at St Andrews, beginning a career as bishop that may have seen the first concerted effort to establish the diocese on a sound footing even though it is generally reckoned to have been during his successor's episcopate that significant advances were made.[36] Amongst Simon's first acts was the securing of a brieve from the king that commanded the royal sheriffs and other officials in Moray to pay their teinds to parsons and to enforce payment by the population at large.[37] Clearly, the new bishop had found that the organisation of his see was in a ruinous condition, and that regular payment or collection of teind income from parishes had fallen into abeyance or been usurped during the long vacancy after William's death. Without teind income, Simon lacked the means to develop – and, critically, to finance – the administration of his diocese. It was probably in response to pleas from the bishop for further aid to enable him to start setting the basic structures of diocesan government in place that King William made a wide-ranging grant to 'the church of the Holy Trinity of the see of Moray' (possibly referring to the church of Spynie which Simon may have made his cathedral) of a teind of royal revenues, income from lawsuits heard in royal courts in Moray, and of his annual tribute in foodstuffs known as cáin from the region.[38]

It has been commented that the appointment of a Cistercian monk to the episcopate represented a significant departure in Scottish bishoprics, where the majority of the men appointed in the middle decades of the twelfth century were drawn from the ranks of the royal clerks; 'such men made undistinguished bishops'.[39] Simon, however, was a distant kinsman of the king and we must be careful not to assume that his election was entirely without royal intervention. Little evidence survives of his impact on his see; certainly few charters survive from his time. The earliest record of his activity in his see is in a royal confirmation of a grant which he had made at the king's request to the hermit John of property at Loch Moy, south of Inverness.[40]

Simon died on 17 September 1184 and it was claimed in the eighteenth century that he was buried in the church of Birnie, which at that time was serving as the cathedral of the diocese.[41] In the disordered conditions of the time, it was to be two and a half years before a successor was appointed.

Richard of Lincoln, 1187–1203

It was only in 1187, at the height of an insurrection led by King William's principal dynastic rival for the Scottish throne, Donald MacWilliam, and with the Scottish grip on the northern part of the kingdom severely tested, that the king secured the election of one of his most trusted clerks, Richard of Lincoln, as bishop of Moray.[42] Elected on 1 March, he was consecrated a fortnight later by Hugh, bishop of St Andrews, at St Andrews; the grant to him of the possessions of the bishopric by King William at Kinghorn in Fife was probably made soon afterwards, given the proximity of the two places.[43] The charter issued to him on this occasion lists only the churches of Elgin with its dependent chapels, and Auldearn with its dependent chapels, which the king had granted to him to augment his see's resources, the sense from this being that he could expect to find the revenues of the bishopric in a perilous state. Although he had been formally vested with his see by the king, he may not have been able to establish himself in his diocese and begin his work of building up the organisation of his diocese until after the defeat and death of Donald at Mam Garvia in July.[44] It was probably in recognition of the still fragile condition of the diocesan revenues that the king assigned to Richard the teind of all his revenues from Moray, including from the exercise of justice within the diocese and from his *cáin*, repeating the grant which he had made to Bishop Simon at the outset of his episcopate.[45] The re-grant of these rights to components of royal revenue probably reflects the chaotic conditions which had prevailed through most of the 1180s when much of Moray was controlled by the MacWilliams and their supporters. This perception of general disorder and irregularity in the collection of teind which may have arisen in the three-year vacancy which followed Simon de Toeni's death is further strengthened by the royal mandate, probably issued shortly after the defeat of MacWilliam, while the king was at Elgin, which commanded the men of Moray

to pay to their churches, parsons and officials all teind as was due to be paid according to the assize of King David I.[46] That William was obliged to repeat this command when he was at Elgin in 1196 or 1197, and order likewise payment to the bishop of the dues which he and his predecessors had made to the bishopric out of royal revenues in Moray, suggests that local resistance to the imposition of a regular system of teinding and royal tribute-gathering remained strong and that Bishop Richard and his clergy were facing difficulties in enforcing payment.[47] A second repetition of the grants of a teind of royal revenues throughout Moray made on 26 December 1199, this time made specifically to the church of the Holy Trinity of Moray and to Bishop Richard, is not simply yet another effort to enforce payment by royal command; the charter provides for commutation of the rents in kind for payments in cash and probably reflects the rapid development of the market economy of the region in the decade since the defeat of the MacWilliam insurrection.[48]

King William made an effort to support his former clerk in his reorganisation of the diocese whenever opportunity arose. Whilst at Elgin during one of his expeditions north to deal with the recurring problem of Harald Maddadsson, earl of Caithness and Orkney, and his troublesome sons, William issued several charters conveying property and rights intended to boost the bishop's finances. By these, Bishop Richard received a toft in the six royal burghs from Banff to Inverness, not to have sites for houses for himself but to give him the rental income from the property and the possible service of the craftsman or trader who took up the burgage.[49] A further toft was added in the 1190s in the royal burgh at Kintore.[50] A second charter granted an annuity of £10 from the burgh ferme of Elgin until such time as the churches of Forres and Dyke fell vacant.[51] Perhaps on the same occasion he granted the bishop leave to build a mill on the Lossie above the salmon cruives below the royal castle at Elgin – not, as has been suggested, the origin of the later settlement of Bishopmill but the site of what became the Sheriffmill (see page 144) – and also granted him and his men extensive rights to timber, fuel-wood and grazing in the royal forests around Elgin, Forres and Inverness.[52]

In the time of Richard's successor, Brice, it was commented that earlier bishops of Moray had moved their see around as was convenient. For most of Richard's episcopate there is no sense of where he had his cathedral or main residence, but in King William's charter issued on 26 December 1199 at Forfar reference is made for the first time to the church of the Holy Trinity of Moray.[53] As that style came to be attached to the church at Spynie north of Elgin which Bishop Brice chose as the fixed location for his cathedral, it is tempting to suggest that towards the end of his life and with the revenues of his diocese on a more secure footing Richard was moving towards regularising the seat of his bishopric and had fixed on Spynie. Indeed, it may have been Richard rather than Brice who was preparing the ground for a formal constitution for his cathedral. Was it perhaps through Richard's personal links to Lincoln that the first moves were made towards securing the details of Lincoln Cathedral's constitution which his successor introduced into the Church of Moray soon after 1203? The rapidity of their introduction by Brice is strongly suggestive that it was Richard who had made the first move in that regard but that the process had been delayed by his death.

There is no formal record surviving of where Bishop Richard died or was buried, but in the early eighteenth century it was stated that both his death and burial occurred at Spynie.[54] The destruction of the medieval church at Spynie in the eighteenth century may have resulted in the loss of any tomb there. A number of fine early-thirteenth-century grave slabs have, however, been found at Spynie and it is possible that one of those once marked the grave of the bishop who seems first to have established the see of Moray on a sound footing.

Brice de Douglas, 1203–1222

The new bishop was Brice de Douglas, a Tironensian monk who had been prior of Lesmahagow in Lanarkshire (Illus 2.2).[55] There is no established connection between him and King William in the manner there had been for his two predecessors. Instead, it is possible that his advance to the see of Moray stemmed from a kinship connection with the de Moravia or Murray family, lords of Duffus, who shared the Flemish origins of the Douglases.[56] If this is the case, his election to the bishopric is a signal of how extensive Murray influence had become within the Church of Moray. The absence of a personal link to the royal household or one of the Crown's chief officers may also explain why, beyond the king's confirmation of the possessions of the bishopric and the expectation of the churches of Elgin and Auldearn on the deaths of the incumbents, and the familiar injunction to the people of Moray to pay their teinds and dues,[57] there is no evidence for a similar level of royal patronage to that enjoyed by Bishop Richard. Instead, there are traces of a much more distant and businesslike relationship from which the bishop did not always emerge as the beneficiary.[58]

A year or so after he became bishop, Brice wrote to the pope to request the transfer of his see to the church of the Holy Trinity at Spynie. His predecessors, he advised the pope, had located their sees in various places – including on occasion Spynie – but recently the clergy and people of the Church of Moray had urgently requested that, since the place where the cathedral was currently located was positioned 'in a certain angle of the sea' which none of his 'parishioners'

2.2   Seal of Bishop Brice de Douglas (Historic Scotland © Crown Copyright)

could cross without difficulty, he relocate his see to a more appropriate place. The description of the location of the cathedral which he had inherited fits Kinneddar at the south-western edge of modern Lossiemouth, which in the Middle Ages stood above the shore of a former inlet of the sea which had turned into a marshy and probably still tidal lagoon. In response to that appeal, in 1207 Pope Innocent III issued a mandate to the bishops of St Andrews and Brechin and the abbot of Lindores instructing them to institute Holy Trinity at Spynie as the cathedral of the diocese.[59] Shortly afterwards, the formal transfer of the see to Spynie was made and then, in what must have been a splendid ceremony attended by the heads of four monasteries and a host of the diocesan clergy, Brice set in place a constitution for his new cathedral which followed the cathedral constitution used at Lincoln in England.[60] The Lincoln precedent provided a blueprint for the chapter of the cathedral; it set up eight canonries supported on prebends funded out of the revenues of several parish churches and portions of property in the diocese.[61]

The first canon was the dean, who was to be head of the chapter, with four of the remaining canonries held in order of importance by the chanter, the treasurer, the chancellor and the archdeacon, with the remaining three being 'simple' canonries. Brice took no place for himself amongst the canons and therefore had no seat in chapter, an anomaly which his successor felt the need to change. In recognition of the fact that clerical duties might require the canons to be non-resident, each canon was obliged under the new constitution to have a priest to deputise for him in the cathedral, to ensure that there was always a complement of eight clergy serving in the church. The constitution also set out the nature of the main services to be held daily in the cathedral, beginning with a mass to the Virgin Mary celebrated with spoken chant, then the chief or morning mass for the dead, celebrated with or without chant, and finally the greater mass or mass of the day, to be celebrated solemnly with chant. It was stipulated that the mass for the dead was to be conducted with a minimum of five priests. This document, together with a large group of texts which Brice had obtained from the bishop, dean and chapter of Lincoln which set out the customs and liberties of their church, the duties of the four senior officials, the places assigned in the choir for the clergy and how services will be conducted, is the earliest surviving constitution of any of Scotland's cathedrals and provides us with a unique insight into the nature of the worship and how mass was celebrated in the early years of the thirteenth century.

As an active reformer and builder of his diocese, it is no surprise that Bishop Brice was one of four Scottish bishops to attend the Fourth Lateran Council in 1215 which Pope Innocent III had summoned to gather in Rome.[62] Amongst the more famous of the provisions of that council was a decree concerning vicarages – 'as those who serve of the altar should live of the altar, let suitable provision be made for vicars' – an enactment which led to a flurry of renegotiated settlements between appropriating monasteries and the affected diocesans which attempted to ensure that proper financial provision was made for vicars in parish churches. As Brice struggled to extract control of parish churches from lay patrons and to set up the prebends for his cathedral's canons, this provision would have been of immense importance to him. It was, however, to be unfortunate for Brice that he returned home immediately at the end of the council for, although he may have been eager to begin to implement the new legal provisions agreed under Lateran IV, he was rapidly drawn into the political and ultimately spiritual crisis which was about to engulf Scotland and England.

In 1215, King Alexander II entered the civil war in England between King John and his opponents, looking to secure the return to Scottish lordship of those parts of northern England which had been held in the time of David I.[63] John, however, had outmanoeuvred his opponents by resigning his kingdom into the hands of Pope Innocent and receiving it back from him as a papal fief. Thus, when Alexander joined in the assault on the English king he found himself in direct conflict with John's overlord the pope. The result was that Alexander and all of his magnates and clerics who had supported or encouraged him to enter the war found themselves excommunicated as a consequence of a decree to that effect pronounced during the Lateran council.[64] Brice would have been aware of that decree and cannot have been ignorant of Alexander's likely stance before he had set out for Rome, yet he still chose to return, unlike the bishops of Glasgow and St Andrews, who remained absent from the kingdom and so largely avoided the effects of the spiritual interdict which was pronounced against Scotland. Until that interdict was lifted – and with it the sentences of suspension from office which the papal legate to England had laid upon certain named individuals, including Brice – the bishop could not even begin to implement the new benchmarks for faith and spiritual standards which were set out in the seventy-one provisions of Lateran IV.

Although the Anglo-Scottish war was over by 1217 and negotiations began to have the interdict lifted, Brice was one of a number of high-profile clergy who remained under suspension until well into 1218. Late in the year he set out for Rome in the company of bishops Walter of Glasgow and Adam of Caithness to secure absolution at the hands of the pope.[65] On 5 November 1218, Pope Honorius III sent a general letter to the people of Moray recalling them to their obedience to Brice, who had been pardoned for the offences he had committed in supporting the war against King John.[66] Brice did not return to Scotland until sometime in 1219, probably not until after the conclusion of the inquest which Pope Honorius instructed on 30 January to examine accusations of extortion and bribe-taking which were levelled against the bishop.[67] This accusation may have left Brice labouring under a cloud and there is little evidence for his actions as bishop in the last years of his life. He last appears in 1221 settling a dispute with John Bisset over the patronage of the churches of Conveth and Dalbutelauch, which King Alexander confirmed on 15 October that year during a visit to Elgin.[68] He died on an unknown date in 1222, probably in the spring given the placing of his obituary at the start of the chronicle entries for the year.[69] His place of burial is unknown, but it is likely to have been in the church of the Holy Trinity at Spynie where he had fixed his seat.[70]

Andrew de Moravia/Murray, 1222–1242

Brice's death in the early months of 1222 was apparently followed relatively swiftly by the election of the well-connected local cleric and probable chancellor of the diocese, Master Andrew Murray (Illus 2.3).[71] Before he had even been consecrated, Andrew was pushing ahead with the process, which Brice may have begun, to relocate his cathedral from Spynie to Elgin, and may have been at Rome in May 1223 when, still described as bishop-elect, he received a papal confirmation of the five churches which were annexed to the episcopal *mensa*.[72] He had certainly visited the curia before April 1224 when he was first described as a fully consecrated bishop and it is likely that he had in fact been confirmed and consecrated during his time in Rome.[73] The document in which he was first styled as bishop was a mandate issued by Pope Honorius III to Bishop Gilbert Murray of Caithness, the abbot of Kinloss and the dean of Ross to investigate the claimed unsuitability of Spynie as a location for the see of Moray which Andrew had laid before him and, if justified, to institute the move. Andrew's complaints focused on Spynie's exposure to the threat of war, its physical isolation and inconvenience for trade, all of which supposedly hindered the canons in the proper celebration of religion. The alternative site which Andrew had proposed to the pope was the church of the Holy Trinity 'next Elgin', a relocation which he claimed had the approval and support of King Alexander and the chapter of the diocese. In July of the same year, Bishop Gilbert reported back that he and his colleagues had found the reasons to move the see to be compelling. Accordingly, on 19 July, in Bishop Andrew's presence, they had formally instituted Holy Trinity as his new cathedral and designated it the seat of the bishops of Moray in all time to come.[74]

2.3   Seal of Andrew de Moravia (Historic Scotland © Crown Copyright)

The language of Pope Honorius's mandate and the report by Bishop Gilbert imply that there was already a church on the new site when it was instituted as the cathedral. What the status of such a church might have been is unknown, for the parish church of the burgh, the church of St Giles, lay in the centre of the town and the locations of its two dependent chapels in the burgh's hinterland are known.[75] The cathedral and its associated chanonry was a late arrival appended to a pre-existing urban centre with its own independent parish church; the cathedral, unusually, had no parish function in respect of the town to which it was attached. It is possible that work may have begun on a new cathedral before the death of Bishop Brice in anticipation of papal approval for a move, but there is nothing in the surviving ruins of the cathedral to confirm that view and, despite modern assertions that there was a pre-existing building, it is probable that Bishop Andrew began to build from scratch on an empty site.[76] Indeed, King Alexander's charter issued at Musselburgh on 5 July, only a fortnight before the bishop of Caithness confirmed the relocation, gives royal assent to the translation, but speaks only of 'a certain place beside Elgin which we have given to the bishop and clergy of Moray for constructing that church'.[77] There is still ambiguity in that statement, however, over which bishop received the gift of land – Brice or Andrew – and when it was given is not made clear. On balance, given that Brice may have begun the process for a second relocation of his see, it is possible that he had obtained the site and started work on his new church in anticipation of retrospectively securing papal approval. Brice, then, may take the credit for the idea and the inception of the plan, but its execution is most certainly the achievement of Andrew.

No record beyond the building itself survives to show how Andrew went about the construction of the church of the Holy Trinity. We do, however, have abundant evidence for how he went about expanding the resources of his see, securing gifts of new land and rights from the king and local magnates, and resolving disputes over property and income to the benefit of his church. At Abertarff at the south end of Loch Ness, for example, a long-running property dispute with Thomas de Thirlstane, lord of Abertarff, was resolved in 1225, when Andrew gave up his claims in return for an annual payment of ten shillings.[78] In another case, on 31 March 1226, Andrew ended a dispute with King Alexander over various portions of land within royal hunting forests in Moray, which he claimed pertained to his see, by giving up his action in return for a grant of the lands of Rothiemurchus on Speyside.[79] A third example concerned the advowsons of eight parish churches in the lordship of Strathbogie and the kirklands attached to them.[80] In a deal with David, lord of Strathbogie, in April 1226, he surrendered his claims to the churches of Essie and Glass, while David surrendered his claims in respect of Botarie, Drumdelgie, Dunbennan, Kinnoir, Rhynie and Ruthven. Andrew's efforts to remove any rival claims to the patronage of these and several other churches involved compromise and the setting aside of other disputes, but this deal and those designed to bring additional revenue to the see formed just part of an ambitious scheme to reconfigure the chapter of his new cathedral.

Shortly after the settlement of the patronage dispute with David de Strathbogie, on 5 May 1226, Bishop Andrew issued a new constitution for his chapter which more than doubled the number of canons from eight to eighteen, one of whom he assigned to be held in future by bishops of Moray, for the constitution of Bishop Brice had given the bishops no seat on their own cathedral's chapter.[81] Several of the prebends created for the support of the new canons drew revenue from churches where Andrew had just recently secured undisputed rights of patronage and possession. His ambitions, however, did not stop at this expanded college, for before October 1232 he had increased the number of canons to twenty-three.[82] This remained the number of canons attached to the cathedral until the early sixteenth century when there was a further reorganisation of the chapter's constitution with the creation in the 1530s and 1540s of two new prebends (see page 124).

Bishop Andrew died late in 1242 – he last appears in a dated document on 18 September[83] – and was buried in his new church at Elgin on the south side of the choir, 'under a large stone of blue marble' according to Robert Keith writing in the early 1700s, but, following some fire damage to the unfinished building in 1244, the Valliscaulian monks of Pluscarden somehow managed to remove his body from its tomb, to bury it in their own church.[84] The Valliscaulians may have felt a particular personal attachment to Andrew, who had been a patron and supporter of their priory, but there is no suggestion that the bishop had intended to be buried there. The slab described by Keith may be the ledger-style graveslab with inset for a memorial brass which still survives in front of the bottom of the first step of the presbytery area opposite the archway through to the south choir aisle. This, however, is either a much later replacement for an older monument or is the tombstone of another later medieval bishop, for its style is not that of the mid-thirteenth century.[85] It may be the gravemarker of one of three bishops, Alexander Bur (d 1397), William Spynie (d 1406) or Andrew Stewart (d 1501), who were said to have been buried in the choir area (see page 108).

Simon II, 1242–1251

The election of Simon, who was probably the 'Simon, dean of Holy Trinity of Elgin' or 'dean of the church of Moray'

named in the time of Bishop Andrew,[86] may have occurred before the end of 1242 or, more likely, early in 1243. A year later, however, he was still described as bishop-elect.[87] He has left very little evidence for his activities as bishop, much of the record of his episcopate perhaps having been lost when the cathedral's muniments were burned in 1390. One important surviving act from his episcopate was the reaching of an agreement with Freskin Murray, lord of Duffus, in 1248, which settled a dispute between the bishops and the lords of Duffus over their respective rights in the woods and moors of Spynie and Findrassie on the north-facing slopes of the ridge that dropped towards the inlet of the sea which separated Duffus from the mainland proper.[88] It was also during his time that an agreement was reached with the monks of Arbroath over the revenues of the two churches in his diocese which they held, Aberchirder and Inverness, whereby the abbey was finally to agree to the proper establishment of vicarages to serve the cure of souls in the parishes.[89] It is a slender record, but it does suggest that he was active in building further upon the secure foundation which his predecessor had given to the Church of Moray at parish level in the second quarter of the thirteenth century. His death was recorded in the list of bishops of Moray compiled during the time of Bishop John Winchester under the year 1251.[90] There is no record of where he died or where his tomb was located, but in Robert Keith's early-eighteenth-century history of the Scottish bishops it was suggested that he was buried in the choir of Elgin.[91]

Archibald, 1253–1298

Following Simon's death in 1251, a certain Ralph, canon of Lincoln, was elected as his successor. Ralph, however, appears to have either died before he was consecrated or had his election rejected, possibly on account of the factional conflict which scarred the minority of King Alexander III and which was causing major controversy in respect of elections to the Scottish bishoprics.[92] Whatever the cause, it led to an extended vacancy which lasted until the election and consecration of Archibald in 1253. Archibald was identified closely with the faction headed by Walter Comyn, earl of Menteith, which had been in the ascendant in the kingdom since 1251 and which had enjoyed broad support from the clergy against their rivals, the faction headed by Alan Durward.[93] He appears to have been close to Bishop Gamelin of St Andrews, one of the chief clerical supporters of the Comyns, and succeeded Gamelin as chancellor of Scotland on his election to the bishopric of St Andrews. On 21 June 1255, Pope Alexander confirmed Archibald in the office of chancellor of the kingdom.[94]

As the rather quiet record of the early part of his episcopate seems to suggest, for nearly two decades after his election Archibald administered his diocese with little disturbance. Whatever minor damage had been done to the cathedral-church in 1244 had probably been repaired soon afterwards by Bishop Simon II and it is likely that the eastern limb of the building at least was complete by the 1260s. That calm start to his episcopate was completely overshadowed in 1270 by a devastating fire which not only inflicted severe damage on the church but also destroyed at least part of the surrounding chanonry. The fire passed without comment in surviving contemporary sources but is noted in Walter Bower's early-fifteenth-century *Scotichronicon*, which drew much of its data from now-lost thirteenth-century sources.[95] Traumatic though this event is likely to have been, Archibald and the chapter seized it as an opportunity to completely remodel the eastern limb of the cathedral as a more commodious setting for the enlarged college of resident clergy and more elaborate liturgical ceremony which had developed through the thirteenth century.

Short-term need to secure revenues to fund the great programme of enlargement which Archibald initiated at Elgin, which saw the doubling in length of the eastern limb, provision of aisles along both flanks of the choir, reconstruction of the central area of the crossing and building of a grand polygonal chapter house,[96] may have seen the bishop begin to pursue litigation over financial matters with greater stringency than before. This greater assertiveness in securing positive outcomes in disputes may be seen, for example, in the quittance made by Augustine, lord of Inveralian (on the Spey south-west of Grantown) of 'a certain particle of my land which is called Fanymartach' which Archibald asserted belonged to his demesne estate of Finlarg.[97] Augustine's formal renunciation of the contested land is made in terms of an amicable settlement 'for good peace', but that is balanced by a statement that it was made for the souls' welfare of his parents, himself, their ancestors and heirs; the threat of excommunication and imperilment of their mortal souls seems to hang in the background as a threat which secured the outcome Archibald wanted. A similar process, but with that threat put into operation, can be seen in 1280 when Archibald raised the stakes in a long court case with William de Fenton, lord of Beaufort in the Aird, and his wife Cecily over land which belonged to the church of Kiltarlity. Having failed to get them to yield up the land peaceably, he first secured pronouncement of excommunication against them by three papal judges subdelegate and requested confirmation of that sentence by the provincial council of the Scottish Church that August.[98] This was the spiritual equivalent of the nuclear option; for excommunication thrust his opponents outside of the Christian community and held over them the risk of eternal damnation should they die without having been

received back into the spiritual fold. Whilst under sentence of excommunication they lacked all protection afforded to them by the Church, including the legal safeguards which canon law provided to them in respect of contracts, oaths and the like; excommunication undermined the basic aspects of lordship and jeopardised their property-owning position. It may have been this kind of action in legal disputes which led to the king beginning to send knights and royal clerks to observe the business of the council and to prevent it from actions which were contrary to the king's dignity and the custom of the kingdom.[99] Archibald complained to Pope Honorius IV in 1285 that royal officials were, with King Alexander's support, 'oppressing' his see and infringing the privileges which he and his predecessors had received from past popes and kings of Scots.[100] He received in response a papal letter to Alexander urging the king to cease his harassment of the bishop and instead defend the rights of the Church of Moray.

While short-term need may have led to spiritual strong-arm tactics to secure quick resolution of property disputes, in the longer term Archibald and the Church of Moray appear to have benefited from the buoyant economy of Scotland in the second half of the thirteenth century. As the rebuilding work at the cathedral suggests, Archibald and the chapter were able to obtain revenue from which to fund the new construction, which allowed them to plan with little thought to economy. Much of this new revenue may have been the product of the booming Scottish export trade in wool, hides and salted fish, much of it destined for the rapidly growing Flemish weaving centres in cities like Bruges and Ghent. The silver flowing in to Scotland funded a great surge in building work as both lay and ecclesiastical landlords maximised the profit from their estates. Moray was a major centre for the production of wool, hides and fish, and Flemish merchants were certainly operating in the burghs along the Moray Firth in the last decades of the thirteenth century, but the principal Scottish export centre was Berwick-upon-Tweed. It is known that the northern Scottish Cistercian monasteries were arranging for the forwarding of their wool production to Berwick for sale through agents and it seems that Bishop Archibald was looking to do the same for the produce of the episcopal estates. It appears to have been in the late 1280s that he bought a property in the commercial district on the Ness in Berwick.[101] This was perhaps a base from where his representatives could oversee the sale of the produce from his demesne estates – probably also from the properties of the diocesan clergy – and the wool and hides received as teinds, and purchase luxury goods in return.

Along with the other political leaders of the kingless kingdom, on 17 March 1290 Bishop Archibald gave his formal consent to the proposal for the marriage of the young Queen Margaret to Edward, son of Edward I of England.[102] Although he was clearly keeping actively involved in the major political developments of the day, there is also evidence that by 1291 Archibald was preparing for his end, receiving papal permission on 13 April to draw up his will.[103] His action may have been triggered by a bout of illness, for by the late autumn he was possibly becoming involved in the political manoeuvring which surrounded the court set up to resolve the competing claims over the succession to the throne of Scotland. There is, however, a tension between perception and reality in suggestions that he had some link to the cause of the count of Holland, who claimed that his ancestress Ada, sister of King William, had been designated as William's heir to the exclusion of their remaining brother, Earl David, and his heirs. According to the dating-clause given in documents supposedly confirming the authenticity of this agreement, it was in mid-November 1291 that Bishop Archibald and the prior of Pluscarden had set their seals to letters affirming that the original document was genuine. The original was said to record Earl David of Huntingdon's surrender of all rights for himself and his heirs to the kingship of the Scots in exchange for lands in the Garioch in Aberdeenshire.[104] Analysis of the surviving text, however, shows that Archibald's authentication of the document has simply been appended to what is now dismissed as a patent forgery. Why Archibald should have been willing to participate in this fraud is unknown.

Archibald, who must have felt that he was drawing closer to the end of his life, probably also submitted to Edward I in the general collapse of Scottish resistance after the defeat at Dunbar. There is no formal record of such a submission, but the issuing of a protection for two years to the bishop, dated 8 September 1296, suggests that he was by then in Edward's peace.[105] He died on 9 December 1298 and, according to the eighteenth-century account of Robert Keith, which records his burial in the choir, he is believed to have been buried in the presbytery of the cathedral beneath the fine gabled monument set into the third bay from the east in the north wall of the presbytery.[106] No effigy survives in the recess, but it is likely to have contained a near life-size figure of the bishop in full mass vestments. It is possible that the splendid but sadly mutilated effigy discovered in 1936 buried on the west side of the chapter house came from Archibald's tomb.[107]

David Murray, 1299–1326

The joint Guardians of Scotland, Robert Bruce and John Comyn, moved to fill the vacancy in Moray and appointed Master David Murray, parson of Bothwell in Lanarkshire, who was probably the younger brother of Sir William Murray of Bothwell and nephew of Wallace's colleague Andrew Murray.[108] A staunch adherent to the national cause, David nevertheless made his formal submission to the conquering Edward I in 1296, but was later reported to have preached to his flock that fighting for the kingdom was equivalent to waging crusade against the Saracens.[109] Throughout his career he would give almost unswerving support to those who opposed Edward I and Edward II in their efforts to conquer Scotland. This commitment to the cause of national independence was shown from the outset of his episcopate when as bishop-elect he travelled to Rome in the company of William Lamberton, bishop of St Andrews, as part of the Scottish diplomatic mission to Pope Boniface VIII; he was consecrated there on 28 June 1299. His hostility to the English Crown was well known and his bishopric may have suffered the consequences for his support for the resistance; a request to Edward I in 1303 for timber to repair the house of the dean in Elgin, burned by the army led through the region by Prince Edward, suggests that damage to the chanonry may have been significant.[110] As Scottish resistance collapsed after the defeat of their French allies and the direction of all of Edward's energies towards the northern war, there is no record evidence that he made any formal submission to Edward I as part of the general Scottish submission in 1304.[111] He was, however, amongst the Scottish bishops notified on 19 February 1304 of the peace settlement with Edward.[112]

Peace with the English king did not last for long and in March 1306 Bishop David was one of five Scottish bishops to declare their support for Robert Bruce's bid for the kingship. He was present at Scone on 25 March to preside with Bishops Lamberton of St Andrews and Wishart of Glasgow in the enthronement ceremony.[113] By late summer 1306, with the newly enthroned king a hunted fugitive, Murray was himself in hiding and being sought by the anti-Bruce earls of Ross and Sutherland. On 11 August 1306 Edward I wrote to his lieutenant, Aymer de Valence, expressing his surprise that Ross had failed to capture the bishop and urging him to ensure that it was done speedily as 'he much desires to have the bishop's person in England'.[114] Around the same time charges were drawn up which accused Murray, Lamberton and Wishart of perjury, irregularity and rebellion.[115] It soon emerged that Murray had fled for safety to Norwegian-controlled Orkney. Edward I then wrote to King Hakon V of Norway to request the arrest and return to him of the rebel bishop who had also been excommunicated by Pope Clement;[116] his see was to suffer a dreadful harrying at Ross's hands as punishment. Murray, however, was not arrested and sent to Edward, possibly through the influence of Isabella, dowager-queen of Norway, who was the sister of Robert Bruce. Nevertheless, after a year in exile in Orkney, Murray appears to have compromised, made his submission to

Edward II, and returned to his bishopric.[117] On discovering the scale of the damage to his property and the possessions of the see he threatened the earl with excommunication unless satisfactory compensation was offered for the losses which he had sustained, but he was warned by King Edward to desist from his threats as the damage had been inflicted whilst the bishop had been a rebel.[118]

David Murray's submission to Edward II may have been very brief, for in September 1307 King Robert began what was to be an extended campaign through northern Scotland which targeted the adherents of the English king and rallied his own supporters throughout the region.[119] By November the king was at Elgin and, although he failed to take the English-held castle there, he had clearly managed to reduce the surrounding district to his submission by early 1308; Bishop David is likely to have reverted quickly to his allegiance to King Robert. Following his victory over the Comyns near Inverurie in early May, resistance to the king collapsed in northern Scotland and on 31 October Earl William of Ross submitted to him at Auldearn; amongst the sureties for the good behaviour and future loyalty of the earl were Bishop David and the dean and chanter of the cathedral.[120]

Murray's staunch adherence to King Robert after 1307 led to his regular identification as one of the leading clerical opponents of peace with England and an instigator of conflict. Complaints against him and his pro-Bruce colleagues reached a peak in 1319 when Edward II's campaign at Rome to have Bishop Lamberton deprived of the bishopric of St Andrews and replaced by a reliable Englishman was at its most strident.[121] Murray had been summoned to Rome by Pope John XXII along with Lamberton and Bishops Cheyne of Aberdeen and Sinclair of Dunkeld, but all four ignored the summons.[122] On 16 June 1320 all four bishops were excommunicated for their defiance.[123] Murray died on 20 January 1326 and, according to Keith in the early eighteenth century, was buried in the choir of the cathedral.[124]

John Pilmore/Pilmuir, 1326–1362

Bishop David's death was fortuitous for John Pilmuir, an active clerical servant and diplomat for King Robert I. Pilmuir had recently been elected as bishop of Ross, a highly strategic but relatively poor diocese in which he would have been an important Crown agent in a territory which had often been strongly opposed to the Bruce regime. On David Murray's death, Pilmuir and his royal patron may have moved swiftly to secure his transfer before his election to Ross was formally confirmed. Pilmuir's election to Moray was certainly approved by King Robert and it is possible that the king had in fact nominated him.[125] The son of a Dundee

burgess and nephew of a prominent Cistercian monk of Coupar Angus, Pilmuir had already had a distinguished career in France and in papal service, and had served the king in peace negotiations with England from at least 1321.[126] Bishop John was firmly identified with the Bruce regime and in February 1328 was one of a high-powered delegation of Scottish representatives who came to York to conclude the peace treaty with England.[127] In 1329 he again served as an envoy, this time travelling to the papal curia as leader of the embassy sent to negotiate for the rite of anointing to be included in the coronation of future Scottish kings, starting in 1331 with the young David II, son of King Robert.[128]

An appointee of the Bruce regime, Pilmuir was deeply involved in the resistance to the invasion of Scotland by Edward Balliol, son of the former King John Balliol, and his associates in 1332 and probably witnessed the first impact of the resulting civil war when Balliol's supporters David de Strathbogie and Henry de Beaumont came north to claim their heritage in Moray and Buchan. With resistance to the invaders in the north being led by the Randolphs and Murrays, it is likely that there was close cooperation between the bishop and these leading northern lords, but little evidence has survived for how Pilmuir contributed to the effort. A lull may have come when de Beaumont was cornered in his castle at Dundarg and forced to surrender and then quit Scotland as he tried to raise his ransom, and when Strathbogie came temporarily into the peace of King David II. Strathbogie's defection back to the cause of Edward Balliol was followed by his cornering and slaying at Culblean in Aberdeenshire late in 1335. The war then returned to Moray in summer 1336 when Edward III led a swift-moving cavalry force on a raid or *chevauchée* through the central Highlands to rescue Strathbogie's widow, the countess of Atholl, who was under siege in the island castle of Lochindorb. From there Edward III burned his way north through Moray, destroying Elgin but sparing the cathedral and chanonry, before turning east to Aberdeen, which he also burned.[129] It may have been the longer-term consequences of this raid which were referred to in King David II's inspection and confirmation on 4 April 1343 of the foundation charter of the Maison Dieu at Elgin, which speaks of the poverty and wasting of the hospital.[130] Pilmuir confirmed and gave the full weight of ecclesiastical authority to the king's charter on 8 April, for as holder of the right of presentation to the office of master of the hospital he had a vested interest in ensuring its financial viability. The scale of his interest was revealed in a sworn attestation made as part of the process authorised by Pope Benedict XIII in the aftermath of the burning of Elgin Cathedral in 1390 (see page 37). Sir John Wylgus swore on oath that during his time at the Maison Dieu Pilmuir gave custody of the hospital to a succession of four men, including his uncle and namesake John Pilmuir, monk of Coupar Angus, and his cousin Master John Kinnaird.[131]

Along with the other Scottish bishops, on 26 September 1357 Pilmuir put his seal to letters appointing ambassadors to treat with Edward III of England for the release of King David II.[132] David's release followed that October. Probably very elderly by the time of David's release, despite the close relationship which he had once had with the Bruce monarchy, Pilmuir played no significant part in the king's first efforts to rebuild royal power upon his return to Scotland. Instead, the last notices of his activities relate almost entirely to his own diocese and some speak of preparations for his own end. On the Feast of St Nicasius and his Associates (14 December) in 1360, for example, Bishop John made a grant of a piece of land, three and a half roods wide at the front and bounded by two lanes lying on the west side of the stone enclosure wall of the chanonry, to be divided equally between four of the perpetual chaplainries in the cathedral as sites for the chaplain's manses.[133] This land, which he had bought from a secular clerk, was described as 'held of the Brothers of St Lazarus next the walls of Jerusalem', or Lazarite Order, who cared for lepers. This was not the site of the 'houses of the lepers in Elgin' which are mentioned in 1391 but which disappear thereafter from the records, but was evidently a piece of land from which the brethren drew rental income.[134] This grant to the chaplains was made specifically for the salvation of his own soul and the souls of his parents; it was clearly intended as a preparation for his own coming end, to secure the masses and prayers of a body of clergy who were already bound to provide such services for the dead, and whose future existence was guaranteed by the generous endowments which their original patrons had given them. Pilmuir died on 28 September 1362 in his castle at Spynie.[135] What may be the effigy from Bishop Pilmuir's tomb survives, relocated in the recess tomb of Bishop Tulloch in the south aisle of the choir.[136]

Alexander Bur, 1362–1397

News of Bishop Pilmuir's death reached King David II in late autumn 1362 whilst he was at the earl of Mar's castle of Kildrummy in Aberdeenshire.[137] Recognising the opportunity presented not only to boost his own finances through seizure of the dead bishop's personal assets and the royal right to administer the temporalities of the see during a vacancy, but also to strengthen Crown influence in northern Scotland through the insertion of a loyal servant into Moray, David moved west and by 28 November he was based in the episcopal palace at Spynie.[138] He was moving swiftly to exploit the first real opportunity to arise since his return from English captivity in 1357 to rein back the regional influence

of his nephew Robert Stewart, his heir-presumptive but also chief political rival who had been expanding his own power north of the mountains.[139] Whilst an extended vacancy in the see was attractive for the revenues which it would bring to him, David understood that it was more important to replace Pilmuir rapidly. Even before leaving Kildrummy he may already have determined who would serve him best as bishop of Moray. The man settled upon was Alexander Bur, a trusted royal clerk and councillor who had held the archdeaconry of Moray since 1350 (Illus 2.4).[140] Indeed, it seems that David must have instructed the chapter to 'canonically elect' their archdeacon under his licence perhaps as early as October, for the bishop-elect was able to reach Avignon by December 1362. There, he was formally provided to his see by the pope on 23 December and had been consecrated before February 1363.[141]

On his return to Scotland Bur began strenuous efforts to recover the extensive jurisdictional powers which his predecessors had enjoyed before King Robert I had created the earldom of Moray for Thomas Randolph. After the death of John the third and last Randolph earl in 1346 the earldom had passed notionally to Patrick, earl of March, husband of one of John's two sisters. The great powers of the Randolph earls, however, had been held by an entail and limited to a succession through heirs male; the regality jurisdiction should have ended with John's death. Earl Patrick, moreover, had to share Moray with his cousin, the husband of the

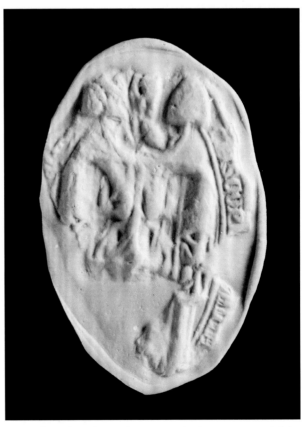

2.4   Seal of Alexander Bur (Historic Scotland © Crown Copyright)

second Randolph sister, while Earl John's widow also had her terce of the earldom lands, controlled since 1355 by her new husband Robert Stewart, the king's nephew. The territorial fragmentation of the earldom, therefore, was well underway by the later 1350s, but it is equally clear that King David had begun to break up the jurisdictional powers that the Randolphs once had held.[142] The road was open for Bur, a university-trained lawyer and royal servant, to recover the ancient ecclesiastical liberties and rights of his see.

Recovery of ecclesiastical liberties and jurisdictional rights meant recovery of income. This was good news for Bur, who in 1363 was desperately in need of boosting his finances to cover the costs of having his provision to the see confirmed at Avignon; by mid-1364 he had failed to pay the first instalment he was due to make, but threats of interdict, excommunication and suspension from office induced him to find the necessary 650 gold florins he owed.[143] With the balance due by September 1365, Bur needed to rebuild rapidly the depleted resources of his see. Some cash may have been raised by an indulgence which he had been granted whilst at Avignon, to encourage pilgrims to come to Elgin and make payment towards the restoration of the cathedral which was ruinous 'by neglect and hostile incursions'.[144] As the last recorded attack on Elgin had occurred in 1336 when Edward III led a *chevauchée* through Moray, on which occasion the cathedral and chanonry were specifically spared,[145] it is likely that the indulgence was intended by Bur to be a general revenue-raising device. More effective revenue generation may have come from royal restoration of the judicial rights of the bishop over his tenants in Badenoch and Strathspey, which redirected the flow of profits from fines and escheats into the episcopal coffers.[146] Success there, however, came at a cost, for the revenue streams that Bur had recovered had been taken from the Stewarts' hands; the bishop was colliding directly with the ambitions of Robert Stewart and his third son, Alexander, who would gain historical notoriety as 'the Wolf of Badenoch'.[147]

With royal backing through the late 1360s Bishop Bur gradually recovered the ancient rights and privileges of his see which had been curtailed by the Randolph's regality powers in Moray. By 1370, however, he had begun to recognise that he needed to come to terms with the Stewarts, Alexander especially, for it was becoming increasingly likely that King David was not going to father a legitimate heir and that the throne was going to pass to Robert Stewart. It was also important for Bur to establish a working relationship with Alexander Stewart, for the ambitious young nobleman was building a powerful lordship for himself in the Moray uplands founded on the employment of mercenary bands of *ceatharn*, warriors drawn from the militarised Gaelic kindreds of the western Highlands and Islands.[148] To safeguard the interests of the Church of Moray from these *ceatharn*, the bishop entered an agreement with Alexander Stewart which placed his property and tenants under the protection of Stewart and his men.[149] It may have seemed like a pact with the devil, but for Bishop Bur the agreement offered some security in increasingly uncertain times.

That uncertainty increased greatly in February 1371 when the childless David II died and his nephew ascended the throne as King Robert II. The new king had moved swiftly to establish his son Alexander formally in the lordship of Badenoch and by March 1372 had also ended the long dispute over the succession to the earldom of Moray by granting the mainly lowland districts of the earldom centred on Elgin, Forres, Nairn and Inverness to John Dunbar, younger brother of George, earl of March.[150] Shorn of the protection which his close relationship with David II had afforded, Bur found himself swiftly drawn into dispute with both Stewart and Dunbar and left isolated and friendless in the new political landscape of early Stewart Scotland. By the late 1380s the conflict was reaching crisis point, with Dunbar's men withholding payment of rents due to the Church of Moray, obstructing teind collection, grazing their livestock on episcopal pasture land and seizing the bishop's property and goods; Dunbar chaplains were even flouting Bur's bans on men against whom he had pronounced interdict and excommunication for their assaults on the bishopric's interests.[151]

In parallel with the deteriorating relationship with Earl John, matters had gone rapidly from bad to worse with Alexander Stewart, who had by then acquired the title of earl of Buchan. Bur had attempted to find legal remedies for his dispute with Stewart, but had eventually sought to sweeten him with the lease to him in April 1383 of the valuable episcopal estate of Rothiemurchus.[152] It resolved nothing, for by February 1387 Bur was complaining that Alexander's men were occupying episcopal estates, withholding rents – including the £8 due annually from Rothiemurchus, part of which had been assigned by Bishop Andrew Murray towards the lights of the cathedral[153] – and were uplifting the teinds payable to the bishopric of Moray from royal law courts in the north of the kingdom for their own uses.[154] With Alexander also in control of those same courts, Bur lacked any forum in which he could mount a legal defence of his rights and, in an effort to at least control the inroads being made into his possessions, chose to grant Alexander the lease of another episcopal property, the lands of Abriachan on the west side of Loch Ness.[155] Having antagonised the two most powerful lay lords within his diocese, Bur lacked the effective support of a politically influential lay patron who could either advance his interests in the royal council or offer him the protection of genuine military strength; his bishopric, consequently, was being plundered almost without challenge.

In December 1388, a glimmer of light appeared in this gloom when the ageing Robert II's politically adept second son, Robert, earl of Fife, staged a *coup d'état* which gave him effective control of the government of Scotland. Bitter rivalry between Fife and his elder brother, John, earl of Carrick, and their younger sibling, Alexander, had characterised their exercise of lordship through the 1380s and, as lieutenant for his father, Fife was determined to dismantle the power bases which his brothers had assembled for themselves. Alexander in particular was on the receiving end of Fife's attack, for Robert had ambitions of his own to build a great lordship for his son Murdac in the Highlands. To achieve that, however, he needed allies in the region, and Bur was quick to seize this opportunity. Fife moved rapidly to construct a new axis of power in Moray and formed a coalition with both Bur and Dunbar between whom in October 1389 he had brokered a settlement.[156] On 2 November 1389, Bur gave a powerful signal of his new alignment when he and Bishop Kilwhiss of Ross – another Fife associate – presided over an ecclesiastical court at Inverness to pass judgement on Alexander's marital relationship with his estranged wife, Euphemia, countess of Ross. Ostensibly a spiritual and matrimonial issue, the court's actions really amounted to an assault on Alexander's lordship and formed part of a concerted attack on him which used his wrongs committed against his abandoned wife as a tool to undermine him.[157] Alexander appeared to have been humbled and in demonstration of how sure he was that Alexander's power had been broken, in February 1390 Bur ended his agreement with him for the protection of episcopal property and entered into a new indenture with Thomas Dunbar, sheriff of Inverness, the son of John, earl of Moray.[158] Made for the protection of episcopal property and tenants 'against all malefactors, caterans [*ceatharn*] and others of whatever status and condition', it was clearly directed against Alexander. The new confidence of Bur and the Dunbars, however, quickly turned sour, as the later rubric which was inserted in the register of the diocese to describe the agreement shows: 'that useless and damnable provision for the lands and teinds of the church of Moray from which followed their final destruction'.

The confidence of February 1390 dissolved in the explosive backlash which Alexander released on the Moray lowlands in May and June of that year. Far from being the blindly violent acts of a man whose only response to political challenges was atrocity and terrorism, what followed were violent but calculated assaults on the property of the men who had united against him; the supporters of Robert, earl

of Fife, but especially John and Thomas Dunbar and Bishop Bur.[159] He was further spurred into action by the need to try to recover some ground in the period of uncertainty which followed his father's death on 19 April 1390, particularly once it became clear that Fife would continue to control the reins of power as lieutenant for their invalid elder brother Carrick, who now became King Robert III. With his enemies' attention focused elsewhere, towards the end of May Alexander's men were beginning to raid into lowland Moray. Their first significant target was Forres, a possession of the earl of Moray and within sight of his residence at Darnaway Castle, but the location also of the church which was the prebend of the archdeacon of Moray – the cleric who had direct oversight of Alexander's marital conduct – and the archdeacon's rural manse.[160] The symbolism of the attack on these targets would have been obvious to all observers, but it would also have provided a shocking warning of the inability of the Dunbars to protect their own property, let alone that of the Church of Moray, as the three-month-old indenture with Bur promised. It was, however, a mere foretaste of what was to come.

On 17 June 1390, Alexander's men poured into Elgin and began to plunder and burn a series of specific properties and buildings. The town was theoretically the chief place of the earldom of Moray and one of the greatest financial assets in John Dunbar's control; its sacking was a personal humiliation and a crippling economic blow. Its parish church was annexed to the episcopal *mensa* and one of the biggest sources of Bur's personal income; its burning was a direct assault on the bishop's resources. The almshouse of the Maison Dieu on the eastern edge of the burgh had been founded by Bur's predecessor Bishop Andrew Murray in the 1230s and the office of Master of the Hospital was in Bur's gift, although in 1390 Alexander Dunbar, younger son of Earl John, had been intruded by his father.[161] Its destruction was a blow to the prestige and the resources of both bishop and earl. The greatest and the most shocking casualties, however, were the cathedral and eighteen of the manses of its canons and chaplains in its surrounding chanonry, which were ransacked and given to the flames. As the cathedral's brief chronicle account records it: 'and what is more bitterly to be grieved, the noble and beautiful Church of Moray, the wonder of the land and ornament of the realm, with all the books, charters and other goods of the land stored therein, were burned'.[162] There may be a certain grim irony intended in the burning of the cathedral given that one of Bur's complaints against Alexander was that he was withholding the rents from Rothiemurchus which had been assigned by Bishop Andrew Murray to the lighting of the Church of Moray.[163]

It had been intended as a demonstration of his power,

but Alexander's attack on Elgin backfired spectacularly. Rather than winning him political support it earned him universal revulsion, for such violence against the Church was still regarded as a heinous act and an offence against God. Excommunicated and politically untouchable, Alexander performed humble penance in the street outside the door of the Dominican friary in Perth and again at its high altar, and swiftly submitted to terms imposed on him by Bishop Walter Traill of St Andrews.[164] Alongside spiritual penance he also promised to make financial satisfaction to Bur, but the bishop evidently deemed the promised money insufficient as reparations. He appealed to Robert III to raise a general tax to cover costs, but the king demurred. Instead, the king issued letters ordering his brother and Earl John not to enter the castle of Spynie, and freeing Bur from any financial obligation to the Dunbars under the terms of the February 1390 indenture, which they had so clearly failed to honour.[165] A second appeal on 2 December 1390 brought a little more success; a grant of £20 annually from royal revenues, but this was suspended on Bur's death in 1397.[166] Pope Clement VII offered additional hope, assigning the fruits of all vacant benefices in the see of St Andrews towards rebuilding costs at Elgin, but this was an unpredictable and irregular source of funding.[167] By early 1391, as Bur and his canons began to piece together the fragments of their records – absolutely essential to them for their struggle to gather and organise the diocesan finances[168] – it was clear to them that the costs of reconstruction were going to fall largely on the clergy and people of Moray.

Instead of promising brighter days ahead, Alexander Stewart's humbling and the rapid contraction of his power in the Highlands between August 1390 and December 1392 added to Bur's woes. Into the vacuum left by Alexander stepped Alexander MacDonald, lord of the Isles, who was allied with Fife. MacDonald ambitions were set firmly on expansion and the owners of land in Lochaber, Badenoch and the Moray lowlands soon found that one predatory neighbour had simply been replaced with another; by September 1394 Thomas Dunbar had entered an indenture of protection for seven years for the lands of regality of Moray with the lord of the Isles.[169] Bur joined Dunbar in the indenture, which extended its protection to church property at further cost to the episcopal purse. MacDonald, however, seems to have done little to enforce his peace and protection; through the 1390s the bishop was powerless to prevent the continued wasting of his lands in the central Highlands and Great Glen. It was a sad end to a career which had started with such high hopes of a restoration of the golden age of power and prestige which the bishops of Moray had enjoyed in the thirteenth century, where the bishops had been the close allies of the Crown in maintaining law and order throughout their diocese. As a creature of David II, Bur's star was already in decline before the king's death in 1371 and was to remain overshadowed by the new Stewart king's promotion of his own candidates for regional authority. Bur had been regularly successful in securing parchment victories which confirmed the jurisdictional powers which had given his predecessors great authority in the past, but in the changed world of the late fourteenth century he lacked the means to exercise that jurisdiction effectively. Isolated amidst political rivals locally, and rapacious and predatory neighbours, he had presided over an era of decline in the prestige of his office which reached its symbolic culmination in the burning of his cathedral. It had been an uneven struggle for over twenty years and its spectacular climax in June 1390 seems finally to have broken him. From the thrusting and ambitious clerk who had set about the recovery of his diocesan liberties with energy and zeal, Bur was at the end of his episcopate truly the tired and dispirited failure he described in his own letter to King Robert, 'sick, old and impoverished'.[170] On 15 May 1397, with work barely begun on the restoration of his cathedral, he died in his castle of Spynie.[171] He is said to have been buried in the choir of the cathedral.[172]

William Spynie, 1397–1406

For the first time since David Murray, the new bishop, if his name is anything to go by, was a local man. He was also, it would appear from what can be pieced together of his career before he became bishop, already extremely elderly by the standards of his day and may have been born around the year that Murray died![173] Between the 1350s and early 1370s he spent most of his time in France, first studying at the University of Paris and then teaching there. During part of this period his studies were supported on the fruits of benefices in St Andrews and Dunkeld dioceses, but by 1362 he had gained the canonry and prebend of Advie and Cromdale in Moray, which he held together with the parsonage of Dunnottar in St Andrews diocese.[174] Opportunities for advancement in the church of Aberdeen were not followed up, presumably because of the prospect of similar opportunities at home in Moray. Soon after May 1372 he had advanced to the office of precentor of Moray, in which he received papal confirmation by September 1373;[175] other canonries and prebends in the churches of Orkney and Caithness followed by the mid-1370s. In 1387, he resigned most of these positions on his elevation to the deanery of Aberdeen, but retained the precentorship of Moray and a canonry of Ross.[176]

On the death of Bishop Bur in May 1397, Spynie, although already in his seventies, was elected by the chapter of Moray. He travelled to Avignon with fellow canon John

Innes to secure papal confirmation of his election and was subsequently to reward Innes for his efforts to that end.[177] Granted papal provision on 1 September 1397, Spynie was consecrated at Avignon by Pope Benedict XIII on 16 September.[178] Letters from the pope to King Robert III on 28 September announced his provision and consecration, requesting that the king admit him peaceably to the Church of Moray, and aid him in the recovery of the spiritual rights of that church;[179] Spynie, it seems, had taken the opportunity to let Benedict know of the continuing tribulations of his see. On 16 January 1398, Robert III issued instructions at Linlithgow to the sheriffs of Inverness and Banff to admit Spynie to the temporalities of his see and to cease any interference in the lands and finances of the bishopric.[180] It took a second letter from Robert on 3 May 1398 directed to his younger brother, Alexander, earl of Buchan, to secure the delivery of the castle of Spynie to the new bishop.[181] It must have been especially galling for Spynie and the canons of Moray that the man responsible for the burning of their cathedral and manses had been given control of the greatest symbol of the temporal power of the bishops of Moray during the vacancy after Bur's death.

It is probable that the chapter at Elgin had turned to Spynie as an experienced, well-connected and highly skilled pair of hands to guide their church through a period of extreme uncertainty. Certainly, he may have been the leading figure in the petition to Avignon and the subsequent legal processes which were intended to help the chapter reconstruct its registers, which had been burned in the destruction of the cathedral in June 1390. References in material in the existing manuscript versions of the register specifically attribute the compilation of part of the work to Spynie.[182] This view of Spynie as a skilled legal investigator is supported by the fact that throughout the 1380s he appears to have acquired a reputation as a canon lawyer of some distinction and had already experience of litigation with some of the see's greater lay opponents, including Buchan.[183] Indeed, he had been one of the tribunal at Inverness in November 1389 where Bur and Kilwhiss had ordered Buchan to put aside his mistress and return to his lawful wife. It has been commented that he was inextricably bound up in the events which led to the burning of the cathedral and he may have contributed significantly to the sense of grievance which Buchan held against Bur and the leading clergy of Moray diocese. As bishop, putting right the damage that Buchan had inflicted became his driving purpose and most of his acts show him striving to recover fiscal and juridical rights that would benefit his church, and opposing claims that would further injure it. His zeal in going about that task may have disconcerted his chapter, for in August 1400 he gave a response to what seems to have been an effort on

their part to limit their own financial responsibility for the rebuilding costs.[184] Indeed, electing a skilled canon lawyer seems here to have rebounded on the canons, who could mount no sound opposition to his case. Spynie's impositions on the prebendaries seem to have continued under his successor, John Innes, and clearly rankled with the members of the chapter who succeeded in the 1420s in imposing limits on the bishop's interference in their revenues (see page 41).

How far the task of rebuilding had advanced by 1402 is unknown, but in that year Elgin suffered from another devastating raid. On that occasion the perpetrator was Alexander MacDonald, third son of Donald, lord of the Isles.[185] The brief chronicle account of this event records that on 3 July 1402 Alexander and his captains had violently entered the chanonry of Moray and 'plundered it totally of all the goods found in it', burning also a large part of the burgh before withdrawing to their own territory. Spynie, however, did not simply bow to this insult and defiance but pronounced sentence of excommunication against him. The result was that on 6 October Alexander returned to Elgin and, after humble submission to the bishop, was absolved of his crimes first 'before the doors of the church … and afterwards before the high altar'. Despite his age, Spynie was evidently more than capable of meeting such challenges to his authority and to the privileges of his church head on, and winning. A great pastor of his church and defender of its rights to the end, he died in the chanonry at Elgin on 2 August 1406 and was, apparently, buried in the choir of the cathedral.[186]

John Innes, 1407–1414

Spynie's successor was another local man, John Innes, a member of the family of Innes of that ilk which took its name from the lands of Innes in Urquhart parish and which was also descended from one of Moray's twelfth-century Flemish colonisers.[187] He was clearly marked out for a high-profile career in the church and by 1396 when Bishop Bur granted him a teind of the issues of the eyres (itinerant judicial hearings) and courts of the bishop of Moray towards the costs of his studies in canon law at Paris he was already archdeacon of Caithness and a canon of Moray.[188] He was certainly in possession of a canonry of Moray by February 1390 when he witnessed the indenture with Thomas Dunbar for the protection of the property of the Church of Moray, but had an interest in the prebend of Duffus from soon after 1395.[189] A close associate of William Spynie, he accompanied him to Avignon in 1397 when securing papal confirmation of Spynie's election and his consecration as bishop, and in return Spynie confirmed his possession of Duffus over his rival for the prebend.[190] His elevation within the Church continued and sometime after May 1399 he secured the deanship of Ross, an office which he retained until his election to the bishopric of Moray.

Like his predecessor, Innes was consecrated at 'Avignon' (probably in fact Marseilles, where the papal court was then based) by Benedict XIII.[191] After the busy evidence for his earlier career, his time as bishop has left little trace in the written records of the diocese. Indeed, he appears only once as a witness to a charter, issued at Perth in 1408 by Robert, duke of Albany.[192] Elgin tradition, however, assigned him an important role in the continuing rebuilding efforts at the fire-damaged cathedral, identifying him as the builder of the great central tower over the crossing. This suggestion is perhaps borne out by the ringing claims which were apparently made for him in the inscriptions on his tomb which identified him as builder of 'this notable work' and that 'for seven years he strongly built and diligently continued' construction efforts.[193] The agreement made in the chapter which gathered in May 1414 to elect his successor, however, suggests that the means he used to raise revenue from his diocesan clergy to pay for the building work had led to conflict. If one of the canons was elected, that canon was to swear to devote one-third of his episcopal income to the building work until it was completed, to in no way diminish the privileges of his canons, to refrain from any interference in the common churches of the resident canons, and to cease from impeding the prebendaries in burying their parishioners at their prebendal churches.[194] To modern eyes these might seem fairly innocuous points, but each one was clearly linked to matters of finance; Innes, it seems, had been attempting to get the canons and prebendaries of the cathedral to pay a higher share of the rebuilding costs than they felt was their due. On 25 April 1414, Innes died in the chanonry at Elgin.[195] His tomb was described by Robert Keith in the early eighteenth century as built 'at the foot of the north-west pillar that supported the great tower or third steeple now fallen';[196] the damaged effigy of a kneeling bishop now placed in the south-eastern nave chapel is believed to have come from his monument.[197]

Henry Lichton, 1415–1421

A kinsman of Robert, duke of Albany, Henry Lichton could count on powerful support for his elevation in the church.[198] University-educated, he was a skilled lawyer and accomplished scholar destined for high office in Crown service or a senior ecclesiastical appointment. He had secured his first benefice, a vicarage in the diocese of St Andrews, by 1392, but progressed to a more lucrative one in Aberdeen diocese within a few years.[199] At Aberdeen he had been provided to a canonry with expectation of one of the prebends in the cathedral and, on the death of the poet John Barbour, succeeded him as archdeacon.

The promotion, however, was challenged and, following litigation, he appears to have given up his claim on the office whilst retaining his canonry. Possibly as compensation for resigning any claim to the archdeaconry, he received the rich rectory of Kinkell in Aberdeen diocese and in the next few years had also added the canonry and prebend of Inverkeithny in Moray diocese and the mastership of the hospital of Rathven.[200] As a canon and prebendary of Moray he was present on 18 May 1414 at the chapter which had gathered for the election of Bishop Innes's successor, where it had been agreed that if one of the chapter was successful in securing election, he would promise to assign one-third of his revenues annually to the task of completing the repairs to the cathedral until the work was finished.[201] It appears to have been Lichton who secured election, for it was he who travelled to the curia – by then driven from Avignon and based at Valencia in Pope Benedict XIII's native Aragon – to gain papal provision before 4 March 1415.[202] Lichton sought consecration at Benedict's hands, which he obtained on 8 March.[203]

By March 1415, the Great Schism was entering its closing stages and Benedict used Lichton as an envoy to Albany to discuss the current negotiations for ending the split in the Church. A memorandum outlining Benedict's instructions to him has survived, but his responses – if any – have not.[204] On his return to Scotland he very much fades from view, possibly engaged busily in his duties in Moray;[205] he attended a general council of the nobility, clergy and burgesses at Perth in March 1416, but only sent an agent to the next provincial council of the Scottish Church in 1420.[206] If Lichton adhered to the 1414 agreement with his fellow canons, then much of his efforts would have been directed towards the rebuilding of the cathedral. It was, however, not to be he who saw the protracted reconstruction brought to its conclusion. Probably in March 1422 Lichton was postulated bishop of Aberdeen by the chapter there and was translated to Aberdeen in early April.[207]

Columba Dunbar, 1422–1435

Lichton's successor at Elgin was Columba Dunbar, third son of George, earl of March, and, therefore, a cousin of the Dunbar earls of Moray and a kinsman of King James I.[208] During his family's exile in England, which arose from their anger at King Robert III setting aside his promise that March's daughter would marry David, duke of Rothesay, the heir to the throne, Columba had been educated at Oxford. Marked out young for an ecclesiastical career, it seemed at first that he would find that career in England and by 1403 he had been awarded a benefice in Shropshire by King Henry IV.[209] He may have returned to Scotland with his family in 1408 and, in 1412, accused earlier of having severely dilapidated his English benefice, he was deprived of his charge. By then, however, he was already holding the deanery of his family foundation, the collegiate church of Dunbar, and over the next decade built up an extensive portfolio of benefices. Most of these were in the East Lothian and Berwickshire heartland of his family's influence, but in 1415 he was granted provision to the mastership of the hospital of Rathven in Aberdeen diocese, providing him with his first northern connection.[210]

On 3 April 1422, he was provided to the see of Moray, which was newly vacant following Lichton's translation to Aberdeen, and on 5 April he was named as bishop-elect.[211] Unlike his predecessors, he did not travel in person to the curia to have his election confirmed and to receive consecration, sending instead a proctor. Although he had received authority on 15 December 1422 to be consecrated by any bishop, he was still unconsecrated on 12 February 1423, but had been consecrated by 10 October when he first appears styled as bishop as a witness to one of his brother's charters.[212]

Little evidence survives for Bishop Dunbar's activity within his see, most material relating to him being more concerned with his role in royal diplomatic activity. It is thought that he may have been the bishop who brought the rebuilding work on the western limb of the church to completion, for what is thought to be his coat-of-arms is located on the west gable above the great west window.[213] Dunbar died in the castle at Spynie before 7 November 1435 when his successor is named as bishop-elect.[214] It was said in the early eighteenth century that he was buried in the chapel of St Thomas the Martyr, which modern accounts have identified as being in the north transept,[215] an identification that seemed to be supported by the presence in that transept of three lay members of the Dunbar family.[216] As discussed below, however, it is probable that St Thomas's chapel lay on the south side of the church, possibly in the south-eastern section of the nave south aisle (see page 113).

John Winchester, 1436–1460

Dunbar's successor was a man who boasted strong ties with the royal household and who almost definitely owed his promotion to King James I. An Englishman and graduate who had come north in the retinue of the freed king and his English wife, Joan Beaufort (who was the niece of Henry Beaufort, bishop of Winchester), Winchester's career in Scotland was made in royal service; he had a rapid rise, appointed by February 1425 as vicar of the church of Alyth and then chancellor of the see of Dunkeld, and he appears as a witness to the king's charters almost from the start of the reign.[217] Although he was appointed around 1434 to the provostship of the Black Douglases' well-endowed and

much-prized collegiate church of Lincluden in Galloway, that appointment was secured through James I's influence.[218] Amongst those benefices gained was a prebend in the Church of Moray and the deanery of Aberdeen, but it was as a canon of Moray that towards the end of 1432 Winchester incorporated himself as an individual in the Council of Basel.[219] It is unlikely that he had travelled to Switzerland on his own initiative to observe the workings of this gathering of leading churchmen who were coming rapidly into conflict with the pope; on 15 December he was described as in the king's service, suggesting his presence at this great reforming council was as a political observer on behalf of James I.

In the last years of James I's reign, Winchester was one of a group of ecclesiastics who were regularly in attendance on the king and provided him with counsel.[220] A regular witness to the king's charters, he was a man who spent much time close to the inner workings of royal government.[221] The opportunity to give a proper reward for his long and loyal service to James came in 1436 when the see in which he held a canonry fell vacant. It is likely that his fellow canons may have seen the wisdom in electing a man who enjoyed a close relationship with the king, so James may have needed to give them little encouragement. Unlike several of his predecessors, he did not travel to Rome in person to seek confirmation of his election, possibly because of his past association with the Council of Basel, but his election was confirmed by the pope at Easter 1436. Winchester was consecrated as bishop at Cambuskenneth Abbey near Stirling on the Feast of the Ascension (9 May) 1437.

Following the assassination of James I at Perth on 21 February 1437, Winchester emerged as an important political figure in the factional manoeuvring for control of government during the minority of the young King James II. He remained close to Queen Joan and was one of her small group of supporters who, on 4 September 1439, put his seal to the 'appointment' forced on her at Stirling by the Livingstons, who had custody of the young King James II,[222] and remained a frequent witness to Crown charters and regular attender of parliament.[223] He was, nevertheless, courted by the Douglases, the most powerful of the political players in the minority years, who were building up their power in the northern part of the kingdom in the 1440s; James, seventh earl of Douglas, secured provision of the precentorship of Moray for his son, also called James, who was at the same time provided to the diocese of Aberdeen.[224] In 1445, William, eighth earl of Douglas, also succeeded in having his younger brothers Archibald and Hugh created earls of Moray and Ormond (named after the former castle of the Murrays near Avoch in the Black Isle) respectively;[225] Winchester had two powerful new neighbours. Both brothers courted Winchester and made gifts to the Church of Moray,[226] but the bishop retained his close allegiance to the Crown rather than becoming identified with the Douglas power base.

This closeness to the Crown brought further rewards. On 24 July 1451, King James II erected the township of Spynie into a free burgh in barony under the lordship of the bishops of Moray.[227] This grant enabled the bishop to establish a market in the township that had grown up beside his castle and gave rights to buy, sell and trade to its inhabitants, chiefly to trade in fish, brewed ale, and meat. The market was to be held weekly on Wednesdays and the burgesses of Spynie were also given the right to hold a fair annually on the Feast of the Holy Trinity. Because there is no town nowadays at Spynie it might seem that this was an insignificant gift, but it represented a major concession to Bishop Winchester for it cut into the overarching rights of the burgesses of Elgin and their monopoly over trade in the district. It also reflected the ambitions of the bishop, for the growth of a market town at Spynie would have given a significant new source of income to the see in the form of rents, teinds and tolls. In 1451, Winchester also obtained royal confirmation of a grant which James I had made to Bishop Dunbar of a property in Inverness High Street which had fallen to the Crown as part of the personal lands of Alexander Stewart, earl of Mar, bastard son of Alexander Stewart, earl of Buchan.[228] Around the same time, the bishop appears to have secured from the king an exemption for himself and his clergy, their lands and their tenants, from the jurisdictions of the earls of Huntly, Moray and Ross.[229]

Winchester's greatest achievement was in securing the erection of the lands of the Church of Moray into a free barony in 1451,[230] a privilege which his predecessors had sought for over a century. This grant freed his episcopal lands from the political interference of some of the greatest regional magnates, including the three younger members of the Black Douglas family who held northern lordships, Archibald, earl of Moray, Hugh, earl of Ormond, and John, lord Balvenie. Winchester in return was to be a loyal agent of James II after the king had overthrown Douglas power in 1455, in consolidating royal authority in the formerly Black Douglas-held lands in the earldoms of Moray and Ormond. In 1457–9, as king's master of works he oversaw repairs to the castle at Inverness which had been taken back into the king's hands following the forfeiture of the Douglas brothers.[231] His close relationship with the Crown, and his reliability in return as a royal servant, had smoothed a path through the political turbulence at the end of the reign of James I and during the minority of his son, and again through the upheavals of the 1450s. He left the bishopric in a more secure condition than any of his predecessors since John Pilmuir.

Winchester died on 22 April 1460, probably at Spynie, and was said by Keith in the early eighteenth century to have been buried in St Mary's aisle in the cathedral.[232] His tomb there survives to the north of the position of the altar to St Mary in the chapel – the position of greatest honour and spiritual benefit as it became almost directly a part of masses and other services performed there – identified by the inscription '*hic iacet recolende memoᵉ johanes Winnechestair dns epus moravien: q obit xxii die me Apl Anno dni Mᵒcccclx*' (here lies of honourable memory John Winchester lord bishop of Moray: who died the twenty-second day of the month of April the Year of the Lord 1460).[233]

James Stewart, 1460–1462

As dean of Moray and treasurer of Scotland, James Stewart was provided to the bishopric of Moray on 19 May 1460 (Illus 2.5). His two-year episcopate has left almost no trace in the diocesan records beyond his presence at a convocation of the diocesan clergy held on 12 December 1460 and continued to 12 April 1461.[234] He resigned from his see in favour of his younger brother and successor on 21 June 1462 in the papal curia. His effective disappearance from the records after that date might suggest that he resigned through ill health which prevented him from taking part in any active public life subsequently. As a former bishop of Moray, however, on his death in August 1466[235] he was brought for burial in his church at Elgin. In the early eighteenth century it was said that his tomb was in St Peter and St Paul's aisle on the north side of the cathedral.[236] The identification of the dedication of the altars where he was buried may well be correct, but Keith, who made that statement, was wrong in locating the chapel on the north side of the church for the tomb recess bearing what are probably his arms is the eastern of the two monuments in the south wall of the south transept.[237]

2.5 Seal of James Stewart (Historic Scotland © Crown Copyright)

David Stewart, 1462–1476

The younger brother of his predecessor, Bishop David Stewart has left few records of his time as bishop of Moray (Illus 2.6). He was provided to the see before 30 June 1462 by Pope Pius II, apparently when he was present personally at Rome, and was consecrated before December 1463.[238] There is little evidence for any particular closeness between Stewart and his royal kinsman; his appearance as a witness to charters issued in the name of the young King James III occurred entirely at Inverness and Elgin on a royal progress through the north in August 1464.[239] Given the circumstances of this event it would have been more remarkable had he not been present when the young king was brought on this northern circuit. His sole surviving other appearance as a witness to a royal charter occurred at Edinburgh in 1469.[240] He attended only three parliaments – in 1467, 1469 and 1471 – and appears to have neither sought nor held high political office in royal service.[241] The impression gained from this is that Stewart spent the majority of his time active within his see, but that impression is not supported by any great volume of evidence surviving for that within Moray.

Still alive on 18 July 1475, he died some time in 1476.[242] According to Robert Keith's early eighteenth-century account, Bishop David Stewart was also buried in the aisle of St Peter and St Paul 'on the north side of the cathedral'.[243] As with James Stewart, Keith has managed to get his orientation 180 degrees wrong, for the Stewart arms on the western of the two recessed tombs in the south wall of the south transept is almost certainly his.[244]

William Tulloch, 1477–1482

Tulloch was a career civil servant in royal service, rising to the office of keeper of the privy seal.[245] He gained his first significant office in the Church when his kinsman, Thomas Tulloch, bishop of Orkney, secured him a canonry of the see of Orkney, and in December 1461 he was provided to the bishopric by the pope on Bishop Thomas's resignation. An able diplomat and well connected at the Danish court through his position as bishop of Orkney (which was then still part of the Scandinavian archdiocese of Trondheim),[246] he was one of the Scottish ambassadors sent in August 1468 to negotiate the marriage of King James III to Princess Margaret of Denmark; a deal was settled by 8 September which resulted in Orkney and Shetland ultimately passing to Scottish control as security for payment of the promised 60,000 Rhenish florins dowry for the princess.[247] Through the 1470s, Tulloch continued to act as a diplomat on behalf of King James III, mainly involved in the young king's efforts to secure a treaty with England to end the nearly two centuries of hostility between the kingdoms.[248] This loyal service to the Crown was rewarded with higher office in the government of James III, including a tack or lease of the newly acquired royal lands in Orkney,[249] in 1470 appointment to the important keepership of the Privy Seal, a post which he retained until about 1481, and finally in 1477 with his translation to the much richer see of Moray. According to Keith, he was buried in St Mary's aisle, possibly in the tomb recess in the north wall of the aisle two bays west of Bishop John Winchester's tomb; the effigy there, however, is from a much older monument – possibly that of Bishop John Pilmuir – and has presumably been relocated here.[250]

Andrew Stewart, 1482–1501

The youngest son of Queen Joan Beaufort, widow of King James I, by her second marriage to James Stewart of Lorne, Andrew Stewart and his elder brothers John, earl of Atholl, and James, earl of Buchan, were to emerge as major political figures in the reign of their nephew, James III. Elected and provided to Moray soon after Tulloch's death, Andrew, with his brother's backing, had far greater ambitions. Probably with his eyes on a greater prize, he was not immediately consecrated and was to remain only bishop-elect until some time between 22 December 1485 (when he last appears as elect) and 24 October 1487 (when he first appears as bishop) (Illus 2.7). During the political crisis of 1482–3 in which James III was almost toppled from his throne in favour of his younger brother Alexander, duke of Albany, and for a time was effectively a prisoner of his uncle Atholl in Edinburgh Castle, all parties manoeuvred to buy power or sell support. Atholl, Buchan and the bishop-elect had a high price; Andrew, who had been made keeper of the privy

2.6   Seal of David Stewart (Historic Scotland © Crown Copyright)

seal by 25 August 1482,[251] was to become archbishop of St Andrews. The incumbent archbishop, William Scheves, was steadfastly loyal to James III, but was persuaded by the imprisoned king to start the process of appointing procurators to resign his see. Indeed, by November 1482 the plan was so far advanced that a pledge of 6,000 gold ducats had been obtained from the burgesses of Edinburgh to pay for the expenses involved in securing Andrew's provision at the curia; this sum would be repaid by the brothers and their allies if the stratagem were successful. By early 1483 it was clear that they had failed; Albany's grip on his brother and on government had slipped, James had regained the initiative and resumed his full powers as king, and his uncles were pushed from power.[252]

2.7   The arms of Andrew Stewart, as carved on the pier in the chapter house (Historic Scotland © Crown Copyright)

There was clearly little love lost between Andrew Stewart and Archbishop Scheves, who had probably much enjoyed the reversal of fortunes which James III's uncles suffered in 1483. Indeed, it is probable that he used his power as metropolitan archbishop and papal legate to interfere in the internal business of his suffragan bishop Andrew's diocese. Andrew's hostility to Scheves was such that once he and his brothers had regained favour with James he became increasingly unresponsive to the archbishop's efforts to impose his authority over his nominal suffragans.

In April 1488, Andrew gained an official exemption from Pope Innocent VIII for himself and his diocese from the metropolitan authority of the archbishop of St Andrews.[253] As a loyal agent of James III, however, Scheves suffered further political eclipse when the king was overthrown and killed in 1488; the new king, James IV, showed much greater favour to his great-uncle. When a second Scottish archdiocese was created for Robert Blackadder of Glasgow in 1492, to which the sees of Argyll, Dunblane, Dunkeld and Galloway were attached as suffragans, Andrew and the see of Moray remained exempt from the metropolitan supremacy of both Blackadder and Scheves, whose truncated archdiocese embraced only Orkney, Caithness, Ross, Aberdeen and Brechin in addition to St Andrews itself.

As for Andrew himself, after a brief period of exclusion from the circle of power around his nephew James III after the king regained the initiative in 1483, by the end of the reign he was riding high in royal favour. It was as part of a strong group of royal supporters that he attended James at Aberdeen and, while there on 16 April, received a royal confirmation of the grant made by James II to Bishop Winchester of a regality jurisdiction for the episcopal lands, taking the blench ferme payment of one red rose annually delivered at Inverness.[254] He was close in his nephew's council and, with his elder brother James, earl of Buchan, was one of the leading figures who had attempted to negotiate with Henry VII of England for an invasion of Scotland to support the king against his enemies.[255] The bishop accompanied James III south and was with him at Blackness Castle on the Firth of Forth in early May 1488 when the king outmanoeuvred the rebel force led nominally by his own heir and so reached Edinburgh.[256] It is not known for certain but it is likely that Andrew accompanied his nephew west to Stirling in June and was perhaps present at the Battle of Sauchieburn on 11 June which ended in the king's death, but it is also possible that he was still absent in the delegation sent to court English support.[257]

Having for the second time found himself on the losing side in a civil conflict, Bishop Andrew was probably well prepared for the political disgrace and disfavour which were bound to follow. Signs of that disfavour came within four months in parliament on 17 October 1488, when legislation specifically to overturn attempts by Bishop Andrew to unite or annex benefices in his diocese was passed, requiring that any unions made were to be dissolved and the subjects returned to their previous state.[258] This was punitive legislation and suggests that Bishop Andrew was viewed with deep suspicion by the new regime, which was to pursue him and his brother Buchan for what was considered treasonable conspiracy to induce an English invasion of Scotland. In early January 1489, the new regime that controlled the young King James IV attempted to bring Bishop Andrew to heel and summoned him to account for his actions in 1488, but he simply defied them and remained in the north.[259] A consequence of that disfavour is that the bishop may have spent more time in his see and in May 1489 he presided over a general convocation of the canons of the cathedral which passed a raft of reforming legislation concerning the cathedral and its resident and non-resident clergy.[260] Amidst this preoccupation with ecclesiastical administration, a rebellion seethed up in the north-east against the narrow clique of nobles around James IV, many of whom were felt to have been complicit in the killing of James III. The young king and his regime may have suspected that his great-uncles Atholl and Bishop Andrew were sympathetic to the rebels, but there is no evidence that either man did anything to support the rising; neither, however, did they come out against it. Their brother Buchan, however, played his familiar duplicitous role, initially making noises in support of the government while conducting treasonable negotiations with Henry VII of England.[261]

Andrew remained out of favour with the new regime and in 1496 was reported to be involved in a conspiracy to depose James IV in favour of his younger brother, James, duke of Ross.[262] How real his involvement in the scheme was we can only conjecture, for our evidence for it comes from letters written by one of James III's embittered familiars who constructed increasingly complex and fanciful plans to secure some kind of revenge against the men who had slain his lord. In favour of his involvement, however, is the fact that the hugely ambitious Andrew had been completely sidelined from political influence for nearly a decade. The bishop's role was to keep his younger great-nephew from joining the army which his elder brother was preparing to lead into England in support of the Yorkist pretender to the English throne, the imposter Perkin Warbeck. The plan, however, came to nothing and there is no sign that the bishop had any direct contact with or influence over the young duke of Ross. It is nevertheless perhaps significant that in summer 1497, when Henry VII of England proposed a royal meeting and peace negotiations, the men whom he suggested should be sent as Scottish ambassadors included Andrew, bishop of Moray.[263] Here, he was probably safe to assume, was a man inclined to be relatively more well-disposed towards England than he was to his own king.

For the last years of his life Andrew Stewart remained a somewhat remote and isolated figure. Any hopes that he might see his dreams of securing the archbishopric he had so clearly coveted in 1482–3 had been dashed finally in January 1497 when Archbishop Scheves died.[264] Passed over by the king in favour of the young James, duke of Ross, who was persuaded to accept that his future lay in being

the greatest prelate in the realm, Bishop Andrew seems to have withdrawn to his diocese for most of the final four years of his life. Keith, in his historical account of the Scottish bishops, identifies his burial place as in the choir of the cathedral.[265] No monument that can be identified as his with any certainty survives in the eastern limb of the cathedral, although the 'blue marble' slab which Keith identified as Bishop Andrew Murray's, and which is of a ledger form with inset for a brass – a style more favoured in the later Middle Ages – may in fact be Andrew Stewart's, the misidentification possibly arising from their shared first names.[266] An alternative and more attractive suggestion for the tomb of a kinsman of the king is the now sadly ruined monument inserted into the opening between the choir and the north choir aisle, directly opposite the entrance to the chapter house which Bishop Andrew Stewart had restored; the link between tomb and chapter house is perhaps compelling support for this identification.[267]

Andrew Forman, 1501–1514

A skilled administrator and royal servant, Andrew Forman expected to rise rapidly in the Church as a reward for his services to the Crown which extended back to around 1489 (Illus 2.8).[268] He worked hard for his reward; in 1496, James set him in place as 'minder' of Perkin Warbeck, the Flemish imposter who was claiming to be Richard, duke of York, younger of the two vanished sons of King Edward IV of England who had been placed in the Tower of London by their uncle, Richard III, and who disappeared into legend as 'the Princes in the Tower'.[269] In 1501, James IV granted him the reward he sought through his election and provision to the recently vacant see of Moray, which has been described

2.8   Seal of Andrew Forman (Historic Scotland © Crown Copyright)

as the source of a 'substantial future salary to [an] invaluable administrator'.[270] Forman's reputation as a diplomat was confirmed in October 1501 when he was commissioned by King James as one of the Scottish negotiators of the Treaty of Perpetual Peace with Henry VII of England which resulted in the marriage of King James IV to Margaret Tudor.[271] For his central role in securing the marriage treaty, Forman received presentation from Henry VII to the rectory of the rich parish of Cottingham in Yorkshire.[272] His success in 1502 in negotiating the deal confirmed him in James's eyes as the most reliable servant whom he could employ to conduct his diplomatic business. That reputation as an able diplomat and a man on whom the king could rely, however, coupled with his personal ambition, ensured that Moray would rarely see its new bishop.

Forman quickly came to be seen as a man with the king's ear through whom business could be channelled. James IV's uncle, King Hans of Denmark, for example, wrote personally to Forman to thank him for helping in his business with his nephew, aided by what he understood to be Forman's 'long association with the royal household'.[273] When James began to conduct more aggressive diplomacy with Henry VII in 1508 and at the same time received at his court leading émigré Scots from the French court, it was Forman whom he employed again to 'play' the English emissaries led by Thomas Wolsey, the future archbishop of York. Forman fulfilled his role with aplomb, leading Wolsey to believe that only he and the queen, Henry's own daughter, were supporting the English treaty at court and that everyone else was clamouring for a renewal of the ancient league with France.[274] From 1509 onwards, the bishop was increasingly active on James's behalf in European diplomacy, seeking to mediate a resolution to the power struggles between the emperor, the king of France, the pope and the king of England in order to unite them in a common enterprise, a crusade against the Ottoman Turks.[275] He was, however, still very much active in support of the English treaty, being commissioned by James IV on 19 July 1509 to treat with Henry VIII to negotiate for a personal meeting of the two kings at which the peace between the kingdoms could be confirmed;[276] on 29 August 1509, he swore 'by these Holy Evangelies and Canon of the Holy Masse, by Me bodily Touched' on behalf of James IV, that his king would 'in the Perill of his Soule' adhere to the 1502 treaty and its renewal by Henry VIII.[277] In October 1510, James IV wrote to the Venetian military commander, the marquis of Mantua, announcing that he had sent Forman on a diplomatic mission to Italy in an effort to achieve reconciliation between the French and the Venetians as a precursor to the proposed crusade; similar notification of Forman's mission was sent to the cardinal of St Mark and Pope Julius II.[278] Forman was first dispatched to France to try to urge King Louis XII there to make peace with Julius II; Louis made excuses and Forman passed on to Italy with nothing in his hands other than a separate commission from the French king to negotiate on his behalf.[279] Through 1511, the bishop was employed in a round of diplomatic negotiations which brought a general European reconciliation no closer;[280] by the end of the year the pope had formed a 'Holy League' with the Spanish and Venetians, soon joined by Henry VIII of England, against the French. In January 1512, Forman returned to Scotland as a representative of Louis to try to persuade James to abandon the treaty with England which the bishop had helped to negotiate and to renew his kingdom's 'Auld Alliance' with France.[281]

At the end of March 1513, Forman sailed on a mission to the French and papal courts.[282] He had hoped that the new pope, Leo X, would make good the hints of a cardinalate that Julius II had offered, but Leo was less willing to bargain for Forman's – or Scottish – acquiescence than his predecessor had been. No cardinal's hat was handed to Forman and Leo stuck rigidly to Julius II's anti-French stance and issued letters to the English which permitted the excommunication of King James if he broke the Treaty of Perpetual Peace and backed the French.[283] Back in Scotland, Forman worked hard to bring Scotland into the impending European war on the French side. His reward was not slow in coming. Recognising the significance of Forman in persuading James to remember his kingdom's ancient league with the French, Louis XII of France began to apply pressure to the chapter of the rich archdiocese of Bourges to elect Forman; his success in securing the archbishopric of Bourges has been seen as a straightforward reward for his success in achieving the desired result.[284]

Forman was one of the pre-eminent pluralists of the age and has been labelled 'a Scottish Wolsey', equating him with Henry VIII's great civil servant, diplomat and accumulator of lucrative offices.[285] Not only did Forman hold the bishopric of Moray, but he was also an apostolic protonotary, rector of Cottingham in England, commendator of the abbeys of Dryburgh and Kelso, tacksman of the royal lands of Dunbar Mains in East Lothian, keeper of the king's castle and forest of Darnaway in Moray, chamberlain of the earldom of Moray which lay in royal hands, and custumar – receiver of customs on traded goods – north and west of the River Spey. These offices, lay and ecclesiastical, concentrated both real sources of wealth and great regional influence and political power in the hands of a man whose primary function was oversight of the spiritual welfare of the people of his see. How well he was able to balance his lay interests with his spiritual duties is highly questionable, and it has been said that Forman's 'contribution to the wellbeing of the Scottish Church can only be considered marginal'.[286] His prominence as a very political bishop and Crown servant, actively employed by the king on his international diplomacy, ensured that Forman quickly acquired a negative reputation after the disastrous outcome of that diplomacy in the war with England. By 1533, twenty years after the event and with Forman long dead, Adam Abell, a former Augustinian canon of Inchaffray and latterly an Observantine Franciscan friar at Jedburgh, wrote a history known as the *Roit or Quheill of Tyme* in which Forman emerges as the evil genius who brought about the popular King James IV's downfall.[287] Abell, influenced by Gavin Douglas, Forman's embittered ecclesiastical rival, helped promote a vision of him as 'yon evyll myndyt Byschep of Morray'. Scurrilous stories concerning Forman multiplied as the sixteenth century progressed, with Sir Robert Lindsay of Pitscottie's chronicle account being full of colourful anecdotes of the bishop's practising of magic, his lack of scholarship – supposedly unable to give a prayer in Latin during a formal dinner with the pope – and his shameful deal-making to gain personal advancement by selling Scottish support to whichever European power promised him most.[288] For the most part it is an undeserved reputation, for it is without any doubt that James IV was very much the man who pulled the strings and instructed Forman in how he wished his affairs to be conducted. The bishop may have sought to benefit as best he could personally, but he was the servant of the king's will. Indeed, had he not still been involved in negotiations with Louis XII in September 1513, it is quite likely that he would have accompanied his master on the fatal march into Northumberland.

James IV's illegitimate son Alexander, archbishop of St Andrews, died in the carnage of Flodden. The favoured candidate to succeed him was Bishop William Elphinstone of Aberdeen, but he was elderly and suffered ill-health. In the light of this, Pope Leo X requested the translation of Bishop Forman to St Andrews. Forman had resigned Bourges in central France, which the pope wished to bestow upon a candidate of his own. In April 1514, Pope Leo's proposal was agreed by John, duke of Albany, the French-born regent for the young James V.[289] On 13 November, the pope quashed any elections or postulations made to St Andrews in the period following the death of Archbishop Alexander Stewart and provided Forman. On the same day he granted the new archbishop the commend of the abbey of Dunfermline, one of the richest monasteries in Scotland. On 8 December, Pope Leo wrote to James Hepburn, the incumbent at Dunfermline, ordering him to quit the abbey in favour of Forman.[290] With the fruits of the various other offices and benefices which he held, Andrew Forman was certainly not leaving his old diocese as a poor cleric.

James Hepburn, 1516–1524

Forman's successor was another political appointee, James Hepburn, often referred to as a younger brother of Patrick Hepburn, first earl of Bothwell, but more probably the son of Alexander Hepburn of Whitsome (Illus 2.9).[291] He was the man whom Forman had displaced as abbot-postulate of Dunfermline. Hepburn, who had not yet entered monastic orders and continued to seek to avoid doing so until at least 1520, had received the abbey at royal request made late in 1513 following the death at Flodden of Alexander Stewart, archbishop of St Andrews, who had also been its commendator.[292] Hepburn at this time held two benefices, the rectories of the parish churches of Parton in Galloway diocese and Dalry (Ayrshire) in Glasgow diocese.[293] In August 1514, the regency council for King James V again wrote to the pope to request confirmation of various requests for clerical appointments, Hepburn's to Dunfermline amongst them; Pope Leo X's response in December was an instruction for Hepburn to yield Dunfermline in favour of Andrew Forman, whom he had just provided to the archbishopric of St Andrews.[294] The keenness to secure a rich benefice for Hepburn reflects his growing importance in royal administration, where from at least June 1515 until October 1516 he held the office of treasurer.[295] On 6 May 1516, James Hepburn, styled rector of the church of Parton in Galloway, was still described as 'postulate' of Moray.[296]

Bishop James appears to have been disinclined to give his obedience as suffragan to Archbishop James Beaton, Forman's successor at St Andrews. In January 1524, the archbishop wrote to the cardinal of St Eusebius to advise him that the king was about to write to Pope Clement VII to warn him about threats to the status of St Andrews as primatial see of Scotland and the archbishop's status as legate, relating particularly to appointments to the vacant see of

2.9   Seal of James Hepburn (Historic Scotland © Crown Copyright)

Glasgow.[297] He also, however, noted that Bishop Hepburn of Moray was seeking an exemption from the legatine authority and metropolitan supremacy of St Andrews, much as his predecessors in the late fifteenth century had done. Archbishop Beaton requested the cardinal's aid in blocking Hepburn's effort and his help in obtaining instructions to the bishop to give his due obedience to St Andrews. Hepburn, however, gained his exemption.[298]

There is no evidence for any significant activity undertaken by Hepburn within his diocese. Indeed, one of the few acts which he carried out was the institution of a rector and prebendary of Duffus at Spynie on 19 April 1524.[299] Five months later he was dead.[300] Writing in the early eighteenth century, Robert Keith identified his place of burial as 'in our Lady's aisle, near to the Earl of Huntly's tomb'.[301] As Huntly's monument is one of the few lay tombs in the cathedral which can be identified with confidence and can be seen occupying a central position in the eastern chapel of the south aisle of the choir, it can be assumed that this was the Lady Chapel.

Robert Shaw, 1524–1527

Shaw, a member of the Clackmannanshire family of Shaw of Sauchie, had succeeded his uncle as abbot of Paisley in July 1498.[302] His career there was long and distinguished, marked by a fresh vigour in the religious life of the community and in the development of the abbey as a cult centre with the new building work to provide a suitable setting for the shrine of St Mirin there. It seems, therefore, that he was not just a royal place-man but a cleric of some quality, although during the minority of James V he grew increasingly prominent in political affairs, witnessing many acts issued under the great seal until the time of his appointment to the bishopric.[303] In a letter to Pope Clement VII dated 11 January 1525, King James – or rather the earl of Angus, who controlled his government – explained how careful thought had been given to finding a suitable successor to Bishop Hepburn and that the chosen successor was Robert Shaw, abbot of Paisley.[304] It was requested that Shaw should have all the privileges of exemption which his predecessors had enjoyed, presumably those freeing them from the metropolitan supremacy of the archbishopric of St Andrews. The royal letter, however, noted that Shaw would be more regularly a part of the king's household and a member of council and it was requested that he therefore should have certain dispensations with regard to the vestments he could wear and how they were worn around court. On 23 February 1525, Henry VIII of England wrote to Pope Clement VII to give his support to his sister, Queen Margaret, and nephew, James V, in their request for Abbot Shaw's promotion to the see of Moray.[305] On 6 January 1526, Bishop Robert was confirmed as one of the ambassadors to

negotiate for an enduring peace with England appointed by the government for the young King James V, which was still dominated by Archibald, earl of Angus.[306]

His tenure of the bishopric was short. Consecrated some time before 29 October 1525, he was dead before November 1527 when the see was described as vacant.[307] In the early eighteenth century, Keith described his tomb as located 'between the sepulchres of Bishop Alexander [sic] Stewart and Andrew Stewart his brother'.[308] Keith located the tombs of James and Andrew Stewart in the aisle of St Peter and St Paul. As what are probably the tombs of the Stewart brothers survive directly adjoining each other in the south wall of the south transept, it is difficult to see how Shaw could have been buried 'between' them, unless his was a free-standing tomb placed in the middle of the floor of the southern half of the transept. There was a vacancy of nearly two years before his successor was appointed.

Alexander Stewart, 1529–1537

On 31 May 1528, Henry VIII wrote to Pope Clement VII in support of a proposal made in the name of his nephew James V, but in reality from the Douglas-dominated clique who controlled government, for the promotion of Alexander Douglas, illegitimate son of Archibald Douglas of Kilspindie, to the vacant bishopric of Moray.[309] That bid failed and the successor to Bishop Shaw was a man of altogether different character. Alexander Stewart was the younger bastard brother of John Stewart, duke of Albany, and therefore a cousin of King James V. The son of Alexander, duke of Albany, and his mistress, Catherine Sinclair,[310] he was probably born following his father's flight into exile after his failed attempted coup against his elder brother King James III in 1483, Alexander's rise to public prominence began in the aftermath of the Battle of Flodden when his half-brother became regent for the child-king James V. With his brother regent and himself of royal blood, he was almost guaranteed to rise high with the support of his royal kinsmen. He first succeeded in 1513 in securing the commendatorship of Inchaffray Abbey in Perthshire, but papal confirmation of this was still awaited in August 1514.[311] A papal letter of May 1515 implies that there had been an attempt to intrude him into the preceptory of the Knights of St John of Jerusalem at Torphichen in West Lothian, the pope's instruction being for his expulsion.[312] In 1516, with his brother now firmly established as regent, he was advanced as a suitable commendator for Whithorn Priory in Galloway, but with a request that he could retain the commendatorship of Inchaffray without limit.[313] It took a long process of litigation to secure Whithorn, but in the midst of this in late 1518 or early 1519 Alexander was also appointed to the commendatorship of Scone Abbey.[314]

These appointments had all resulted in protracted litigation against powerful vested interests, but Albany was keen to ensure that richer rewards followed without such difficulties again being encountered. On 18 May 1518, he secured a supporting letter from King Francis I of France which noted that James V was to be writing to the pope to request a legatine commission for Alexander in Scotland, with the same powers as had been enjoyed by Andrew Forman, and that he should be promoted to the first archbishopric, bishopric, or valuable abbacy that became available.[315] He had, however, several more years to wait before the dignity of a bishopric was settled on him; he was only nominated to Moray shortly before May 1528 and secured provision on 13 September 1529.[316] On 10 January 1530, James V wrote to thank the cardinal for his support in securing the promotion of Alexander Stewart to Moray, with permission to retain possession of the other benefices which he already held.[317]

Although he was bishop of Moray for only eight years, he succeeded in leaving his mark on Scotland in more ways than one. In November 1547, the regency government of the child Queen Mary granted letters of legitimation to the young monarch's distant cousin Margaret Stewart, widow of John Aitoun of Kinnaldy near Kirriemuir in Angus, who was the illegitimate daughter of Bishop Alexander.[318] Although her late husband was only a substantial tenant rather than a member of then titled nobility, she had clearly fallen heir through him and, presumably through her father's generous provision of a dowry, to a sizable fortune which would pass to the Crown on her death since children born illegitimate in the eyes of the law could not transmit their inheritance to their children, regardless of their legitimacy. Three years later Margaret's younger brother, Alexander Stewart, likewise received letters granting him legal legitimacy.[319]

Sometimes said to have died in 1534, he was still alive in early December 1537.[320] The Chronicle of Fortingall records his death (wrongly naming him Andrew) on 21 December 1537;[321] given that this source was recorded by a Perthshire cleric and it seems likely that Alexander died at Perth or his monastery of Scone, there seems no reason to doubt this date. He was dead certainly by 12 January 1538.[322] At the time of his death he was still holding the commendatorship of Scone and it was there, according to Keith in the early eighteenth century, that he was buried.[323]

Patrick Hepburn, 1538–1573

To accommodate his policy of placing royal illegitimate sons in possession of some of the wealthiest commendatorships in the kingdom, James V had to make space for them by promoting incumbents elsewhere. The king wanted the commendatorship of the priory of St Andrews, the richest monastery in Scotland, for his bastard son John, so the prior,

2.10   Seal of Patrick Hepburn – original red wax seal with vellum tapes attached (Historic Scotland © Crown Copyright)

Patrick Hepburn, an exceptionally worldly cleric who had himself fathered more illegitimate children than King James, was compensated with the commendatorship of Scone and the bishopric of Moray (Illus 2.10).[324]

Often wrongly identified as a younger son of Patrick Hepburn, first earl of Bothwell, he was in fact son of the head of a junior branch of that family, Patrick Hepburn of Beinstoun, and his wife, Christian Ogilvy.[325] The young Patrick formed a number of irregular relationships by which he had his several illegitimate children. Not all of his energies were spent on fathering sons, for he was also successfully promoting his own ecclesiastical career. Described as a secular clerk and nephew of John Hepburn, prior of St Andrews, he was appointed by Pope Clement VII on 10 June 1524 as his uncle's coadjutor (formal deputy or assistant).[326] On John Hepburn's death in January 1526, he succeeded him as prior of St Andrews, at first holding this office in conjunction with the office of secretary to the young King James V.[327] For the next twelve years he ruled as prior in a manner which saw him already the target of accusations of ungodliness, profligacy and luxury by 1529; he was hardly a model of ecclesiastical propriety.[328]

Possession of the wealthiest monastic benefice in the kingdom, however, was not going to be permanently his. On

1 March 1538, King James wrote to the cardinal of Ravenna to advise that he was going to inform the pope of the death of Alexander Stewart and that, therefore, the bishopric of Moray and abbacy of Scone were vacant.[329] James wished to confer both on Patrick Hepburn, prior of St Andrews, 'a man of great ability and learning'. In his letter to Pope Paul III, James described Hepburn as having a record of 'wise, just, and highminded administration' as prior, perfectly suiting him for the bishopric; it is doubtful if many of the canons at St Andrews would have agreed with this assessment. It was duly noted in papal consistory on 14 June 1538 that Patrick Hepburn had been promoted to the bishopric of Moray and abbacy of Scone, both vacant through the death of Alexander Stewart.[330] In return, Hepburn resigned possession of the priory of St Andrews.[331]

By the mid-1540s, Bishop Patrick was manoeuvring to win local support and to consolidate his position against powerful local rivals headed by the earl of Huntly. Much of this was achieved through the alienation of large portions of the landed property of the bishopric and his abbacy of Scone.[332] Although these alienations have often been seen as a device to secure him the income to fund his lavish lifestyle, they also reflect a growing trend in the Scottish Church generally where ecclesiastical landowners were feuing out property in an effort to raise the cash needed to pay the tax on clerical incomes which the pope had conceded to King James V. In 1545, for example, he gave a favourable feuferme grant of lands around Keith to George Ogilvy of Milton,[333] binding him into a dependent relationship for lands which were sandwiched awkwardly between the earl of Huntly's core estates in Strathbogie and the Enzie.

After becoming bishop, Hepburn retained the prominent role in political life which he had carved for himself in the 1520s and 1530s, serving as a member of the privy council of the Regent Arran, governor of Scotland during the minority of the young Queen Mary. A strong opponent of Arran's proposed marriage of Mary to the future King Edward VI of England, he emerged as a staunch supporter of the regent's principal adversary David Beaton, cardinal-archbishop of St Andrews. As popular support for Protestant reform in the kingdom grew, Hepburn joined with his fellow bishops in tackling the calls for reform and in directly challenging their critics. There is much that smacks of hypocrisy in his participation in the reforming councils of the Scottish Church which proposed internal revival as a means of staving off the threat from the Protestants.[334]

The clergy of his own diocese were hardly exemplars to be used as models for how to conduct suitable religious lives, many of them being as heavily secularised as their bishop. An illustration of the full integration of the prebendaries of Moray into local lay politics came in 1555 when the peace of the cathedral was shattered by a bloody affray within the inner part of the church during the service of Vespers on 1 January between two rival local factions headed by the Dunbar and Innes families who had been feuding for a number of years.[335] William Innes of that ilk arrived at the cathedral with thirty-two men and up to eighty other followers while James Dunbar of Tarbert had himself come with twelve of his own following and another sixty men intent on killing Innes. While many men were injured and blood, it was reported, was shed 'in the presence of the sacrament', we know little else about the fight other than that amongst the men involved were Alexander Dunbar, prior of Pluscarden, David Dunbar, dean of Moray, and four other clerics.

It was with no sense of the incongruity of his participation in a process calling for reform and revival of spiritual standards amongst the clergy while taking action to safeguard the economic wellbeing of his brood of illegitimate children that through this same period Hepburn sought letters of legitimation for many of them. With thirteen children by at least five different mistresses, he had many demands on the resources of his see to ensure that they were provided for adequately.[336] In May 1550, for example, Bishop Patrick secured letters of legitimation for two of his natural daughters Janet and Agnes, possibly as a preparatory move in arranging good marriages for them.[337] He was, however, in good company, Master John Thornton, precentor of Moray, having two bastard sons Henry and Gilbert, for whom letters of legitimation were also procured.[338]

Given his later reputation as a trimmer who showed little adherence to any religious principles,[339] it is surprising to find Hepburn blamed by John Knox in his 'History of the Reformation in Scotland' for securing the burning as a heretic in 1558 of the aged priest Walter Myln, vicar of Lunan in Angus.[340] If true, it is even more remarkable that by April/ May 1559 Bishop Hepburn was promising his support to the Protestant Lords of the Congregation of Christ,[341] although to what extent that arose from religious conviction rather than political considerations needs little guesswork.[342] Like many of the leading Roman Catholic lords and prelates in Scotland (including his all-powerful neighbour George Gordon, fourth earl of Huntly), Bishop Hepburn was compelled to support the Congregation. This was a necessary move to counterbalance the growing French influence in the kingdom. Hepburn's dalliance with the Reformers, however, was short-lived, for in June 1559 a mob from Perth sacked Scone Abbey, of which he was commendator, despite promises from the Protestant lords that they would protect his property, and he at once withdrew his support from their cause.[343] He did not attend the Reformation Parliament of

1560 and soon emerged as a leading figure in the attempted political-religious fight-back against the new Protestant regime. When Queen Mary began arrangements for her return to Scotland in 1561, Hepburn joined with the earl of Huntly in urging her to land in the north-east of the kingdom where support for the old ecclesiastical hierarchy was strong, rather than at Leith, and that with their support they could lead a Roman Catholic army south to overturn the recent religious revolution.[344]

Given even the distant kinship of Patrick Hepburn, bishop of Moray, with James Hepburn, fourth earl of Bothwell, it was unlikely that the Protestant lords who controlled the centre of government in Edinburgh would do much to disturb the bishop's continued possession of the lands of his see. The alienations of episcopal properties that he had begun to make in the 1540s, however, continued apace in the immediate post-Reformation years, but some were still wrapped up in the fiction of pious intentions. In 1566, for example, he feued a substantial block of episcopal properties at Dyke west of Forres to Alexander Brodie of that ilk for 80 merks 'paid towards the repair of the cathedral church of Moray', probably supposedly to modify the internal structure of the building to bring it into line with the reformed style of worship.[345] Even if Hepburn had truly intended to spend the money raised on the care and maintenance of his cathedral, more serious damage was almost simultaneously being inflicted upon it as the Privy Council in Edinburgh began to asset-strip the physical fabric of the old Church hierarchy.

As early as 1561, the cathedral may have already been 'purged' of many of the more accessible and visible symbols of the old faith. Lord James Stewart, the queen's half-brother and aspirant to the earldom of Moray, was active in the northern part of the kingdom targeting the religious images, altars, glass and the like at several major churches.[346] At Elgin, however, the main body of the church was not seriously affected by this action and it remained basically complete but presumably stripped of the altars and images which had decorated the chapels in the nave aisles and transepts as well as the greater altars at the rood screen and in the presbytery at the east end. The first major assault on the main structure came within a year of Bishop Patrick's desultory efforts to set the Church in order and following his involvement in supporting his kinsman James, fourth earl of Bothwell, in the brief civil war which had toppled Queen Mary. Late in 1567, the Protestant-dominated Privy Council ordered the stripping of the lead from the roofs of the cathedrals of Aberdeen and Elgin;[347] there is an air of vindictiveness in this order, presumably punishing the bishop for his rebellion. Although the order was reversed in 1569 and instructions given for the re-leading of the cathedral's roof – with Hepburn himself offering to contribute to the cost – the

work does not seem to have been carried out.[348]

Following the collapse of the queen's position at Carberry Hill outside Edinburgh in June 1567, Bothwell had fled north and first of all found refuge with Bishop Patrick at Spynie. On 21 July, the Privy Council found that the bishop had received him at Spynie and had reportedly encouraged him to continue in his 'wickitnes, to the apperand danger of the Princes person [King James VI]'. On 20 December 1567, Bishop Patrick was cited in the judicial summons proclaimed against Bothwell and his associates, requiring them to compear in parliament to answer charges of involvement or complicity in the murder of Henry, lord Darnley, the second husband of Queen Mary.[349] The citation also laid charges against all who had provided Bothwell with shelter, identifying specifically shelter given to him at Elgin, Forres and Spynie. Although there is no formal parliamentary record of the bishop's submission, a confirmation of a 'benefit of pacification' whereby he was returned to the king's peace was issued in December 1585, presumably to remove some question mark over actions by him after 1568.[350] The price for having sheltered his fugitive kinsman came the following spring when the victorious Protestant lords extracted enormous and clearly punitive concessions from the bishop. In April 1568, Patrick granted away the core of the bishopric lands in feuferme to James, earl of Moray, regent for the young James VI.

Amongst the properties which his charter conveyed were some of those most closely associated with the

2.11 A painting of the coat of arms of Bishop Patrick Hepburn from Spynie Palace

bishopric for over four hundred years; the toun and lands of Spynie (but not the episcopal palace) and their renders in kind, the fishery on the Lossie, the toun, lands and renders of Aldroughty, the lands of Kinneddar with the rabbit warren, meadow and garden, the ruined palace (*palatium dirutum*) and port called Stotfield, and various portions of land around Birnie.[351] Although Bishop Patrick continued to occupy the palace (Illus 2.11), by a second charter of April 1568 he granted to Earl James and his heirs the hereditary bailliaries and justiciarships of all of the lands, baronies and regalities pertaining to the bishopric of Moray throughout Scotland, and also the hereditary captaincies and keeperships 'of the castle, tower, fortalice and palace of Spynie'. As fee for those offices the bishop made over to the earl the loch and wood of Spynie, with the rabbit warren, gardens, orchards, small park, and pleasance (*viridarium*) around and near to the castle, together with £200 of the first-paid fermes of the bishopric lands. In return, the bishop was reserved the use of the place (*locus*) of Spynie, loch, doocot, rabbit warren, orchards, gardens, herb gardens, and '*lie garding*', the wood or park, and the Laverock-moss, during his residence at the palace.[352] Further alienations followed; for example, in January 1569/70 it was his lands of Cluny in the barony of Rafford south-east of Forres which were feued to Norman Dunbar, son of the locally powerful Sir Alexander Dunbar of Cumnock.[353] Further substantial inroads were made on the bishopric revenues in September 1570 when Hepburn was unable to object to the award of a pension of £500 from the future fruits of the diocese to James Haliburton, provost of Dundee, to be paid from the time of the bishop's death.[354] Although Patrick is often seen as having succeeded in retaining possession of his see until his death in June 1573, it is clear that he failed to keep its landed resources intact and was obliged to alienate some of its choicest portions to powerful lay interests nationally and locally. He nevertheless clung on to the end, refusing to give up physical possession of the palace which symbolised the broken power of the bishopric of Moray. According to Keith, the bishop died in his beloved palace at Spynie and was buried in the choir of the cathedral, the last of the pre-Reformation prelates to be interred there.[355]

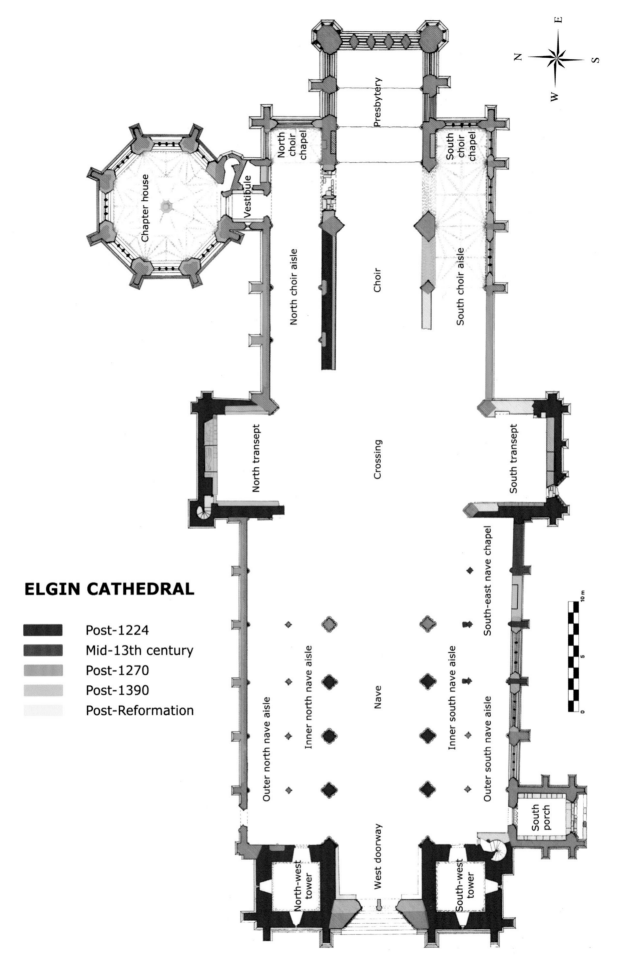

ELGIN CATHEDRAL

Post-1224
Mid-13th century
Post-1270
Post-1390
Post-Reformation

3.1 Plan of the cathedral (drawn by Scott Hamilton, Historic Scotland © Crown Copyright)

3 THE BUILDING

The Layout of the Cathedral

Before discussing the architecture of the cathedral in detail, brief accounts are given of the form of the building, of the stages by which it achieved its final form, and of the types of stone that were used in its construction. At all stages of its history Elgin Cathedral was a cruciform structure (Illus 3.1). In its ultimate state it consisted of the following parts, starting from the east and working westwards:

1   Two shallow aisle-less bays terminating the eastern limb formed the eastern part of the presbytery, the ceremonial area around the high altar.

2   Five further bays of the eastern limb were flanked by a wide vaulted aisle on each side, with the easternmost of these bays being shallower than the others. Within the central vessel the two eastern bays of this aisled section were essentially a westward continuation of the presbytery, leaving three bays for the choir of the canons; the division between the presbytery and choir was marked by massive responds (half piers). Within each of the aisles the shallow east bay was fitted out as a chapel; it appears from references to burial places that the southern chapel was dedicated to Our Lady (the Virgin Mary) and the northern chapel to St Columba. The side entrances into the presbytery from the aisles were in the bay to the west of the chapels. Although the evidence is incomplete, the south aisle appears to have opened towards the main vessel through an arcade of four arches, whereas on the north side there was a solid wall separating the choir from the aisle, the only arched opening on the north side being that already mentioned in the west bay of the presbytery.

3   Off the north side of the north aisle, opposite the entrance from the aisle into the presbytery, is an octagonal chapter house which is covered by a vault carried on a central pier; the chapter house is separated from the aisle by a small rectangular vestibule. On the east side of the vestibule is an irregularly shaped annexe of late construction that may have been used as a sacristy, and between that annexe and the chapter house

itself is a spiral stair, entered from the chapter house.

4   Between the eastern limb and nave was the crossing, which was surmounted by a tower; projecting laterally outwards from each side of the crossing is an aisle-less rectangular transept, extending the equivalent of one bay beyond the choir aisles. There was a spiral stair at the north-western corner of the north transept. The south face of the south transept and the north face of the north transept were subdivided into three narrow bays by buttresses, with a doorway in the western bay of the south transept. On the east side of the crossing would have been a timber screen with a central doorway, which separated the canons' choir from the rest of the building.

5   The nave was seven bays long, with a pair of towers flanking the western bay. In their final form the other six bays of the nave were flanked by two aisles on each side, each of those aisles being narrower than the aisles flanking the eastern limb. There was a doorway in the western bay of each of the two outer aisles, that on the south side being covered by a porch of two shallow bays. The great processional entrance to the cathedral is in the west bay of the central vessel, between the two towers. The towers are walled off from the central vessel and aisles, the only access into them being a single doorway in the east face of each tower. The stair giving access to the first floor of the towers is at the south-eastern corner of the south tower.

The Stages of Construction

We begin with a short summary of the stages by which it appears that the cathedral reached its final state, with brief discussion of the wider architectural context of each phase of the plan. The main discussion of the cathedral's architecture is then set out in the chronological sequence by which the evidence suggests it was built, rather than area by area.

The first cruciform plan as built after 1224

As first planned after the move from Spynie to Elgin in 1224, the cathedral appears to have been laid out with an aisle-less eastern limb possibly corresponding to no more than the area of the three bays of the central vessel of the later canons' choir. The only identifiable survivor of this first eastern limb is a stretch of its north wall that was retained in the later building. West of this was the crossing, which was probably surmounted by a tower from the start, but of which nothing remains. Projecting on each side of the crossing were aisle-less rectangular transepts, which survived later rebuilding to remain part of the final cathedral and which still partly survive. It is possible, though not likely, that the north-western stair turret of the north transept represents a secondary modification, since its base course differs from that around the rest of the transepts. The nave may have been initially intended to be only six bays long with a single aisle along each flank, that single aisle being of the same width as the inner aisle in the final arrangement. If this interpretation is correct, the aisle-less eastern limb was internally about half the length of the aisled section of the nave. The three western piers of each nave arcade, together with the western responds, survived later rebuilding; those piers now survive as no more than truncated stumps, though the responds survive complete because they were incorporated into the fabric of the towers.

The closest parallel for this cruciform plan at a Scottish cathedral is to be seen at Dornoch. The cathedral of the diocese of Caithness was relocated to its present site at Dornoch in the time of Bishop Gilbert de Moravia (1222–1245), and it was presumably he who commenced its construction.[356] It may be significant that Gilbert was a kinsman – perhaps a cousin – of Bishop Andrew de Moravia, the builder of the first cathedral at Elgin. The scale of Dornoch Cathedral, however, was considerably less ambitious than that at Elgin, which is hardly surprising since the diocese was far less well endowed.

The construction of the western towers

The two western towers may not have been part of the very first plan for the cathedral (Illus 3.2). The reason for suggesting this is that the base course that runs around the foot of their walls is different from that of the transepts, the only part of the first building from which outer walls have survived unchanged. Nevertheless, it is certain that the decision to add those towers must have been taken while work on the nave was still in progress, since, as has already been mentioned, the western responds of the two arcades are fully integrated into the north-east angle of the south tower and the south-east angle of the north tower. The towers, which projected sideways well beyond the original line of the outer walls of the aisles, were fully enclosed by solid walls, apart from a single doorway in each. The stair turret at the south-east angle of the south tower may have been initially entered both internally through its north face

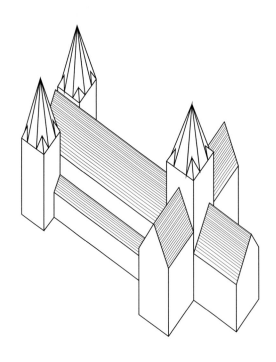

3.2   Block sketch of the likely appearance of Elgin Cathedral when first completed (drawn by Scott Hamilton, Historic Scotland © Crown Copyright)

and externally through its east face, but the latter doorway was blocked when a pair of outer aisles was added to the nave at a later stage.

The decision to give the cathedral two western towers as well as a tower over the crossing is perhaps the clearest indication of the high aspirations of its bishops. The only other Scottish cathedrals known to have had three towers were at Aberdeen[357] and Glasgow,[358] where the full complement was eventually achieved only towards the end of the Middle Ages and thus much later than at Elgin. St Andrews[359] and Kirkwall[360] Cathedrals may have been intended to have a pair of western towers as well as a central tower at an early stage of their planning, though in neither case were the western towers built. At monastic churches triplets of towers were built at the twelfth- and thirteenth-century royal abbeys of Arbroath,[361] Dunfermline[362] and Holyrood,[363] and they were evidently planned at the abbeys of Kilwinning[364] and Paisley.[365] But triplets of towers were always exceptional in Scotland, and those at Elgin must have expressed more clearly than anything else the importance attached to the cathedral of the diocese of Moray.

The addition of the south-eastern nave chapel

After the towers, the next addition to the original plan was a chapel in the re-entrant angle between the south transept and the south aisle of the nave, which extended alongside

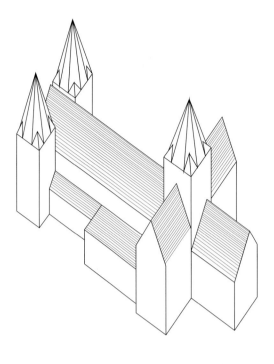

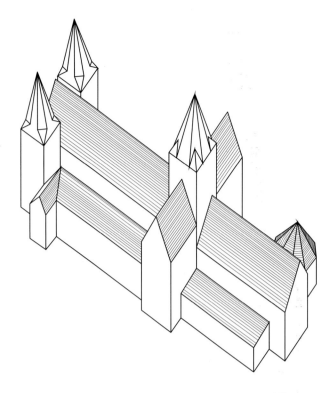

3.3   Block sketch of the likely appearance of Elgin Cathedral after the addition of the south-east nave chapel (drawn by Scott Hamilton, Historic Scotland © Crown Copyright)

3.4   Block sketch of the likely appearance of Elgin Cathedral after the post-1270 augmentations (drawn by Scott Hamilton, Historic Scotland © Crown Copyright)

the three eastern bays of the nave (Illus 3.3). No precisely comparable chapels are known to have been built at any other Scottish cathedrals, and its function and dedication are unknown. It was later absorbed into an added outer south nave aisle.

The post-1270 augmentations

The late-thirteenth-century works, carried out after the fire of 1270, involved very much more than repairs to the existing building, and they brought the cathedral almost to its final full extent (Illus 3.4). The eastern limb appears to have been doubled in length, resulting in four full-depth bays in its western part and three shallower bays at the east end. At the same time a single wide aisle was added along each side of five of its bays, leaving the two easternmost bays to project beyond the aisles, meaning that it was possible to have windows on three sides of the high altar. On surviving evidence, virtually the only part of the first eastern limb to have survived this rebuilding was its north wall, though that wall was extensively remodelled. The octagonal chapter house with its vestibule was added on the north side of the eastern limb, possibly as a slight afterthought.

The late-medieval rebuilding of the central tower, and the subsequent collapse of both the tower and its supporting piers, means we are uncertain of the full extent of post-1270 rebuilding in the crossing area, though the

form of surviving fragmentary responds from the choir and nave aisles into the transepts suggest the crossing area had to be extensively rebuilt. However, the two transepts were themselves retained as first built after 1224 with only relatively minor modifications.

In the nave the towers were retained, but were probably heightened by an additional storey. It seems that at least four bays of the original nave arcade walls to the east of the towers were also retained, but otherwise the rebuilding and augmentation of the nave was almost as extensive as that of the eastern limb. The central part of the west front between the towers was also partly reconstructed, but most remarkable of all was the addition of an outer aisle along each flank between the transepts and west towers, with a two-bay porch over what was probably the main entrance for the laity being provided in the western bay of the south aisle. The line of the external wall of the new outer south aisle was taken from that of the three-bay chapel previously added on the south side, which was embodied within the new work, and the same width was adopted for the outer north aisle.

Moving on to consider briefly the architectural context of the post-1270 works, the plan of the augmented eastern arm, with an aisled section terminating in a short but full-height aisle-less section, had a well-established history in the major churches of Scotland. The first Scottish cathedral to be laid out to such a plan was probably that of St Andrews, started by Arnold who was bishop between 1160 and 1162,[366] though it is likely that there was an earlier example of the type at Jedburgh Abbey, where the eastern limb was set out soon after the abbey's foundation in about 1138.[367] Variants of the plan had also been employed in the late twelfth century for Arbroath[368] and Dryburgh.[369]

Elgin's is the only chapter house at a Scottish cathedral known to have been of centralised polygonal form, though there is an earlier thirteenth-century example at the Augustinian abbey of Inchcolm,[370] and another Augustinian example has been traced through excavation at Holyrood Abbey.[371] The type must certainly be seen as having been inspired by prototypes in England, where there were about thirty chapter houses of centralised plan.[372]

The most unusual feature of the nave as remodelled after 1270 was the double nave aisles, and it is hard to think from where the patrons of Elgin may have taken the idea, particularly since within Scotland the idea was not taken up elsewhere. It is true that at Melrose Abbey the south aisle, on the side away from the cloister, was asymmetrically doubled up by an outer chapel aisle in the rebuilding after the English destruction of 1385,[373] but there the idea was probably borrowed from Continental Cistercian houses, where this was one of the means sometimes adopted for providing space for larger numbers of altars within a relatively simple architectural framework.[374] The only parallel for multiple aisles at a Scottish building of what might be called 'cathedral scale' was at St Giles' parish church in Edinburgh, which was eventually elevated to cathedral status in 1633, though there the final plan was a consequence of the late-medieval piecemeal addition of chapels rather than of a deliberate decision to double up the aisles to a unified design (Illus 3.4).[375] Within Britain the only other cathedral at which the aisles were systematically doubled up, so far as the existing fabric would allow, was Chichester, where the work was probably carried out around the second and third quarters of the thirteenth century, almost certainly under the inspiration of Continental prototypes.[376] Since it seems unlikely that Chichester was the source of the idea at Elgin, is it possible that the designers of the extensions at Elgin were also looking directly to Continental prototypes?

The post-1390 repairs

The architectural evidence leaves little doubt that major rebuilding at Elgin was required after the attack of 1390, and perhaps also after that of 1402. In general, however, this was carried out within the framework of the existing ground plan, the only minor augmentation being the addition of the small annexe on the east side of the chapter house vestibule, which is likely to have been used as a sacristy (Illus 3.5).

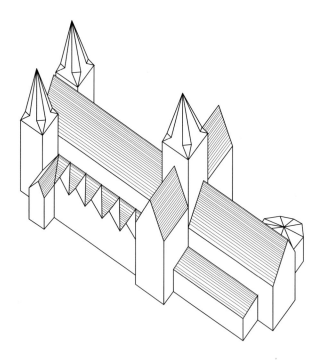

3.5   Block sketch of the likely appearance of Elgin Cathedral after the post-1390 repairs (drawn by Scott Hamilton, Historic Scotland © Crown Copyright)

The Building Stones of the Cathedral

There is no known documentation to tell us where the building stones used in the various phases of building the cathedral were quarried. The earliest surviving parts of the building were constructed of brown to buff-coloured sandstone rubble with freestone dressings, but buff-coloured carefully squared ashlar was introduced for the externally visible parts of the western towers towards the end of that first operation. Rubble was again employed briefly for the walls of the chapel added at the south-eastern corner of the nave, perhaps for the sake of architectural homogeneity with the adjacent earlier parts of the building. But in all later stages of the building work, from the augmentations and rebuilding that followed the fire of 1270 to the end of the Middle Ages, fine ashlar was used, sometimes even in parts that could never have been visible, such as the walling between the aisle vaults and roofs. Indeed, despite the decay – and consequent need for modern replacement – of some of the stonework, the overall quality of the masonry at Elgin Cathedral must always have been one of the most striking features of the building (Illus 3.6).

The area of Moray within easy reach of Elgin is unusual for northern Scotland in having been well provided with good sources of stone that is suitable for use as ashlar as well as for rubble. The sandstone formations around the Moray Firth were briefly discussed in the catalogue of building stones held by the Sedgwick Museum in Cambridge, with particular

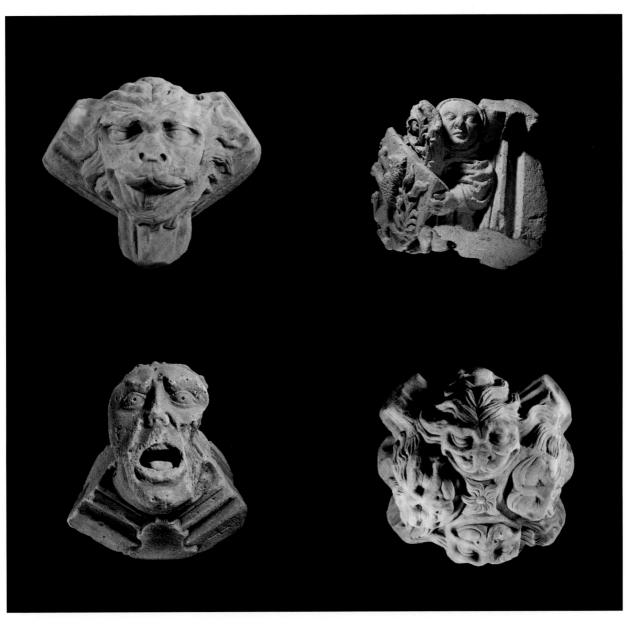

3.6   Examples of some of the finely carved vaulting bosses from Elgin Cathedral (Historic Scotland © Crown Copyright)

reference to samples from quarries at Rosebrae and Newton, as well as to Triassic stones from the Greenbraes quarry at Hopeman.[377] The Permo-Triassic sandstones of the Elgin area are of the New Red Sandstone formation, and have been characterised as 'typically yellow to buff coloured, laminated and composed of well rounded quartz grains with feldspar'.[378]

Unfortunately for us in trying to identify the likely sources of stones, medieval quarries which did not continue in long-term use often left little more evidence of themselves than indentations in the ground, together with associated spoil heaps. But there are many quarry sites in the Elgin area that were worked within recent history. Indeed, two quarries are still being exploited on a commercial basis: the Clashach Quarry at Hopeman, which produces stone of the Hopeman Sandstone Formation, and the Spynie Quarry near Elgin itself, which produces Upper Triassic sandstone. Both of these could in fact perpetuate workings of considerable

antiquity,[379] and both produce stone that shows clear similarities with that used in parts of the cathedral.[380]

Bearing in mind the ready local accessibility of good stone and the natural wish to avoid the greatly increased costs that arose when heavy building materials had to be transported any distance,[381] it seems likely that quarries would have been opened on lands as close to the cathedral as possible, perhaps on the estates of the bishop or chapter. Indeed, Mr Ashley Bartlam, who has carried out research into the building stones of the Elgin area, has suggested that the most likely source of stone for much of the cathedral could be quarries in the Bishopmill part of the burgh, with some of the other stone being perhaps from Spynie.

4.1   Elgin Cathedral, view into the east limb, showing the retained section of the first north wall (© Richard Fawcett)

4 THE EARLIEST PARTS OF THE CATHEDRAL

The North Wall of the Eastern Limb

As has been noted, the earliest part of the first building campaign (started around 1224) to survive *in situ* is probably the north wall of its eastern limb, although this has been so extensively modified on more than one occasion that the evidence it embodies could be open to varying interpretations. This wall now extends alongside the second and third bays from the west of the area later occupied by the canons' choir, the westernmost bay presumably having been destroyed by the collapse of the tower in 1711 (Illus 4.1). While the evidence is certainly not conclusive, a change in the character of the masonry at the end of the third bay suggests that the first eastern limb may have extended no further eastwards. This would mean that the first eastern limb was relatively short by comparison with those set out at a number of other thirteenth-century cathedrals, including Dunblane and Dunkeld, and it must be seen as possible that at Elgin the canons' choir would have initially extended down into the crossing area.

The clearstorey which runs above this section of wall, despite slight differences of treatment to the inner arches by comparison with the parts further east, is manifestly part of the building campaign that involved construction of the eastern bays of the eastern limb, and must therefore be an addition dating from the post-1270 extensions. While it cannot therefore be concluded beyond doubt that the original eastern limb rose little higher than the string course below the later clearstorey, there appears to be a strong possibility that this was the case. Perhaps the most convincing reason for assuming that the wall-head of the first eastern limb was near the level of the string below the later clearstorey is the residual indications of windows set within a continuous internal wall arcade, immediately below the later clearstorey. On the south side of the wall, towards the central vessel, are traces of two wide arches separated by a narrower arch, with part of another narrow arch to the west (Illus 4.2). The ashlar masonry in the spandrels of those arches is differently coursed from the masonry within which it is set. Corresponding to the eastern of those wider arches on the north side of the wall, and now within the area of the north

4.2 Elgin Cathedral, traces of cut-back arcading in the retained section of the north wall (© Richard Fawcett)

4.3 The retained section of the north wall of Elgin Cathedral seen from the north, with the traces of a blocked window (© Richard Fawcett)

choir aisle, traces of an arch head can be seen rising through the wall rib of the later aisle vault, with vertical breaks of bond in the masonry below which seem to have been part of an opening descending to beneath the later wall shaft capitals (Illus 4.3). There are no traces of the narrower arches having passed through the wall thickness.

The combination of evidence for wider arched openings passing through the wall thickness, with narrower arches confined to the inner face, may indicate an arrangement similar to that surviving in restored form in the choir of Dornoch Cathedral, where there were small blind arches between the arched heads of the lancet windows of the side walls (Illus 4.4). At Elgin it seems that we still have the facing masonry which ran around the internal hood-moulds of two windows and of two of the blind arches which alternated with them, while at the springing of the arches are trapezoidal blocks of stone which could represent cut-back capitals or corbels. Comparison with Dornoch, where there was only one tier of windows in the choir, supports the idea that there may similarly have been only a single tier at Elgin. It should be noted, however, that if the wall had indeed risen little higher than the base of the later clearstorey at Elgin, the eastern limb would have been lower than either the transepts or nave, whereas at Dornoch they were all of the same height.

4.4   Dornoch Cathedral, the choir interior looking towards the north-east (© Richard Fawcett)

The evidence that windows pierced this wall down to a relatively low point above ground level also demonstrates that it was an outside wall and that in its first form the eastern limb was therefore without aisles. On the north side of the wall it may be noted that the bases of the wall shafts inserted together with the later aisle vaulting after 1270 rise from a slightly higher level than those further east, and the wall below the bases is of rougher construction than elsewhere. Although there can be no certainty, one reason for this could be that there had been an external base course, which was removed during the later works in order to achieve a flat wall surface which could then be plastered over.

On the south side of the retained wall further changes of masonry should be noted. At the base of the wall the masonry projects beyond the wall-face, which seems likely to indicate the original internal floor level. For about 1.7 metres above this is rubble masonry that has clearly been badly damaged by fire, and above that is ashlar masonry of varying bed depths rising up to the lower sides of the arched masonry that survived from the original windows. The damaged masonry at the wall base presumably dates from the first building campaign, and it could be argued that the fire damage dates from either of the disasters of 1270 or 1390. The way in which the fire damage continues unbroken for the full length of the wall and into the lower parts of the responds that were built at the junction of choir and added presbytery, however, indicates that at least some of the damage must have been caused in 1390. It is possible that it was the proximity of burning timber choir stalls that caused such intense damage, while, by the same token, it would have been the replacement of those stalls that made refacing of the lower masonry unnecessary, since they would have covered the lower part of the wall. A considerable extent of the intermediate stretch of wall above that damaged section had to be refaced, however.

If a relatively low aisle-less eastern limb seems a rather unambitious setting for the liturgically most important functions of a major cathedral, it should be remembered that this was by no means unusual for a Scottish cathedral. The eastern limbs of Brechin, Dornoch, Dunblane, Dunkeld, Fortrose and Lismore remained aisle-less throughout their history,[382] and it seems likely that Whithorn was similarly aisle-less,[383] while there is some archaeological evidence that Glasgow's eastern limb may have been aisle-less until the mid-thirteenth century.[384] Of these, the unaisled eastern limbs of Brechin, Dunblane and Dunkeld rose to a lesser height than the aisled naves, though the absence of any central tower and transepts at those churches may have made the difference in height more acceptable. But perhaps it was more common than we might think for a major cruciform church with a central tower to have an eastern limb rising to a lesser height than the rest of the building. This is likely to have been the case at the Cluniac abbey of Paisley and the Benedictine priory of Coldingham, for example.

The South Transept

The architectural qualities of the first building campaign are now best appreciated in the south transept (Illus 4.5). It is built of rubble masonry that is brought to courses at irregular intervals, with ashlar dressings to the quoins and openings. A number of changes in the character of the masonry are to be seen. This is particularly clear in the west wall, where larger stretches of unpierced and unarticulated masonry than on the other sides of the transept mean that masonry changes are more evident. At the lower levels, courses of large, roughly squared brown and buff-coloured sandstone alternate randomly with courses that are much thinner in the bed. Between the two string courses that define the sill and arch springing level of the clearstorey windows, however, the masonry becomes predominantly thinner in the bed, while above the upper of those two strings there is a higher proportion of roughly squared stones. But it is unlikely that these changes are linked with any significant changes of design or of personnel, and it is perhaps more likely that they simply correspond to the seasons of work and to the beds of the quarries that were being worked in the course of those seasons. On the other hand, the change from rubble in the main walls of the transept to ashlar in what remains of the gable may be more significant, since the proximity of the roof timbers would have made this part more vulnerable in the fires of 1270 and 1390, with a consequent need to carry out more extensive rebuilding after those disasters.

The exterior of the transept will be described before the interior. The walls rise from a two-stage deeply chamfered base course, and the faces are articulated by buttresses and by string courses running below the windows. The buttresses give a strongly vertical emphasis to the walls, having no intakes and terminating with gablets below the wall-heads. Since the buttresses are set back from the angles, the salient quoins give additional lines of vertical emphasis. The south face has four buttresses, creating a three-bay division, while the west face had at least one buttress in the section that projected beyond the line of the original nave aisle; insufficient survives to know if the east face had any intermediate buttresses.

As might be expected, the greatest architectural emphasis was given to the south front of the transept. At the lower level, in the west bay there is a doorway surmounted by an asymmetrically-set triangular gable and there is a vesica window above a stepped string course, while the central and eastern bays each have a tall lancet.

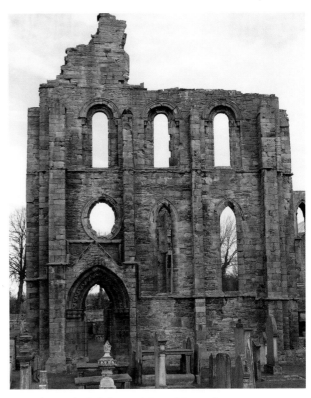

4.5 Elgin Cathedral, the south face of the south transept (© Richard Fawcett)

At clearstorey level there are round-headed windows, one to each bay, which, since they are clearly part of the same campaign as the lancets below, offer an interesting demonstration that round-headed windows might still be preferred for certain situations even after pointed lancets had become more common. At gable level, only the masonry at the south end survives, incorporating the flank of one window; early views suggest it had a three-light traceried window in its final state.

The basic design formula seen here, with its superimposed tiers of triplets of single-light windows, is one that had a long history before its use at Elgin. An early version of the idea had been favoured in the gable wall elevations of the great eastern English cathedrals and abbeys from the turn of the eleventh and twelfth centuries, as at Norwich and Peterborough, for example, and in the course of the early twelfth century it had gained a fresh lease of life at the hands of the Cistercians, for whom it offered an attractively straightforward solution to the treatment of terminal walls. Its use by the Cistercians of northern England, as seen in the north transept of Kirkstall Abbey (Illus 4.6),[385] foreshadowed its adoption in the east gables of several of the major Scottish churches of the second half of the twelfth century. Amongst these were St Andrews Cathedral after 1160 and Arbroath Abbey after 1178,[386] and very probably the presbyteries of Jedburgh and Dryburgh Abbeys. What is seen in the south transept at Elgin is therefore a variant on what was by then a well-established theme, that was to be

4.6   Kirkstall Abbey, the north transept (© Richard Fawcett)

4.7   Elgin Cathedral, the capitals on the west side of the south transept doorway (© Richard Fawcett)

4.8   Elgin Cathedral, the capitals on the east side of the south transept doorway (© Richard Fawcett)

4.9   Holyrood Abbey, a capital of the blind arcading in the south nave aisle (Historic Scotland © Crown Copyright)

yet further exploited in the course of the thirteenth century, and that was eventually to culminate in the later east end of Elgin Cathedral itself.

The external details of the lower parts of the south transept south front are boldly handled. The lancets at that level have broad continuous chamfers below a thin hood-mould, while the vesica has a reveal consisting of a hollow framed by a roll and a chamfer. The mouldings of the doorway are of relatively large scale: each of the jambs originally had three major shafts alternating with two lesser shafts set in front of a broad diagonal plane and there was a continuous inner order; the central order of the arch has a band of massive dogtooth framed by a hollowed roll on one side and a rather squashed filleted roll flanked by hollows and chamfers on the other side. Such treatment of filleted rolls has parallels in a number of early-thirteenth-century works in northern England, as seen perhaps most notably in the new choir of Rievaulx Abbey.[387] Framing the arch is a shallowly cut scalloped border.

Of the capitals of this doorway, those to the west have simple leaves in U-shaped combinations, while those to the east have groupings of stiff-leaf foliage between which hang berries (Illus 4.7, 4.8). A partial parallel for the west capitals may be seen in a number of capitals of the decorative wall arcade below the windows in the south nave aisle of Holyrood Abbey, except that at Holyrood those capitals have additional leaves below and between the basic U-shaped combinations (Illus 4.9). As throughout the whole of the south transept, the abaci of the capitals are of rounded form. The mouldings of the windows at the upper level are more delicately detailed. Nook shafts (now gone) with bell caps supported an outer order of a roll flanked by hollows, and there is a continuous inner order of double curvature.

Little now survives of the east face of the transept, and the overhanging masonry at the north end of the upper level is supported by a massive early-nineteenth-century buttress. One of the few surviving features on this side is the south reveal of a clearstorey window, which has continuous mouldings of double curvature and which, unlike the windows of the south gable at this level, appears to have had a pointed arch springing from a slightly lower level than the arch springings of the south gable windows.

More survives of the west than of the east wall of the transept, and it is of added interest for embodying evidence for the successive changes that took place in the adjacent part of the nave (Illus 4.10). Although the section of the transept that projected beyond the original single south nave aisle, which is the only part of the west wall to survive, was divided into two equal bays by a buttress, the arrangement of the windows was more irregular. At the lower level there was no window in the southern bay, and only a single window in the next bay. That single window appears to have risen from a higher point than

4.10 Elgin Cathedral, the west face of the south transept, seen from the west (© Richard Fawcett)

its counterparts in the south front on the indications of the string course in the adjacent bay, though much of the evidence for the window was lost when the south-east nave chapel was added. In adding that chapel the whole window opening was blocked, leaving only part of the southern arc of its head externally evident in the masonry. At clearstorey level there is a single lancet in the southern bay, set well to the north of the central axis of the bay, while the surviving reveal of the window in the adjacent bay to the north appears to have been set over the outer wall of the original aisle wall, thus not being vertically aligned with the window below it. The position of this latter window suggests that the part of the transept corresponding to both the width of the original nave aisle and the first section projecting beyond it were treated as a single broad bay. The clearstorey windows rest on a continuous string course, and a second string course is taken around their heads as a hood-mould, while the window reveals take the form of a continuous broad chamfer. At the wall-head is a series of regularly spaced corbels which must have formed the lower part of the corbel table of a projecting cornice.

Within the transept, the lowest part of the south wall has been much modified to allow the insertion of two canopied tombs, though a piscina at the east end of the wall was left clear (Illus 4.11). Above the tombs are two widely splayed unmoulded pointed rear arches to the lower level of windows, with a taller and wider, but equally plain, rear arch to the vesica above the doorway in the west bay. Window seats within the vesica rear arch suggest that there may have been a gallery of some kind within the transept – presumably of timber – to give access to that level, though nothing remains to indicate how it would have been reached or how it was supported. At clearstorey level the three south windows are set back behind a mural passage. On the inner side of this passage it appears there was a continuous arcade of five arches, those corresponding to the windows being round-arched, like the windows themselves, and those corresponding to the piers of masonry between the windows being narrower and pointed. Only the two western arches of this arcade survive complete, but there can be little doubt that the others once existed. The small piers supporting this arcade have a quadrangular core fronted by three-quarter shafts flanked by hollows, and the capitals of the shafts are decorated with a range of basically stiff-leaf foliage (Illus 4.12, 4.13). A second, higher mural passage ran across the gable, but insufficient remains to be certain how it was treated towards the interior. There are no indications of how the transept was covered internally, other than that it was clearly not vaulted; it may be that there was a curved or polygonal barrel ceiling that would have left the gable windows internally visible.

4.11 Elgin Cathedral, the south and west internal walls of the south transept (© Richard Fawcett)

The inner face of the east wall of the transept, like its outer face, is so fragmentary that it is difficult to be certain of its original treatment, but at the lower level there appears to have been a wide arch rising from the floor up to near the string course below the clearstorey. The survival of a trifoliate-headed piscina and aumbry in the south-east corner demonstrate that, as might be expected, there was an altar against the east wall, and the arch may have been intended to frame both that altar and a window above it. At clearstorey level, on the inner side of the mural passage, there are the remains of what appears to have been an echelon grouping of three arches, the wider central one framing a single window. That central arch was carried on triplet shafts, while the surviving outer jamb had two orders of free-standing shafts; all the capitals are bell-shaped.

The inner face of the west wall of the south transept, like its outer face, was of a less regular design than either of the other two transept walls. At the lowest level, above a stone bench, was a continuous blind wall arcade with a prominent subordinate order of cusping. Traces of cut-back capitals or corbels are visible below the arch springings. On the indications of the detailing, this arcading is more likely to have been inserted as part of the post-1270 repairs than to have been a primary feature. It is also evident from the character of its mouldings that the southern respond of

4.12 Elgin Cathedral, a capital of the south transept clearstorey arcade (© Richard Fawcett)

4.13 Elgin Cathedral, a capital of the south transept clearstorey arcade. This capital and the one shown in Illus 4.12 are probably the work of the same mason. (© Richard Fawcett)

the arch into the nave aisle was rebuilt at that time, though much of what is now seen of the respond was rebuilt along with the early-nineteenth-century masonry buttress which supports the overhanging upper parts of the wall. Above the blind arcading is the rear arch of the single window at the lower level of this side of the transept, which was blocked when the south-east nave chapel was added. Its rear arch was originally of a similar form to those along the south face, and descended down to a short distance above the wall arcading, where there are traces of a cut-back string course. The lower part of the rear arch is now blocked through the full thickness of the wall, though the inner reveal of the window itself was left exposed, with the blocking confined to the daylight opening of the window at that level. At clearstorey level, although the mural passage continues around this side, there was no attempt to create an inner arcade like those along the south and east faces, and the remaining arches corresponding to the windows are simply separated by stretches of walling that is unarticulated other than by string courses at sill and arch springing level. Clearly the attention of those within the cathedral was expected to be concentrated mainly on the more important east and south faces of the transept. The two orders of the inner arches of the west clearstorey were similar to the outer jambs on the east side of the transept, being carried on free-standing shafts, which are now lost, set against jambs of stepped profile; the capitals are bell-shaped.

The North Transept

The north transept is less complete than its southern counterpart, having lost the greater part of its gable wall (Illus 4.14). Nevertheless, it can be seen to have had the same deeply chamfered two-stage base course around its walls, except at the north-west corner, where the square projection for the stair turret has its upper chamfer at a higher level. This stair must have been the main access to the clearstorey wall passages of the transept and also to the upper levels of the central tower; it would presumably also have been one of the means of access to the nave clearstorey passage. The north transept has essentially the same provision for buttressing as its southern counterpart, with buttresses set back from the angle at the north-east corner (Illus 4.15), two intermediate buttresses on the north front, and a single intermediate buttress on the west flank. The only slight but significant difference from the buttressing of the south transept is that the surviving examples of the north transept have an intake some distance below the level of the clearstorey string course.

Despite the loss of much of the north wall, a combination of the surviving evidence at the north-east angle, and of Slezer's view of 1693, shows that the basic formula was essentially the same as for the south wall of the south transept, other than that there was a stair turret and no doorway. Two levels of three windows, between the buttresses, occupied the main part of the face, but in the

4.14 View of the north transept and chapter house of Elgin Cathedral in 1791 (Francis Grose, *The Antiquities in Scotland*)

4.15 Elgin Cathedral, the north-east angle of the north transept (© Richard Fawcett)

of the lower tier of north windows can be seen to have been simply splayed, as was the case in the south transept. The inner arches of the north clearstorey passage had reveals with two shafts set against a jamb of stepped profile, and bell-shaped capitals, all of which is closer in type to the east and west clearstoreys rather than to the south clearstorey of the south transept. As in the south transept, the main feature of the lower level of the east wall appears to have been a major arch to frame the altar against this wall, but the lower part of the arch was rebuilt and partly infilled at a later stage. There is an arched aumbry on its north side within the inserted masonry. At the upper level of the east wall the northern end of the clearstorey wall passage is still in evidence; there is no trace of an arcade to its inner face, suggesting it was more like the west than the east clearstorey of the south transept, and raising at least a possibility that the north transept could have been started earlier than its southern counterpart (Illus 4.16). The west wall has the remains of what appears to have been a single inserted tomb canopy towards its northern end, and to the south of this, at a slightly higher level, is the north side of the widely splayed rear arch of the single window on this side. Nothing survives of the west clearstorey.

gable Slezer shows a tightly set triplet of windows rather than the three-light window which appears to have been the final fenestration of the south transept gable. Above a height corresponding to sill level of the lower windows we know from early views that the stair turret was taken in at the angles, resulting in an engaged octagon above the square base. The surviving eastern reveals of the two levels of windows show that the lower windows had a similar broad chamfer with a thin hood-mould at the head as in the south transept, and there was also a similar shafted reveal with bell-shaped capitals to the upper windows.

Insufficient survives of the east wall to be able to say anything about its external fenestration, while only part of the lower level of the west wall still stands. From the fragments of the west wall, however, it can be seen that, as in the south transept, there was just one window at the lower level, outside the line of the original single north nave aisle, and this would have been blocked when the outer nave aisle was added after 1270. Part of the original external base course of this wall survives within the added outer nave aisle, where it may once have been concealed behind the base of an altar.

Moving on to the interior of the north transept, the evidence at the base of the north wall has been disturbed by the insertion of two canopied tombs east of the doorway into the stair turret. But the surviving fragmentary rear arch

4.16 Elgin Cathedral, the east wall of the north transept, seen from the south-west (© Richard Fawcett)

The West Bays of the Nave

Within the nave, the bases and the lower courses of several piers of the three western bays (east of the towers) of the first church survive, albeit as partly reconstructed in 1935–9. More important survivors are the complete western arcade responds and the arcade arch springing above them, which are engaged with the two inner eastern corners of the towers. Above those responds and arch springings are the western reveals of the windows and the inner arcade responds of the clearstorey, which make clear that the nave had a two-storeyed elevation. From the towers there are openings at two levels towards the arcade walls of the nave; the lower ones would have led into the clearstorey passage on each side and the upper ones on to the walks along the wall-head gutters, which were at the same level as those in the transepts. From this intimate inter-relationship between the nave arcade walls and the towers, it may be concluded that if, as perhaps suggested by the change of base courses, the decision to add western towers was only taken after the first cathedral had been laid out in about 1224, that decision must have been made before the western parts of the nave were under construction (Illus 4.17).

The arcade piers had a core of basically cruciform profile, with a major engaged filleted shaft on the cardinal axes and an engaged three-quarter shaft on each of the diagonal axes. The arcade bases are of characteristic thirteenth-century water-holding type. The capitals of the western responds – the only ones to survive – have deep bells surmounted by simple mouldings. The arcade arches were of three orders, the outer orders having slender rolls separated by hollows, and the axial order having a triplet of rolls separated by hollows; some of these rolls were filleted and others plain. The clearstorey windows had broad continuous chamfers both internally and on the south side, but a pair of narrower chamfers on the north side. The jambs of the inner clearstorey arcade had three orders of rolls separated by hollows and they terminated in engaged rolls, the middle roll being filleted. The arc of the arch springing of the clearstorey window on the south side indicates that there was probably space for three closely spaced windows to each bay, and this is supported by what is shown on Slezer's views.

As in the transepts, the high central vessel of Elgin's nave was unvaulted, but the evidence for the covering of the nave aisles is less clear. Certainly there are wall ribs against the towers at the west end of the aisles, which might suggest that the aisles were always vaulted. Against this, however, is the slightly uncomfortable relationship of those ribs with the abaci of the arcade respond capitals, while the weather moulding of the original roof-line of the north aisle, built into the east face of the north tower, appears to descend too low to have co-existed easily with the vaulting unless there was

4.17 Elgin Cathedral, the junction of the south nave arcade wall with the south-west tower (© Richard Fawcett)

some form of complex roof configuration. The problems of interpreting the evidence are further complicated by the fact that the roof weather moulding over the south aisle is of much shallower pitch, and could fit easily over the vault indicated by the wall rib; however, this weather moulding appears to be of a different section from that over the north aisle and is apparently a later insertion. One final piece of evidence is the curious feature of a much remodelled window that opens out from the first floor of the north-west tower. This would have looked into the narrow space between the vault and roof of the north aisle if the two had co-existed in the form we now see, whereas it seems more likely that it had been meant to provide a view down the aisle. It should be noted that there was originally a similar window in the east face of the south tower, and in each case the existence inside the towers of an embrasure of primary construction points to the intention that there was always to have been a window in this position. On balance, all of this appears to suggest that the wall ribs, and therefore the vault, are of secondary construction. In further support of a later date for the vault represented by those ribs is the fact that they have the same profile as those in the vault springings associated with the outer north aisle that was added after 1270. It therefore seems very likely that the aisles, like the central vessel, were initially unvaulted.

Assuming that, once the foundations had been laid out, the building of the cathedral had started with the more liturgically important parts at the east end, and had then progressed westwards, the decision to have a two-storeyed elevation in the nave was clearly anticipated in the transepts and probably from the very start of the work. There is sometimes an assumption that a two-storeyed elevation was in some way inferior to one with three storeys, and some support for this view could be derived from the fact that the eastern limbs of Scotland's two most architecturally ambitious cathedrals, at St Andrews and Glasgow, which were started around 1162 and about 1240[388] respectively, had three-storeyed elevations. At Elgin, however, the outstanding quality of the work throughout the first building campaign makes it extremely unlikely that the choice of elevation type was anything other than the expression of positive preference.

In trying to understand what lay behind the choice of a two-storeyed elevation by Elgin's patrons and designers, we should remember that, since the late twelfth century, there had been a growing number of experiments with ways of reducing the impact of the triforium or gallery at the middle stage of three-storeyed elevations. This was at first particularly the case in Wales and the English West Country, as at St David's Cathedral and Llanthony Priory.[389] But by the 1220s and 1230s fresh approaches to two-storeyed designs were being worked out by leading masons elsewhere, as in the choirs of Pershore Abbey, Worcestershire,[390] and Southwell Collegiate Church, Nottinghamshire (Illus 4.18).[391] There was also an interest in suppressing the middle storey in parts of Continental Europe at this time, notably in Normandy, as in the choir of Coutances Cathedral and the partly reconstructed nave of Bayeux Cathedral of around the 1230s and 1240s respectively.[392] Designs such as those of Pershore and Southwell show significant parallels with what we can understand of Elgin's nave, particularly in the way that inner clearstorey arcades of two or three arches were designed to correspond to each bay of the main arcade. The main difference between those English churches and what we see at Elgin is that there was no vaulting over Elgin's central vessel, so that the arches of the clearstorey arcade did not have to be grouped in an echelon formation to accommodate the lateral severies of the vaulting. But in Scotland high vaults had always been rare, so we need not be surprised that it was decided not to have them at Elgin. Admittedly more unusual was the apparent absence of vaults over the aisles, though this had the advantage that there was no need to elevate the sills of the clearstorey windows over a sloping aisle roof angled to rise above the vaulting.

The master mason of Elgin was not alone in Scotland at this time in investigating the range of possibilities inherent in two-storeyed elevations. In the nave of Dunblane Cathedral, where vaulting was evidently originally intended to be placed over the aisles, that vaulting was eliminated after

4.18   Southwell Minster, the interior of the east limb (© Richard Fawcett)

building had started,[393] and the arcades were heightened, possibly taking over the part of the overall height that had originally been allocated to a gallery or triforium (Illus 4.19). Other variants on these experiments are seen in the transepts of Pluscarden Priory, where building was started after the foundation of the house in about 1230,[394] though at Pluscarden the chapel aisles were vaulted, with implications for the height of the clearstorey window sills at the back of the wall passage. Later in the century, other ways of reducing the impact of the middle storey were to be explored in the nave of Glasgow Cathedral, where the clearstorey and gallery were conjoined within pairs in each bay,[395] and there may also have been an intention to create something similar to Glasgow's nave in the nave of Paisley Abbey.[396] The two-storeyed design of Elgin's nave must therefore be understood within a wider context of developments both within Scotland and further afield.

The 'Scottishness' of the approach taken in Elgin's nave is, however, particularly evident in the approach to pier design, with its engaged shafts around a core of stepped profile; piers of this type had become increasingly common in Scotland since the first years of the thirteenth century, the earliest examples possibly being in the nave of Holyrood Abbey.[397] As might be expected, the closest parallels for the

4.19 Dunblane Cathedral, the nave (© Richard Fawcett)

4.20 Elgin Cathedral, the west towers (© Richard Fawcett)

Elgin pier type date from the second quarter of the century, and include the north nave arcade of Dunblane Cathedral, where all the shafts are simply rounded, the Blackadder Aisle at Glasgow Cathedral[398] and the north nave arcade at Inchmahome Priory.[399] Construction had probably started at all of those buildings around the 1230s and 1240s, though it may have been several years before work reached the parts in question, and it was presumably around the same years that work at Elgin had extended into the nave.

The Western Towers and the West Front

The western towers are faced with carefully cut ashlar which is generally of relatively shallow courses (Illus 4.20). The only exceptions to this are the parts of the east faces of the towers which were enclosed by the original single aisle on each side of the nave, and the inner flanks of the towers that faced into the central vessel. The latter were refaced above arcade level after the fire of 1390, but the lower parts are of rubble which shows extensive traces of burning.

As already said, the towers have a different base course from that around the transepts, suggesting that the decision to build them may have been made after the earlier parts of

the first phase of the building had been laid out. Although modified through later consolidation in a number of areas, in its original form the base course of the towers consisted of two levels of chamfers and an upper string course. As completed, the towers rise through four storeys, with string courses below the windows. Most of the corners of the towers are reinforced by pairs of slender buttresses slightly set back from the angles, but both buttresses are omitted from the north-east corner of the south tower and the south-east corner of the north tower, while that on the east face of the north-east corner of the north tower has also been omitted. The buttresses rise without break up to the string course below the windows of the top storey, where they are chamfered back at the angles behind a gablet, and they terminate below the wall-head with a second tier of gablets.

The towers have windows at all four stages. At the lowest level are single small slit-like lancets in the west and south faces of the south tower and in the west and north faces of the north tower. At the second storey there were two-light Y-traceried windows in the same faces, though the tracery of those in the north tower was modified at a later date when that stage was internally subdivided. The most complex windows were to the third storey, in the west, south and east faces of the south tower, and the west, north and east faces of the north tower. Within a semicircular arch there were four lights grouped into pairs within two asymmetrical arches. Putting aside comparisons with inner clearstorey arcades in the upper parts of a number of English cathedrals, such as those at Salisbury, which are not directly relevant, there is nothing quite like this ramping arrangement of lights. However, within Scotland there are partial parallels with the asymmetrically arched window at the east end

4.21 Dunblane Cathedral, the east windows of the sacristy range (© Richard Fawcett)

of the north choir annexe of Dunblane Cathedral, which probably dates from not long after the start of operations there in the late 1230s (Illus 4.21).[400]

The most elegant treatment is reserved for the top storey of each tower, with slight differences of treatment between the two towers. On three of the four faces of each tower a single lancet with continuous reveal mouldings is set within the central arch of an arcade of three arches. Flanked by the top section of the buttresses, which have chamfered angles and gablets at both top and bottom, this gives an attractive sense of lightness to the storey as it rises above the nave roof apex. In fact, however, the delicacy of detailing of this top stage of the towers has very much more in common with the work produced as part of the post-1270 operations elsewhere in the cathedral. Taking account of the length of time it usually took to complete towers, it may simply be that the original scheme was only completed, albeit to a modified design, in the later decades of the century. However, in view of the emphasis given to the windows of the third stage, is it possible that the towers were originally intended to rise through no more than three storeys, and that a decision to add a fourth stage was only taken as part of the proposals to repair and enlarge the cathedral in the 1270s? This possibility will be considered further when looking at the interiors of the towers. It is unclear if there was ever a parapet above the top stage in either form, but it

is perhaps more likely that the intention was to have spires rising directly from the wall-head.

The only access to the lowest storey of each tower is by a doorway at the west end of the inner nave aisles. Each doorway has a continuously chamfered surround, but while the doorway into the south tower is round-arched, that into the north tower is of slightly depressed form. The lowest storey in each of the towers was covered by a quadripartite vault with heavy chamfered diagonal ribs and wall ribs with an edge roll. This was the only storey to be vaulted when the towers were first built and, indeed, probably the only part of the whole building in its earliest form to have vaults. The lancet windows at this level have unmoulded splayed rear arches. The second storey of the towers was reached by way of the single spiral stair at the south-east angle of the south tower. Above that level there were spiral stairs at the north-west angle of the south tower and at the south-west angle of the north tower. Access between the two towers was provided at three levels: across a mural gallery above the west doorway; by a parapet walk that was open to the interior at the base of the west window; and by a wall-walk across the west gable. In their present form, however, these connections date largely from the post-1390 repairs. As already indicated when discussing the nave, there was also access from the towers into the nave clearstorey passages and onto the wall-head walkways above the clearstorey. The evidence of extensive fire damage, which is particularly prominent within the south tower, is a useful indicator of which parts of the internal masonry are original and which parts had to be repaired after one or other of the fires. It is worth noting in the south tower that, while there is much fire damage at second-storey level around the doorway from the lower stair, the masonry encasing the stair to the upper levels is undamaged, suggesting that it had to be extensively rebuilt.

The first flight of stairs within the south tower, from the lowest to the second storey, has been modified on more than one occasion. It is now entered through a doorway from the inner south nave aisle, in the north face of the stair turret. But it seems also to have been entered initially by a doorway in the east face of the stair turret, which, before the addition of the post-1270 outer aisle, would have been outside the building. The wall of the turret has been extensively refaced in this area, while the steps of the spiral stair are now mainly made up of roughly recut ledger slabs of both medieval and post-medieval date, demonstrating that the stair was rebuilt some considerable time after the Reformation.

There has also clearly been major reconstruction at the second-storey head of the stair turret, evidently as part of the post-1270 modifications. Externally, this is seen along the south and east faces of the turret, where there are blind arcades that are evidently of the later thirteenth century.

4.22 Elgin Cathedral, the east wall of the south-west tower at second-storey level (© Richard Fawcett)

4.23 Elgin Cathedral, the fragmentary vault over the south-west tower stairwell (© Richard Fawcett)

4.24 Fire-damaged inward-sloping masonry in the south tower that may have been intended to support a stone spire (© Richard Fawcett)

Internally, the stair appears to have been initially intended to enter the second-storey chamber at a higher level than the present doorway, and the arch of the doorway that was first constructed is still to be seen at the east end of the south wall of the chamber. It also seems that there was an intention to give access from the stair to a short corridor at a mezzanine level in the east wall.

The most puzzling aspect of the level indicated by the original doorway from the stair is that it should be so high above the floor level within the tower, since that floor level is fixed by the extrados of the ground-floor vault, and is also tied to a wide embrasure in the east wall within which is a blocked window that would have looked down into the south nave aisle (Illus 4.22). It is one possibility that the vault was only inserted after the fire of 1270 and that in doing so it was decided to lower the floor level of the second storey, although, since the east window embrasure also shows signs of fire damage, that seems unlikely (Illus 4.23). The changes to the stair will be discussed more fully below. In the north tower, the evidence for the original treatment of the chamber on the second storey has been largely obscured by alterations which, on stylistic evidence, must be attributed to the post-1390 rebuilding.

Below the sill level of the top storey of windows in the south tower are fire-damaged traces of three courses of inwardly sloping masonry set diagonally across the north-east, south-east and south-west corners. The most likely reason for the provision of this masonry is to support diagonally directed faces of a spire, and its relatively low location may be seen as affording further support for the suggestion made above that the fourth storey of the towers was not part of the original design (Illus 4.24).

As the frontispiece of the cathedral towards the outside world, every effort would have been made to ensure that the twin-towered west front was as impressive as could be achieved, though nothing survives in place of what first stood between the two towers, at the end of the central vessel of the nave. But it is almost certain that, as was later the case, the principal processional entrance to the building occupied much of its lower part, and it is possible that its most prominent feature above that doorway was a great rose window of which fragments were found during works on the vault of the south choir aisle in about 1936 (Illus 4.25). It should be stressed that the original location of this window cannot be identified with absolute certainty, though it is clear that it can have had no place in any of the gable walls of the cathedral in their final medieval state, and on balance it seems most likely that its location was at the centre of the west front until the repairs carried out after the fire of 1390. Elgin would not have been the first major Scottish church to have been designed to have a twin-towered west front with a large-scale circular window above the processional entrance. There was another example of this approach at Arbroath Abbey, which is probably slightly earlier in date than Elgin, though it is not known what – if any – tracery there was in the Arbroath window. The design of the window at Elgin has been shown to be of a type found in a group of major Yorkshire churches, including the Cistercian abbey of Byland, but with the only complete surviving example being in the gable of York Minster's south transept.[401] While the Byland and York windows each had two rings of twelve and twenty-four radiating arches, however, that at Elgin appears to have been more complex in having three rings of six, twelve and twenty-four radiating arches. The likelihood that the Elgin rose was cut by masons who had worked in Yorkshire provides further evidence that there was a continuing active channel of communication for architectural ideas with that part of northern England throughout the thirteenth century, as there had also been in the previous century.[402]

4.25 A reconstruction study of the fragmentary rose window of Elgin Cathedral (© Stuart Harrison)

The South-eastern Nave Chapel

Assuming that the decision to build the towers was taken in the course of constructing the nave, the chapel that extended along the three eastern bays of the south nave aisle was probably the next addition to the cathedral once work on them was either complete or nearing completion. So far as can now be judged from the surviving fragments that were absorbed into the outer south nave aisle, the masonry was of rubble that was roughly brought to courses at intervals. The south wall of the chapel was built slightly beyond the intermediate buttress on the west side of the adjacent transept, and the lower part of that buttress was cut back so that it would not project into the chapel. The wall rises from a two-stage chamfered base course, which takes a partial lead from that of the adjacent south transept. Above the lower part of the base course the walling of the two eastern bays has been largely lost, while much of the western bay was extensively rebuilt in both the post-1270 and post-1390 campaigns. The chapel was separated from the south aisle by an arcade of three arches carried on slender piers constructed on what would have been the original line of the south aisle wall. These piers are composed of four filleted half shafts separated by three-quarter hollows. On the indications of the springing that has been set into the west wall of the transept, the arches carried by those piers were made up of four orders of rather compressed filleted rolls separated by deep hollows. The bays of the chapel were demarcated by transverse arches of the same form, some of the springings of which remain in place along what remains of the south wall. There was also a wall arch at the east end of the chapel of the same type, which presumably framed the altar. The compressed filleted rolls of these arches show some affinities with the details of the south transept doorway.

An attractive feature of the chapel is the way in which the arcade arch of the east bay and the east wall arch interpenetrate. The vogue for interpenetration of the individual mouldings of arches probably first developed towards the end of the twelfth century, and is seen in an essentially late-Romanesque idiom in the wall arcading of the north aisle of Holyrood Abbey of around 1190. Looking further afield, an example of a type of interpenetration that is closer to what is seen at Elgin is to be found in the blind arcading within the north porch of around 1210 at Wells Cathedral, Somerset,[403] though this is evidence of nothing more than that this fashion had its followers over a wide area. Scottish examples of such treatment of mouldings closer in date to that at Elgin are to be seen in the doorway arch and vault ribs of the partly rebuilt north porch of Paisley Abbey,[404] and in the south transept aisle at Pluscarden Priory, where the vault ribs and arcade arches interpenetrate. In neither of those cases, however, was the interpenetration such a prominent feature as at Elgin.

4.26 Elgin Cathedral, the capital and arch springing of the east wall arch of the south-east nave chapel (© Richard Fawcett)

4.27 Elgin Cathedral, a capital and part of a transverse wall arch in the south-east nave chapel (© Richard Fawcett)

The east wall arch at Elgin is received at its southern end by a corbel in the form of a capital with a short section of respond terminating at its base with undercut foliage (Illus 4.26). The corresponding wall arch at the west end of the chapel was received at its southern end by a respond in the form of a quarter pier. The transverse arch between the second and third bays appears at first to have been carried on a respond in the form of a half pier, though the respond was later removed and the capital provided with support in the form of a rather inadequate triplet of simple conical corbels (Illus 4.27). The capitals and corbels of these arches are decorated with deeply undercut and widely spreading leaves of various types. Among the leaves of the capital between the second and third bays, delightful wyvern-like creatures disport themselves. Once established, the taste for mythical creatures took firm hold at Elgin, and charming examples are to be seen on several of the post-1270 vaulting bosses that were found during the early-nineteenth-century clearance of collapsed overburdens.

The slenderness of the piers and the absence of vault springings associated with the transverse arches make clear that there was no intention to place vaulting over the south-eastern chapel; indeed the stump of the outer wall as it emerges from the south transept appears to have part of a decorative blind arch in an area that would have had

to be covered by any vaulting placed over the chapel. A horizontal row of corbels above the east wall arch suggests that the chapel was covered by a flat ceiling above a wall plate, while the roof moulding inserted into the west wall of the south transept, at the time that the window in that wall was blocked, shows that the roof was pitched at a very shallow angle.

5.1   Elgin Cathedral, fragments of tracery in one of the lower level windows of the east gable (© Richard Fawcett)

5 THE REBUILDING AFTER THE FIRE OF 1270

The Extended Presbytery and Choir

So far as can now be judged, no trace of the first unaisled eastern limb was left externally in evidence after the post-1270 augmentations. Indeed, as already said, the only part to have been retained appears to have been its north wall, which was entirely enveloped by the new work. If the original eastern limb in its final state corresponded to no more than the three western bays of the eastern limb's central vessel, the eastward extension after the fire of 1270 effectively doubled the length of this part of the cathedral. But the overall floor area of the eastern limb must have been almost quadrupled, when account is taken of the great width of the new choir aisles. Clearly it was intended that this new phase of work should provide an altogether more magnificent setting for the daily services and rituals of the cathedral clergy, with that setting located within a fully self-contained part of the building rather than extending down into the crossing. Yet, at the same time, it appears to have been decided that the new work should sit as sympathetically as possible with what already existed elsewhere in the building. Although in its Scottish context the repertory of architectural detailing is unquestionably of the later thirteenth century, when seen against that of the earlier work, there would have been no jarring differences of scale or of relative proportions in the elevations towards the central vessel or in the view down the church from the nave into the eastern limb.

Starting with the exterior of the new work, the east front of the extended eastern limb was designed as its great climax, and its markedly vertical appearance is emphasised by the way the aisle ends are set back from the central vessel. The parts intended to be visible were faced throughout with finely cut buff-coloured ashlar. The two main tiers of windows, corresponding in relative height to the arcade and clearstorey inside the building, have groupings of five equal-height lancets to each tier, which occupy most of the space between massive octagonal buttresses at the angles, with the residue of the wall being articulated by thin vertical shafts and string courses. Within the area of the gable at the top of this front there are now the relics of a great rose window flanked by a blind arch on each side, and with the remains of a further pair of blind arches at the gable apex. The stubs of the tracery in the rose window, together with the inner mouldings of the reveal, evidently date from the post-1390 repairs, though it seems certain that there was always a rose window in this position, since the outer mouldings of the reveal show a repertory of elements similar to that of the rest of the post-1270 work. The mass of the octagonal buttresses is relieved by two tiers of deeply recessed cusped blind arches at the level of the lower tier of windows, with one arch to each face. By contrast, the parts of the buttresses corresponding to the upper tier of windows and the base of the gable are plain, perhaps largely because the existence of the stairwell at this level meant that the walls were very thin, and the only piercings are the windows that light the spiral stairs interconnecting clearstorey and wall-head. The pinnacles which surmount the buttresses at the height corresponding to the upper part of the gable again have a cusped blind arch to each face, all faces being capped by a tall gablet that runs back into the facets of the spirelets that once rose steeply through the pinnacles.

The character of the change from the work of post-1224 to the work of post-1270 is apparent in the mouldings, those of the latter phase being significantly more complex and minutely detailed. In the window and internal clearstorey arcade jambs the repertory is chiefly composed of combinations of engaged shafts, many of which have narrow fillets that in some cases look almost more like keeling, alternating with hollows or with bands of dogtooth or square-flower decoration. The arch mouldings are generally particularly finely detailed, with combinations of as many as five double- or triple-filleted rolls separated by half or three-quarter hollows to each order. The lower windows of the east front, for example, have two bands of square flower on each side of a filleted engaged shaft to the jambs, with triplets of shafts between the windows. The upper windows are slightly simpler, having a band of dogtooth between two shafts as the principal elements. But the greatest difference between the two levels of windows was the provision of simple bar tracery in the window heads at the lower level which, on the indications of the remaining stumps, consisted

5.2   Sweetheart Abbey, windows on the north side of the presbytery (© Richard Fawcett)

of no more than a circlet above a sub-arch (Illus 5.1). Having been introduced from France into England in the 1240s,[405] bar tracery was a relatively late arrival in Scotland, and these examples at Elgin were part of the first Scottish generation. Among other early examples are windows in the last phase of works in the nave of Dunblane Cathedral, in the transepts of Glasgow Cathedral, which probably date from the 1270s, and in the choir of Sweetheart Abbey, which was started soon after 1273 (Illus 5.2). There were also examples of uncertain date nearer to Elgin in the choir of Pluscarden Abbey.[406]

In the fundamental approach to design, with its superimposed tiers of lancets, the east front of Elgin represents a later – and considerably more sophisticated – stage of the tradition of façade composition that had already been taken up in the south transept. The particular approach to design seen in the east front had its immediate origins in northern England, and especially in Yorkshire, where there had been several developments on the theme of tiered groupings of lancets in the course of the first half of the thirteenth century. The way in which the lancets have come to occupy virtually the whole of the available space in the Elgin east front, together with the use of massive octagonal pinnacles at the angles and an oculus in the gable, is reminiscent of early-thirteenth-century work at Whitby Abbey, as seen particularly in the north transept gable (Illus 5.3). But the design is even closer in spirit to the south front

of the great transept at Beverley Minster, Yorkshire, in the greater lightness of the mouldings and also in way that the rose window in the gable is flanked by blind arches, and in this there are also some parallels with the vast south transept front at York Minster. Elgin differs from those, however, in its larger number of lancets and also in the use of simple bar tracery at the lower level. There appear to be no parallels in the lancets of the English members of this group for the use of tracery, except as secondary insertions, though there does seem to have been a growing wish to reduce the mass of the wall as far as possible and to fit in a larger number of lancets. Southwell Collegiate Church, which has already been referred to in connection with the two-storeyed elevation of the nave, has four lancets to each storey of its east front, while the west front of Ripon Minster, Yorkshire, has two levels of five lancets to its wide nave between the two towers. In all of this we are reminded of the continuing exchange of ideas that was taking place between Scotland and England throughout the thirteenth century. Yet Elgin was not simply a derivative copy of architectural solutions that had been worked out south of the Border; it is a highly creative contributor to a pool of ideas that extended widely across parts of the two kingdoms.

Apart from the east front, the most complete part of this phase of work at Elgin to have come down to us is the south side of the eastern limb, of which five of the seven bays still

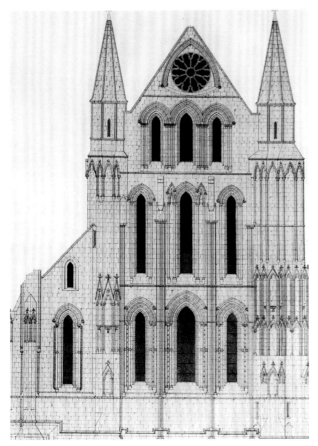

5.3 Whitby Abbey, the north transept (Edmund Sharpe, *Architectural Parallels*)

stand to almost full height, a state of preservation at least partly attributable to the fact that much of the aisle which runs along three of those bays was adapted for use as a burial place by the dukes of Gordon and their ancestors (Illus 5.4).

The two shallow aisle-less bays at the east end of the presbytery are subdivided by a buttress running up to the wall-head corbel table, with intakes at the level of the sills and arch springings of the lower level of windows, and with chamfered angles and a gabled top. The lower level of this flank had windows of two lights, each light having had a sub-arch and circlet like the lower lancets of the east window, and with a circlet at the head of the tracery field (Illus 5.5). Because of the existence of sedilia inside the cathedral at this point, the sill of the western of these two windows is at a higher level than that of the eastern window. The upper level of windows to this pair of bays, which rises from a string course with semi-dogtooth decoration, has two lancets to each bay, with a band of dogtooth between a pair of filleted shafts to the jambs.

The third bay from the east, which is the easternmost of the aisled bays and which houses the south-east chapel at the east end of the aisle, is also shallow. It has a pair of lancets to the clearstorey; but west of that the bays are deeper and there are triplets of lancets to each bay at clearstorey level, taking a lead from the earlier work in the nave (Illus 5.6).

5.4 Elgin Cathedral, the south flank of the east limb (© Richard Fawcett)

5.5   Elgin Cathedral, fragments of tracery in one of the lower level windows of the south flank of the presbytery (© Richard Fawcett)

5.6   Elgin Cathedral, the south choir arcade wall (© Richard Fawcett)

It seems that the usual demarcation of bays at clearstorey level of the aisled section of the eastern limb was by a thin pilaster-like buttress, capped by a gablet. But between the fourth and fifth bays from the east, perhaps marking both the junction of the old and new work at the lower level, and also the divide between choir and presbytery, is a buttress with chamfered angles of similar dimensions to that between the first and second bays from the east. Since this buttress penetrates the wall-head cornice, it is likely that it was capped by a pinnacle. The outer walls of the three surviving aisled bays on the south are substantially of the post-1270 campaign, having the same type of base course as that below the aisle-less section of the presbytery. However, there has clearly been much remodelling of the aisle walls after the fire of 1390, and the three- or four-light windows now seen, with their broadly chamfered reveals, are part of the repairs carried out after that disaster and will be discussed more fully with that phase of work.

Less survives of the aisled portion of the presbytery and choir on the north than on the south side. The outer wall of the aisle has been lost above the base course except at the east end of the aisle, where much of the east and north walls of the north-east choir chapel stand to full height apart from their buttresses, and at the adjacent entrance to the chapter house. Indeed, in the third bay from the east the liberal incision of the monogram 'AM'[407] on many of the individual stones suggests that much of the masonry now seen there is modern. As if in compensation, the north clearstorey of the central vessel extends about a half bay further west than its southern counterpart. The clearstorey on the north side of the presbytery is essentially similar to that on the south, with the three eastern bays having two lancets each and the deeper fourth bay having three. By contrast, the surviving section of clearstorey over the north side of the choir bays takes a rather different form, and it will be remembered that this is the section that extends over the retained earlier

wall. As on the south side of the eastern limb, the division between presbytery and choir at clearstorey level was marked by a massive buttress, but west of that there were no buttresses or pilasters to indicate bay divisions, and on the surviving evidence it seems that this side of the clearstorey was lit by a sequence of paired lancets which took little account of what happened below, and which may not have closely corresponded to the bay rhythm on the opposite side of the choir. The easternmost surviving pair of lancets over the retained wall is very like the pairs of lights to be found further east in both detail and scale. Yet, while the next pair to the west, and the reveal of the window that remains at the broken west end of the clearstorey, have external mouldings that are related to those of the other windows, the windows themselves do not rise quite so high, and they are both broader and set more closely together. While there can be no certainty, what seems likely is that the clearstorey over the retained section of north wall was built before the rest, perhaps because this wall was ready to take its clearstorey at an earlier stage. Subsequently, modifications were introduced into the design on the south side and further east as the work progressed, presumably as the new design was more completely worked out and its full implications came to be grasped.

Moving on to the interior of the eastern limb, the wish to ensure continuity of proportions from the nave into the eastern limb is most evident on the south side. There it can be seen that the underlying principle of the two-storeyed design, with three lancets in each bay of the clearstorey corresponding to one bay of the arcade, takes the nave elevations as a starting point. As has already been seen externally, however, the greatest change from the nave is in the complexity of the mouldings, which are again characterised by closely set concentrations of shafts or rolls alternating with hollows, with even greater intricacy of detailing in the arches than in the piers, responds and reveals. The arcade piers have triplets of shafts on the cardinal axes, the axial shaft being filleted, with an almost monotonous sequence of shafts alternating with salient quadrant hollows to the diagonal faces. Mouldings of the same kind extend into the massive responds which divide choir from presbytery, and which terminate at clearstorey level in three-tiered pinnacles with square-flower decoration to the gablets, and with trifids of simple stiff-leaf foliage as crockets. These pinnacles are such an unusual internal feature that it must be asked if the original intention might instead have been to throw a diaphragm arch across the central vessel between the responds, in order to demarcate the presbytery from the choir. The pier bases are of refined water-holding type, while the capitals have closely spaced tiers of mouldings covering the greater part of the bell, an approach to design which shows some similarities with the caps in the nave of Glasgow Cathedral (Illus 5.7). A notable refinement of detail in those arcade arches that have not been subjected to later modifications is the way in which the mouldings emerge from the vertical line of a springer block above the capital. A certain number of parallels for this detail are to be found throughout England and Europe,[408] and in Scotland comparisons may be drawn with the clearstorey arcade and gable wall windows of the north transept at Dryburgh Abbey, which date from around the mid-thirteenth century (Illus 5.8).[409]

At clearstorey level, the majority of arches to the arcade on the inner side of the wall passage have narrowly filleted shafts to each side of a band of dogtooth as the main

5.7   Elgin Cathedral, a choir arcade capital (© Richard Fawcett)

5.8   Dryburgh Abbey, the north transept windows
       (© Richard Fawcett)

element in the jambs. Over the retained earlier north wall the clearstorey passage is at a slightly higher level, though the eastern pair of arches over that wall is essentially like those on the south side. The lower and wider arches in the west bays of the north clearstorey have jambs of related type, while the arch mouldings are significantly simpler, though the basic vocabulary is broadly akin to that in the rest of the clearstorey. The design of the clearstorey throughout the eastern limb, in which all of the arches in each bay reach up to the same height, demonstrates that the central vessel of the eastern limb was never intended to be covered with stone vaulting. The arched profile of masonry around the rose window in the gable suggests that there was probably a timber barrel ceiling over the central vessel in its final state, and it is reasonable to suspect that this would always have been the way in which the most important of the high spaces throughout the cathedral were covered.[410] With the notable exceptions of St Andrews and Kirkwall Cathedrals, stone vaults were not employed over the central vessels of Scottish cathedrals, timber barrel ceilings probably being the norm. We certainly know from the wall rib against its east wall that Glasgow Cathedral had a timber barrel ceiling of slightly cusped profile by the time Elgin was ready for roofing (Illus 5.9). In fact the ribbed ceiling there, which is largely modern but whose design is based on evidence of what had been there, may provide a good general pointer to

5.9   Glasgow Cathedral, the timber ceiling over the east limb
(© Richard Fawcett)

what we have lost at Elgin.[411] The circle of the existing rose window would have fitted well within such a barrel ceiling and, while the stumps of the rose we now see are mainly of late-medieval date, it is important to note that, like its outer reveal mouldings, the rear arch is manifestly of the post-1270 campaign on the evidence of the engaged shafts and bands of dogtooth to the jambs and the arch mouldings.

It must be assumed that the differences between the two sides of the choir, with one side having arcades opening into the aisles and the other having a blank wall, would have been rendered less obvious by the plethora of furnishings required in this part of the cathedral. Many of these furnishings would have been of timber and have left little trace except where their burning damaged the masonry. The likelihood that it was the burning choir stalls that caused such intense damage at the base of the north choir wall has already been mentioned. A pointer to the site of the bishop's throne is the way in which the leading triplet of the massive south respond between choir and presbytery has been cut back, presumably to allow the insertion of a suitably imposing flèche-like canopy. The east end of the south bank of stalls is the location that would be expected for this feature, though the fact that the respond had to be cut back suggests that the superstructure of the late-medieval throne was more

5.10   Elgin Cathedral, the fragmentary remains of the sedilia (© Richard Fawcett)

ambitious than had been its thirteenth-century predecessor. Around the choir enclosure there would have been screens. The western of those screens would have been in the east crossing arch, where it faced towards the nave, and the paintings associated with it, which were only destroyed as late as 1640, are discussed below. Initially, there would probably also have been screens behind the choir stalls in the three-bay south choir arcade, but in at least one bay this was later replaced by a low stone wall that accommodated a canopied tomb on the side towards the aisle. There would also have been screens at the entrances to the presbytery from the aisles through the arch on each side; the northern of those two arches was later filled with a tomb capped by three arches, with the two eastern arches covering the tomb chest and the western arch covering the doorway from the aisle into the presbytery.

The most important liturgical furnishings within the cathedral were those in the presbytery, with the high altar as their focus. The altar itself, with the retable behind it, was presumably destroyed in the first phase of the Reformation, but one of the stone-built fixtures associated with it survives. In the second bay from the east, on the south side of the aisle-less section of the presbytery, are the fragmentary remains of the sedilia, on which the priest and his assistants sat during parts of the celebration of the mass. These sedilia had four seats recessed into the thickness of the wall, the seats stepping upwards from west to east (Illus 5.10). The recesses were covered by miniature quadripartite vaulting, and were fronted towards the presbytery by arches and gablets, with pinnacles between, all of which was lavishly enriched with square--flower decoration and stiff-leaf crockets. In the third bay from the east on the north side of the presbytery, where the wall of the lower storey is blank because of the presence of the chapel in the aisle behind it, is a tomb recess which is an integral part of the post-1270 work (Illus 5.11). Its design, and the possibility that it served a supplementary liturgical purpose, is discussed along with the other tombs.

The windows piercing the aisles along the five western bays of the remodelled eastern limb were replaced after the fire of 1390, though what survives of the shell of the aisles and their chapels is essentially of the late thirteenth century. Both aisles have a stone bench along the outer wall, and the position of the principal altar within the shallow bay at the east end of each is marked by the provision of a piscina in the adjacent south wall. Internally, the most notable surviving original feature of the aisles is the tierceron vaulting, with finely carved bosses at the multiple intersections; this vaulting survives over the full length of the remaining section of the south aisle and over the chapel of the north aisle (Illus 5.12). Tierceron vaults had perhaps been first developed

5.11 Elgin Cathedral, the tomb recess on the north side of the presbytery (© Richard Fawcett)

at Lincoln Cathedral in the 1230s[412] and, bearing in mind Elgin's debt to Lincoln for the constitution of its chapter, it is attractive to think that it may have been at Elgin that this more complex type of vaulting was introduced to Scotland (Illus 5.13). It was a type of vaulting that was to become very popular for major ecclesiastical buildings, though all of the other Scottish examples appear to be at least a century later than those at Elgin, with the late-fourteenth-century vaults over the south chapel and nave aisle at Fortrose Cathedral (Illus 5.14) and that over the main precinct gate at St Andrews Cathedral Priory[413] possibly being next in date. The date of these examples might be taken to suggest that the Elgin vaults were also of the fourteenth century, and that they were inserted along with the enlarged aisle windows, and it is true that repairs to the vaults were probably required at that time. Nevertheless, both the vault springings and the supporting wall shafts are evidently an integral part of the post-1270 design and, bearing in mind Elgin's close architectural and ecclesiastical contacts with England, there is no reason to see the choir aisle vaults as secondary insertions.

5.12 Elgin Cathedral, the tierceron vaulting over the south choir aisle (© Richard Fawcett)

5.14 Fortrose Cathedral, the south aisle vault (© Richard Fawcett)

5.13 Lincoln Cathedral, the nave vault (© Richard Fawcett)

Works in the Crossing and Transept Areas

The collapse of the central tower in 1711 almost totally destroyed the crossing area, and we therefore have very little physical evidence for the building chronology of this area of the cathedral. However, the partly surviving outer responds of the arches into the two choir aisles from the north and south transepts have mouldings of the type found in the choir piers. This is also the case with the extensively rebuilt outer respond of the arch from the south transept into the inner south nave aisle, though insufficient survives of the west wall of the north transept to be certain if there was a similar respond on that side. The survival of these responds indicates that there was extensive rebuilding in the crossing area after the fire of 1270, and it must be a strong possibility that the central tower itself had to be rebuilt at the same time.

The Outer Nave Aisles and South Porch

Less survives of the post-1270 works in the nave than in the eastern limb, and from the limited remaining evidence it appears that much of what was done after 1270 had to be extensively remodelled after the fire of 1390. Nevertheless, there can be no doubt that the post-1270 works had a major impact on the nave. Amongst the main changes for which there is certain evidence was the addition of outer aisles along the full length of each side of the nave, incorporating the earlier three-bay south-east chapel within the new aisle on the south side. At the same time, a porch was built against the west bay of the south aisle, and the west doorway was reconstructed.

The addition of a symmetrical pair of outer aisles along the nave of a medieval cathedral in any building within the British Isles was most unusual; even in Continental Europe before the wholesale addition of private chapels in the later Middle Ages, double aisles were relatively unusual unless there were particular structural reasons, as at Bourges,[414] and to a lesser extent at Paris. Probably the only British cathedral to foreshadow the Elgin double aisles was Chichester in Sussex, where outer aisles were added along the nave in stages over the central decades of the thirteenth century. It is hard to think that the minor cathedral of Chichester can have been an influence on Elgin, however, though it is worth noting that initially the Chichester aisles appear to have had a gable to each bay,[415] since Elgin in its final state also had such gables to some or all of the bays of the outer aisles.

The date of the Elgin outer aisle gables is uncertain, however. It must be borne in mind that lateral gables had been employed in the twelfth and thirteenth centuries in England. Apart from at Chichester, they are still to be seen in the transept chapels at Fountains Abbey, Yorkshire, for example, and they were almost certainly employed in the nave galleries of Durham. Beyond Britain's shores they were widely used across much of Continental Europe, where they were to be a particular leitmotif of what has been identified as the thirteenth-century Parisian 'court style'.[416] On this basis it cannot be ruled out that they had been first provided as part of the post-1270 operations.

Lateral gables only survive over the third and fourth bays from the east of the south aisle, that is, in what was the western bay of the earlier south-east chapel and in the bay to its west,[417] and in both cases the gables are structurally associated with major four-light windows that are clearly part of the post-1390 modifications (Illus 5.15). It is true that the remaining fragment of cornice of the western of those gables is decorated with semi-dogtooth and miniature intersecting arcading that on first sight looks to be of thirteenth-century type. But semi-dogtooth was also used archaistically in the late-medieval work in the chapter house, and it does seem unlikely that late-thirteenth-century gable cornices would have been retained when the greater part of the gables was having to be rebuilt to accommodate new windows. The evidence for the date of the gables is given further consideration when considering the interior of the south aisle.

The only surviving fragments of nave aisle windows dating from the post-1270 building campaign are in the fifth bay from the west, where there are the east reveal and part of the west reveal of fenestration with lavishly moulded surrounds.

5.15 Elgin Cathedral, the surviving bays of the outer south nave aisle (© Richard Fawcett)

With their filleted shafts alternating with bands of dogtooth and square flower, there can be no reasonable doubt that these reveals were designed by the same mason who was responsible for the remodelling of the eastern limb, or by someone who had worked closely with him. While there is the possibility that the reveals were associated with a pair of lancets like those in the east gable of the presbytery, since traceried windows were being installed in the flanks of the presbytery and the chapter house it is perhaps more likely that they were associated with a single traceried window.

There were three doorways into the remodelled nave: one in the west bay of each of the outer aisles, and one in the centre of the west front where it is framed by the two towers. The simplest of these doorways was that on the north side, which appears in its final state to have had mouldings consisting of no more than a pair of chamfers to the inner order and a slightly more complex outer order. Its southern counterpart, which would have been the principal entrance to the cathedral for the laity, was considerably more richly detailed. A very similar repertory of mouldings was employed for this doorway as for the window in the adjacent bay. Framing the doorway opening was a pair of continuous chamfers, beyond which were three shafted orders, with a band of dogtooth between the first and second engaged shafts. The centre line of the doorway is slightly offset from that of the porch and, since the blind arch over the doorway is centred on the porch vault rather than the doorway, there is a misalignment of axes. Covering this doorway was a porch of two shallow bays, of which only the lower walls survive, but there is clear evidence that it was covered by tierceron vaulting, and there are fragmentary remains above a bench along its internal flanks of blind arcading, which had mouldings emerging from springer blocks like those in the choir arcade. Very little remains of the outer doorway of the porch, but it can be seen to have had three orders of engaged shafts, two of which were separated by a band of dogtooth.

This south porch was two-storeyed, with a doorway at the upper level towards the aisle, and it is possible that there was some form of access from the nearby stair at the south-east corner of the south tower (Illus 5.16). It has already been said that there is evidence of extensive remodelling of that stair as part of this campaign. Externally, the remodelling is seen in the triplet of trifoliate-headed blind arches set within sunken gablets on the two faces at the south-east angle, where the stiff-leaf foliage decoration of the capitals, the semi-dogtooth of the gablets and the lack of through coursing with the adjacent walls allow little doubt that this is post-1270 work. Regrettably, the post-Reformation refacing of the east face of the stair turret below the arches of the blind arcading, together with the reconstruction of the stair itself, has confused the evidence of how any connection with

5.16   Elgin Cathedral, the south doorway (© Richard Fawcett)

the first floor of the porch might have worked. Nevertheless, there are traces both externally and internally of a blocked doorway off the stair which has its sill at about the level of the nave arcade arch springing, and which may have opened on to a timber gallery that gave access to the upper storey of the porch. The blocking within this doorway is evidently of a late date, and externally incorporates a winged angel head likely to have come from a seventeenth- or eighteenth-century memorial.

Internally, the remodelling of the south-east stair into the second-storey chamber carried considerable structural implications, although the modifications may never have been completed. A number of steps at the head of the stair were roughly cut back, leaving their stumps projecting. As we have seen, a new doorway into the second storey of the tower – the one that is now in use – was formed at a lower level in the south-east corner, while leaving the blocked head of the original doorway in place in the south wall. Above the truncated stairwell a handsome miniature ribbed vault was started, through the missing central part of which it can be seen that the weight of the superincumbent masonry of this corner of the tower was carried by a higher cross-shaped formation of relieving arches. While it is readily understandable why the head of the re-formed stair-well should have been afforded the widely visible fine display of decorative blind arcading that was created externally, it might seem profligate to have such impressive miniature vaulting over a stair which is perhaps unlikely to have been put to extensive use. But it should be remembered that medieval patrons and masons were very fond of having elaborately detailed vaults above spiral stairs, as may be seen over a stair in the north-west corner of Dunblane Cathedral or over the stair turret of the free-standing bell tower of Cambuskenneth Abbey, for example. Elgin is by no means unusual in having relatively hidden work of such high quality.

Moving on to the interior of the nave as remodelled after 1270, new piers would have had to be built for the outer aisles. There are also the fragmentary remains of augmentations to the slender piers into what had been the south-east chapel: the original piers were doubled in thickness by additions on their north side in the form of a triplet of shafts attached to a rectangular section with chamfered angles. It is likely that at least some of the eastern main arcade piers were rebuilt at this time on the evidence of the respond – now heavily renewed – that was constructed at the entrance to the inner south aisle from the south transept. The most easterly arcade pier stumps to survive in anything approaching an authentic state are the second ones from the east. These, together with the surviving pier stumps of the north outer arcade, which are smaller in scale, are all of a type related to those in the choir. They had triplets of shafts on the cardinal axes, while the diagonal flanks had a single axial shaft flanked by salient quadrant hollows. However, the bases of the eastern main arcade piers are unlike any others found in this campaign, suggesting that they had to be repaired, or possibly even more extensively replaced, after the fire of 1390.

As has been mentioned above, it can be seen from the wall ribs against the towers that tierceron vaults like those over the choir aisles were inserted over the original aisles and that they were also placed over the new outer north aisle, all of which, on the evidence of the moulding details, was most probably carried out as part of this phase of works. There is greater uncertainty over the form of the covering provided over the new outer south aisle. Above the south-east chapel that was to be absorbed into the new outer south aisle, it has already been seen that transverse arches had been constructed. Those transverse arches were evidently retained after 1270 and, although the evidence does not permit complete certainty, on balance it appears unlikely that stone vaulting was ever constructed over those three bays. It can be seen that a related arrangement of transverse arches was extended down the three new bays of the south outer aisle in the course of the post-1270 work, with those arches rising from triplet wall shafts. There is, however, a rather puzzling feature in the first of the new outer aisle bays west of the old chapel, where a vault springing with details datable to the post-1270 campaign was formed within an excavated pocket in the

wall thickness of what had been the west wall of the chapel. But there is nothing to demonstrate that a vault rising from that springing was ever completed, particularly since the surviving portion of the west wall of the old chapel above it was never taken down, as would have had to be done if the vault was built. It was therefore presumably at this stage that it was decided to extend the transverse arches down the outer south aisle rather than to construct vaulting. When vaulting was eventually added over the west bays as part of the post-1390 remodelling, it will be seen that it sprang from well above the transverse arches so that it could embrace the head of the later windows. It might be added that a vault which rose from the height indicated by the abandoned vault springing could not have co-existed with the gables now seen in the third and fourth bays from the east, although it must be conceded that those gables could have co-existed with the transverse arches.

The West Front

Changes to the west towers after the fire of 1270 have already been touched upon, including the modifications to the stair turret at the south-east corner of the south tower, and the possibility that the fourth storey of each was an addition made to the original design at this stage. Between the two towers, the new west doorway, which was the great processional entrance to the cathedral, was one of the most ambitious doorways ever built in thirteenth-century Scotland (Illus 5.17). It occupies the full space available between the buttresses of the flanking towers, and is surmounted by a trio of gables. As part of the post-1390 operations, a pair of sub-arches carried on a trumeau (central pier) was inserted on the inner plane of the doorway. We have no way of knowing if this reflected the original arrangement However, the west doorway of Glasgow, which is close to that of Elgin in scale and had probably been only recently completed when Elgin's was built, also has a trumeau, so it is likely enough that the inner arches we now see were a later replacement of what had been provided after 1270 (Illus 5.18).

The greater part of the doorway survives unchanged, with jambs composed of eight orders of engaged shafts, the outer shafts on each side being grouped as triplets; as in the choir piers, there are quadrant hollows cut into the projections that alternate with the shafts. The capitals have the multiple mouldings characteristic of this phase of work, while the bases were of water-holding type. The arch springs from a relatively low level for a doorway of such great width and depth, possibly because its overall height was constrained by the retention of the rose window that it has been suggested was the focus of the upper level. The orders of the arches are composed of combinations of tiny filleted

5.17   Elgin Cathedral, the west doorway (© Richard Fawcett)

5.18   Glasgow Cathedral, the west doorway (© Richard Fawcett)

5.19   Elgin Cathedral, detail of the west doorway arch
        (© Richard Fawcett)

rolls and deep hollows, as in the presbytery arcades; the outer orders are further enriched, two of them having paired bands of dogtooth, while another has paired stiff-leaf trails. The decoration of the outermost order has been lost, but the hood-mould is also decorated with dogtooth (Illus 5.19).

On each side of the doorway arch is an image niche (Illus 5.20). The jambs of these niches have engaged shafts flanked by a band of dogtooth, and they carry capitals with stiff-leaf foliage that can be seen to have been deeply undercut but that has now largely broken away. The niche arches have cusps which have yet more stiff-leaf foliage. The three gables above the doorway march across the space between the towers with no correspondence to the relative widths of the doorway and its flanking niches. They rise from a string course that dies into the hood-mould of the doorway at about two-thirds of its height; the cornice mouldings, which only survive on the two outer gables, have stiff-leaf decoration. Within each gable is an image niche, with jambs similar to those of the lower image niches, but with trifoliate arches that fit tightly below the gable apex. Flanking each side of the niches in the two outer gables is a sunken quatrefoil. The image niche of the central gable, which is smaller than its neighbours because of the way that the apex of the doorway impinges into the gable, is flanked by ramping trifoliate arches.

Elgin's was not the first processional doorway to be surmounted by a trio of gables. At Jedburgh Abbey, in the later years of the twelfth century, the west doorway had been set in a salient section of wall capped by a trio of gables, each gable having an image niche (Illus 5.21). More recently, perhaps in the years around 1200, the west front of Arbroath Abbey had been built with a triple-gabled gallery between the two towers and over the west doorway.

5.20 Elgin Cathedral, the arch of one of the tabernacles flanking the west doorway (© Richard Fawcett)

5.21 Jedburgh Abbey, the west doorway (© Richard Fawcett)

The Chapter House and Vestibule

The chapter house, which projects off the second bay from the east of the north presbytery aisle, is separated from the aisle by a square vestibule (Illus 5.22). There can be no doubt that the chapter house was built as part of the post-1270 building operations, since its walls rise from a base course of the same form as that which runs below the eastern limb and nave aisles, and its primary details relate closely to those of the other parts of the building dating from this campaign. There is, however, a possibility that the decision to build it was only taken after the aisle from which it is entered had already been started, since there are some slight clues that the doorway leading from the presbytery aisle into the chapter house vestibule was modified to give it the form we now see. Above the outer side of the doorway, towards the vestibule, is a triangle of ashlar facing framed by what appears to be a cut-back moulding; around this there is rubble extending out to the raggle line of the vestibule roof, beyond which, on the east side at least, there is the ashlar of the aisle wall-face. This triangle of ashlar would have been hidden between the vault over the vestibule and the roof above it, and it is therefore hard to imagine why it was so carefully formed. One possibility could be that the original intention was to have an external doorway at this point, perhaps giving access to the presbytery from those canons' manses that were to the north and east of the cathedral, and that this triangle of ashlar is the relic of a gable over that door (Illus 5.23). Nevertheless, it must be conceded that, if there was any intention to have an external doorway here, it must have been abandoned at an early stage of the

5.22 Elgin Cathedral, the chapter house from the south-west (© Richard Fawcett)

5.23   Elgin Cathedral, possible traces of a gable over the outer face of the doorway from the south choir aisle into the chapter house vestibule (© Richard Fawcett)

operations, because the doorway from the aisle that is now seen was clearly intended to open into a space beyond the aisle, since it has its principal mouldings on the side towards the aisle.

Putting aside as implausible the possibility that the chapter house was not part of the post-1270 building operations, it is likely enough that it would only have been started once the liturgically more important alterations to the presbytery, choir and nave were nearing completion. It was set out as a regular octagon with buttresses at all but its south-eastern angle, where a spiral stair within a polygonal turret gives access up to the wall-head. Cordiner's view of the cathedral published in 1780 shows that the cap house above the stair rose a full storey above the wall-head, and had gablets around the base of a spirelet pinnacle, very much like the pinnacles flanking the east gable (Illus 5.24). For the upper half of its height the stair within the turret is now a post-Reformation reconstruction for which, as in the south-east stair of the southern tower, abandoned memorial stones have been pressed into service. At the wall-head the survival of runnel stones and spouts above a corbelled cornice demonstrates that there must have been a wall-walk and parapet, though what is now seen may be at least partly the result of later alterations. The buttresses have a single intake at the level of the arch springings of the windows. They have chamfered angles terminating with trifoliate moulding stops, and are finished with gablets. They are thus essentially similar to those of the presbytery and are evidently the work of the same master mason. The traceried

windows which now pierce seven of the eight sides of the chapter house date from the late-medieval repairs, though most of the tracery now seen was restored between 1972 and 1986. Around the existing windows there are the traces of the original window openings, which show that the first windows were larger than those now in place, extending to occupy virtually the full space available between the buttresses and up to the wall-head cornice. As can be seen by comparison with the windows in the flanks of the aisle-less section of the presbytery, however, the complex reveal mouldings are likely to have considerably reduced the actual daylight opening of the windows.

The doorway from the presbytery aisle into the chapter house vestibule was subdivided by two sub-arches carried on a trumeau, which is now gone, and there was an open quatrefoil between the heads of those sub-arches (Illus 5.25). The sub-arches were framed by inner jamb mouldings consisting of a chamfer and roll, while the jambs of the main arch have two shafts with slender fillets alternating with salient hollow chamfers. Towards the vestibule this doorway has mouldings to the rear arch which die into splayed jambs. The vestibule was covered by a quadripartite ribbed vault carried on shafts rising from benches along the side walls. It is lit by a lancet in the west wall, which has shafted reveals to the exterior and continuous mouldings to the interior, and there are slight traces of a corresponding lancet head in the east wall, but this was suppressed when an annexe was added on that side, with a door opening off the vestibule.

5.24 View of the choir and chapter house of Elgin Cathedral from the west in 1769 (Thomas Pennant, *A Tour in Scotland*)

5.25 Elgin Cathedral, the doorway from the south choir aisle into the chapter house vestibule (© Richard Fawcett)

5.26 Elgin Cathedral, the chapter house doorway (© Richard Fawcett)

5.27   Elgin Cathedral, east capitals of the chapter house doorway
(© Richard Fawcett)

The doorway from the vestibule into the chapter house itself now has continuous inner mouldings dating from the post-1390 repairs; thus there is no way of knowing if the opening was initially subdivided by sub-arches like its counterpart on the other side of the vestibule (Illus 5.26). But its outer mouldings show that it was even more ambitiously conceived than that outer doorway, having two engaged filleted shafts separated by a band of dogtooth to each jamb. The capitals of these shafts were embellished with deeply undercut stiff-leaf foliage, the leaves of which appear to have been more three-dimensionally modelled on the western jamb, while those of the eastern jamb had rather flattened individual leaves (Illus 5.27). The arches had the combinations of triple-filleted rolls separated by deep hollows that are characteristic of this phase of works.

The interior of the chapter house was extensively remodelled in the later Middle Ages, when seven of its eight walls were encased in new masonry above window sill height, and the central pier and vault were rebuilt. As a consequence little now survives of the original design. The only significant evidence for the interior as first built is to be seen above the entrance doorway, on the upper part of the south wall, which was only partly refaced, presumably because no new window was required (Illus 5.28). Although this wall, as the only one not to be pierced by a window, was in most respects atypical, it does give us some idea of the highly enriched decorative repertory of the post-1270 design in this part of the building. Within the arch of the vault is a blind arcade of four cusped arches carried on responds in which engaged shafts alternate with bands of dogtooth, and between the heads of the central arches rises a fifth smaller arch. Embracing all of these arches is what appears to be a cut-back wall rib, indicating that the chapter house as first built was almost certainly vaulted.

5.28   Elgin Cathedral, the south internal wall of the chapter house entrance wall interior (© Richard Fawcett)

It would be hard to think of a more effective expression of the high corporate aspirations of a college of canons than the octagonal chapter house we see at Elgin. It was not uncommon for the chapter houses of the thirteenth-century secular cathedrals to be buildings of high quality. Glasgow's was a splendid two-storeyed square structure projecting from the north-east corner of the eastern limb,[418] while at Dunblane and Fortrose it was incorporated within a two-storeyed range on the north side of the choir that housed a number of administrative functions.[419] At Dunkeld the same functions were also housed in a two-storeyed building, in this case a square block that was added on the north side of the choir in 1457.[420] In England, however, it had became increasingly common for major religious institutions to have centralised chapter houses of polygonal or circular plan, starting perhaps with that at Worcester Cathedral Priory, of the early twelfth century.[421]

Of the English secular cathedrals, those at Hereford, Lincoln, London, Salisbury, Wells and York all eventually had centralised polygonal plans, while Lichfield had an elongated octagon (Illus 5.29). In Scotland this fashion for centralised buildings was reflected at the Augustinian abbeys of Holyrood and Inchcolm though, as far as we know, Elgin was the only secular cathedral to take up the idea. Similarities with English chapter houses are also evident in the form of the subdivided outer entrance doorway, with a quatrefoil

5.29 Lincoln Cathedral, the chapter house (© Richard Fawcett)

between a pair of arches, which reflects the type of entrance found earlier at Salisbury Cathedral and Westminster Abbey,[422] where the quatrefoil was unpierced. The idea was later further developed at Wells Cathedral and Southwell Collegiate Church (Illus 5.30).[423] In all of this we are again reminded how close was the interchange of architectural ideas with England throughout the thirteenth century.

5.30 Southwell Minster, the chapter house entrance
(© Richard Fawcett)

6.1   Tain Collegiate Church (© Allan Rutherford)

6 THE REPAIRS AFTER 1390

The Presbytery and Choir

Despite the widespread evidence of fire damage to the masonry, at least some of which must be attributable to the fire of 1390, there is relatively little in the central vessel of the presbytery and choir to indicate that major reconstruction of those parts followed that fire. Apart from some refacing and minor repairs, the most identifiably rebuilt feature is the rose in the east gable, of which no more than the outer form pieces survive. In its final form it appears to have had twelve cusped bowed triangles around the perimeter, with their bases resting on the outer ring; the heads of these triangles would presumably have alternated with twelve lights radiating out from a central foiled figure.

The evidence for rebuilding is more extensive in the aisles of the eastern limb than in its central vessel. Within the south aisle, where the vaulting is best preserved, a few bosses are perhaps more likely to be of post-1390 than of post-1270, suggesting that partial rebuilding of the tierceron vaults was required. The most obvious insertions, however, were the aisle windows. Most of these were of four lights, but in the north aisle bay through which there is also the entrance to the chapter house there was a narrow window of two lights, and there were windows of three lights to the flanks of the shallow chapel in the east bay on each side. For reasons that are no longer clear, the three-light window to that chapel on each side rose to a lesser height than the others and above that on the south a small trefoil window was inserted. The simply chamfered reveals of the inserted windows are very different from those of the original windows of the eastern limb, which have more enriched mouldings. The slight sense of baldness this gives to the aisles is now further increased by the loss of the wall-head cornices. Nevertheless, it is a striking feature of all phases of work at Elgin that efforts were made to attune the vocabulary of the work in progress to what was to be retained in adjacent parts of the building, as far as the requirements of tastes of the time would allow. Thus, although the new windows inserted in the aisles were larger than any known to have been built earlier at the cathedral, with the possible exception of those of the chapter house,

their tracery took the earlier windows in the presbytery as a starting point. As we have seen, each of the lower level of late-thirteenth-century lancets of the east wall had a circlet above a sub-arch at its head, while the presbytery flanks had Y-tracery with circlets above sub-arches at the light-heads and between the Y-forms. The new three- and four-light windows in the choir aisles were given intersecting tracery, within the interstices of which circlets were placed. There must thus have been a striking sense of thematic continuity.

Despite the fact that they were hybrids of two periods, the remodelled Elgin choir aisles were to have some influence on other churches in the north-east. At Fortrose Cathedral, for example, in the south nave chapel we find the remains of a four-light window comparable with those in the Elgin aisles, together with similarly chamfered and gabled buttresses, and there is comparable tierceron vaulting over the internal spaces. There is perhaps an element of irony in this, since the chapel was built for Euphemia, countess of Ross, the estranged wife of the earl of Buchan who had put Elgin to the torch in 1390.[424] But evidently the relative age of the constituent parts was a less important consideration for Euphemia and her master mason than the overall architectural prestige of the finished building at Elgin. Another building with some similar tracery and related buttresses, albeit without the angle chamfers, is the smaller pilgrimage church of St Duthus at Tain (Illus 6.1).[425]

The Central Tower

Once the liturgically most important eastern parts of the cathedral had been brought back into a state of good repair, work would have moved westwards. According to the inscription recorded from the tomb of Bishop John Innes (1407–1414), which was against the north-west tower pier, it was he who started the rebuilding of the central tower,[426] suggesting that work on the eastern limb had been completed by then, and that work was moving westwards. However, the work on the tower may have consisted of little more than repairs to the damaged structure, because it is said that it partly collapsed in 1506, and had to be rebuilt over a period of about thirty years.[427] Since its final collapse

6.2 The partial figure of a bishop said to be from the central tower of Elgin Cathedral (© Richard Fawcett)

6.3 The partial figure of a knight said to be from the central tower of Elgin Cathedral (© Richard Fawcett)

in 1711, no part remains in place above ground, and the only known evidence for the form of the tower in its final state are the views of John Slezer, which show it rising a single storey above the surrounding roofs, evidently with one window lighting each stage of that storey. A stair to the wall-head rose into a square cap house at its north-west corner.

Flanking the nave roof, at the corners of the tower Slezer shows high image tabernacles, and two portions of large-scale images currently set up against the east wall of the south-east nave chapel are believed to have come from those tabernacles. One portrays a bishop almost complete from knee height upwards (Illus 6.2). He is wearing a cope with a richly jewelled morse and has a mitre on his head. His right hand appears to have been raised in blessing, while his left hand holds the fabric-draped staff of a crozier. The other image is very much more damaged, and only survives from the top of the legs to the shoulders. It is of an armoured figure grasping the hilt of a dagger which hangs from an elaborately decorated and prominently buckled belt (Illus 6.3). Arm-pieces and thigh-pieces of plate are worn over chain mail, and the scalloped edge of a mail aventail hangs over a surcoat. It seems possible that these figures represented two of the three estates, the clergy and nobility;

if they did indeed come from two tabernacles on the tower, the other tabernacles could perhaps have contained representations of the burgesses and the king.

The Nave

Once work on the central tower had been completed, work would then presumably have extended down into the nave. It has been suggested above that in their present state the two lateral gables in the third and fourth bays from the east of the south outer chapel aisle are almost certainly of the post-1390 campaign, and could belong to a relatively late phase of those works.

Although lateral gables had been widely used elsewhere in Britain and Europe in the twelfth and thirteenth centuries, in Scotland it was only in the fifteenth century that there appears to have been a certain vogue for them, as in some of the chapels added on to the flanks of the burgh churches at both Edinburgh[428] and Stirling, for example.[429] At those churches, each of which served one of the country's great trading burghs, the idea was perhaps brought in from the Low Countries, where such gables were to be a prominent feature of the aisles and chapels of a large number of late-medieval churches.[430] Assuming that the gables in their

STIRLING PARISH CHURCH

LINLITHGOW PARISH CHURCH
MELROSE ABBEY

LINLITHGOW PARISH CHURCH

PERTH PARISH CHURCH

IONA ABBEY

6.4 A sketch of some windows with tracery of related types to that in the south aisle of Elgin Cathedral (© Richard Fawcett)

final state ran the full length of the Elgin outer aisles, the saw-tooth effect must have been a striking part of the overall massing of the building, the aesthetic impact of which must have been very like what is still to be seen in the early-fifteenth-century nave at the church of Onze Lieve Vroukerk at Aarschot,[431] or the aisles of the abbey church at Saint-Hubert as rebuilt after the fire of 1526,[432] both in what is now Belgium. It has been noted that the fragmentary cornice on the eastern side of the western of the two bays has what on first sight appears to be a thirteenth-century vocabulary of intersecting arches and a band of semi-dogtooth. Yet if that detail had been reused from an earlier gable, it must have required a quite disproportionate effort to reshape the stones into which it is cut to fit the head of the inserted window. It must instead be a real possibility that it was provided as part of the post-1390 works, and that an effort was being made to ensure that the new work would sit easily with what was being retained elsewhere in the aisle, and we shall see that similar mouldings were to be employed in the chapter house at the end of the fifteenth century.

Of the windows within these two surviving gables at Elgin, although only the eastern one remains in a relatively complete state, it is clear that they were in most essentials of a similar design. The western of the two, however, was

6.5 Elgin Cathedral, the inner face of the surviving bays of the outer south nave aisle (© Richard Fawcett)

narrower than its partner because there is a greater width of masonry on its eastern side, which may be the partly retained buttress of the west wall of the south-east chapel. The form pieces of the western window were also slightly more finely detailed than those of its neighbour. It may be observed that the profile of the reveals of these windows is different from that of the windows inserted into the choir aisles, suggesting that a new master mason was responsible by this stage of the operation, a change of personnel that is hardly surprising in such a protracted operation. In each of the windows four lights were grouped into pairs by major sub-arches which are rather uncomfortably deflected sideways in the eastern of the two windows; above each of the round-arched light-heads are lesser sub-arches with daggers between their heads, and at the head of the window was a spiralling grouping of four mouchettes within a circlet (Illus 6.5). Rather unusually, the top mouchette of the western window broke the circlet, something that does not seem to have happened in the other window. Variants of windows having spiralling mouchettes within a circlet at the head of the tracery field were to be particularly popular in late-medieval Scotland, being found as far afield as Iona Abbey, Linlithgow St Michael, Melrose Abbey, Perth St John and Stirling Holy Rude (Illus 6.4).[433] At many of these a date around the middle years of the fifteenth century is most likely, though there were to be later examples of tracery showing variants on this basic type. It was probably at this stage of the operation that slightly ungainly gargoyles were added at the tops of some or all of the buttresses between the outer aisle bays. That on the buttress adjoining the south transept was probably a winged beast, while that between the fourth and fifth bays from the east was a recumbent human figure.

On the inside of the outer south aisle, corbels and springings for stone vaulting were provided during this phase of works in the fourth, fifth and sixth bays from the east. The corbels are at the same level as the base of the window arches, which is well above the transverse arches that had been built between those bays as part of the post-1270 campaign. Rather enigmatically, there are also small corbels at a similar level on the west side of the second and third bays from the east, within what had been the south-east nave chapel. However, there are no other indications of vaulting having been either constructed or contemplated in these bays and, since it must be assumed that vaulting would have left clear evidence at the east end of the chapel, where the wall survives to full height, it can perhaps be safely concluded that the three bays of the absorbed south-east chapel continued to be without vaults (Illus 6.6).

The remains of the few nave arcade piers replaced during this phase of work present a considerable problem

6.6   Elgin Cathedral, the junction of the south-east nave chapel and the outer south nave aisle (© Richard Fawcett)

of interpretation, particularly since we cannot be certain how much of what we now see is medieval and how much dates from the partial re-assembly of masonry carried out in 1935 and 1939. The three western arcade piers on each side, along with the western responds built into the eastern corners of the tower, have already been described as part of the first building campaign. Little that is reliable is now known of the easternmost arcade piers or of the eastern pier of the outer chapel aisle on the north, all of which were presumably destroyed by the final collapse of the tower, and the two western piers of the outer chapel aisle on the south have also been lost. However, the main arcade bases of the second piers from the east on each side, together with all of the surviving pier bases of the north outer aisle, are of a type that is not found elsewhere in either the post-1224 or the post-1270 building campaign (Illus 6.7). Above a sub-base with a chamfer and roll, the bases themselves have three rolls separated by spur-like arrises. As has already been said, however, the piers they support are related to the pier type in the choir in having triplets of shafts on the four cardinal axes, with single shafts flanked by salient quadrant hollows to the diagonal faces. While certainty is impossible on such inadequate – and seemingly contradictory – evidence, the balance of possibilities suggests that what we see are piers that are essentially of the late-thirteenth-century campaign but which had to be extensively repaired after the attack of 1390, at which stage the bases were replaced, a difficult but

6.7 Elgin Cathedral, the junction of the north nave arcade wall and the north-west tower (© Richard Fawcett)

by no means impossible process.

At the west end of the central vessel of the nave, within the bay defined by the west towers, the inner flanks of the towers were refaced with ashlar above a pair of steeply pointed wall arches, which were presumably intended to extend something of the rhythms of the nave arcades along the tower flanks. Where they adjoined the nave arcade responds, the eastern of those wall arches on each side is carried on a shaft that had been built along with the arcade responds in the first building campaign, but that was now finished off with a new capital. Otherwise the arches are carried on inserted corbels. Both capitals and corbels are decorated with bands of rather coarsely executed foliage. It is possible that the refacing of the flanks of the towers was intended to support a barrel vault between the towers. The masonry corbelled out above a string course appears still to be slightly arched, and it is shown to be even more prominently arched in the background of the view of the west front interior by Robert William Billings. Since there is no physical evidence of a vault against the west gable, however, whatever the original intentions, it is doubtful that one was ever built. Indeed, the masonry above the string course now has recesses for roof timbers.

The West Front and West Towers

The west front is dominated by the mid- and late-thirteenth-century west towers and the late-thirteenth-century doorway, and the only clearly late-medieval features are the inner skin of the west doorway and the west window and gable above it. The inner skin of the doorway, which presumably had to be replaced because of internal fire damage, has two sub-arches, which were originally cusped, and which are carried on a trumeau. Framing the arches, and rising from engaged bases, are continuous mouldings, within the hollows of which are foliage trails. The tympanum within the main arch of the doorway has a large blank vesica between the two door arches, with a foliate corbel to carry

6.8 Elgin Cathedral, the remodelled tympanum of the west doorway (© Richard Fawcett)

6.9 One of the angels carved on the remodelled tympanum of the west doorway of Elgin Cathedral (© Richard Fawcett)

6.10 Elgin Cathedral, the stubs of tracery in the west window (© Richard Fawcett)

an image, and the fixing holes for that image are still to be seen on the masonry within the vesica (Illus 6.8). Although the central image has been lost, the carved field of the tympanum remains: kneeling on a foliate corbel to each side of the vesica is a censing angel against a field decorated with vine trails (Illus 6.9).

Above the retained main body of the doorway and its trio of gablets, the central part of the west front was completely rebuilt. Virtually the whole space available was taken up by a vast seven-light window, framed by a deep reveal with continuous mouldings, with square-flower decoration to the principal hollow of the reveal and also to the hood-mould. Only the stumps of the tracery form pieces around the edge of the window have survived, and it is not possible to be certain of the original design of the tracery (Illus 6.10).

Nevertheless, it is clear that the main motif was a rose with twelve bowed triangles around its perimeter, which was presumably intended to reflect the reconstructed tracery of the rose window in the presbytery east gable. Below the rose, it seems that the outer pair of lights on each side was contained within a sub-arch, and there were trefoils above some of the light-heads themselves, a motif perhaps intended to continue the themes of the circlets of the tracery in the choir aisles (Illus 6.11).

The window arch rises up into the gable, and thus into what would have been the roof space over the nave. This would be consistent with the possibility that the nave was covered by a curved barrel ceiling resting on the wall-heads, similar to that which is indicated for the presbytery by the arched masonry around the rose of the eastern gable. Above the window arch, the west gable is treated in a way for which there is no close parallel in Scotland. On each side of the upper part of the arch the gable steps inward and upward to a horizontal section of walkway running across the apex of the window, and there are the remains of a richly carved foliate cornice marking both the steps to either side and the

6.11 A reconstruction sketch of the possible form of the west window of Elgin Cathedral (© Richard Fawcett)

central flat section of walkway. The apex of the gable was set back behind the wall-walk and was pierced by a rectangular basket-arched window which may have opened into the roof space above the ceiling. On the cornice in front of that window are carved the royal arms of Scotland, while to the north of the main window arch are the arms of Moray hanging from the branches of a tree;[434] to the south of the arch are arms assumed to be those of Bishop Columba Dunbar, with a pastoral staff.[435]

Internally, the west front between the towers was entirely remodelled as part of the post-1390 works (Illus 6.12). At the lower level, and above a wall bench, it is refaced with ashlar that is unpierced apart from the twin arches of the doorway, and which thus makes no reference to the single embracing arch of the doorway on the exterior. Running at some height above the doorway arches, and below the sill of the west window, is a mural passage which interconnects the second storey of the towers. This passage opens on to the nave through four arches alternating with narrower arches, the latter being blind at jamb level but open at arch level; all of these arches are carried on engaged shafts.

The only clearly identifiable changes within the towers dating from this stage of operations are at second-storey level of the north tower. These involved the insertion of a stone barrel vault, carried on an inner skin of masonry, and of a mezzanine timber floor, carried on corbels which still survive in the north wall. Access between the two levels thus created was presumably by way of a timber stair, since there was no door to the mezzanine level from the main stair.

6.12   Elgin Cathedral, the inner face of the west wall (© Richard Fawcett)

The subdivision of the windows at this level in the west and north walls that has already been noted externally was to take account of the inserted mezzanine floor. As part of the modifications a fireplace was formed at the northern end of the east wall, with a mural closet to its south within the window embrasure corresponding to that in the south tower. The vaulted construction of this insert hints at the possibility that it was used as a strongroom or treasury in the later Middle Ages. It is easily understandable that the attacks of 1390 and 1402 should have left the chapter more than a little nervous, and the slightly tortuous access route to this chamber would have made it additionally attractive for such use.

The Chapter House

The sole addition to the plan of the cathedral in the course of the later medieval works was a small chamber on the north side of the chapter house vestibule, in the space between the stair and the north presbytery aisle. This was added only after the two-light aisle window that it now blocks had already been remodelled, as can be seen from the reveals and tracery stumps of that window. This reminds us that it was not until well after the attack of 1390 that the rolling programme of repairs eventually reached the chapter house. Indeed, the arms of Bishop Andrew Stewart (1482–1501) on the capital of the chapter house pier make clear that it was over ninety years after the attack that the work on the chapter house was carried out.

The added chamber is internally of irregular plan because of the way it was fitted in between existing walls and buttresses. It has a fireplace on its south side, in front of the blocked aisle window, and below the window in its east wall is an elongated basin which presumably served some function in connection with the ablutions of the liturgical vessels used at the altars of the cathedral. Such basins are found at a number of cathedrals within chambers that were presumably used as sacristies, one example of which is to be seen in the chamber in the re-entrant angle between the south-east transept and the south choir aisle at Lincoln Cathedral.[436]

The most obvious external change brought about by Bishop Stewart's remodelling of the chapter house itself was the insertion of new traceried windows in seven of the eight faces of the chamber, all of which can be seen to have been of significantly reduced daylight opening from the original windows. Only one of the windows retained a significant part of its late-medieval tracery into modern times, that in the north-east face, and its state in the early nineteenth century is shown in W Clark's views of 1826, and in a partly restored state by Robert William Billings (Illus 6.13). The missing mullions and form pieces were reinstated in 1904. The design of this window is essentially the same as that of a window in the south nave aisle of St Michael's Church at Linlithgow, but since that window is probably a secondary insertion, it is of little help in any attempt to confirm the date

6.13 The chapter house interior of Elgin Cathedral in the mid-nineteenth century (Robert William Billings, *Baronial and Ecclesiastical Antiquities of Scotland*)

6.14 Linlithgow St Michael, the window of the same type as one in the Elgin chapter house (© Richard Fawcett)

of the remodelling of the Elgin chapter house (Illus 6.14).[437] The tracery of the other six windows was restored between 1972 and 1986, the designs being based on the evidence of the stubs of the form pieces that were embodied within the reveals. In most cases it was possible to restore the windows beyond reasonable doubt, though it must be conceded that in some cases the evidence was open to more than one possible interpretation. The window in the south-west face was related to the surviving windows in the south nave aisle, raising the possibility that they were considerably later in date than the west front, while the others are of types for which there are no precise parallels.

The interior of the chapter house was extensively refaced in the work carried out for Bishop Stewart. The chief exception to this was the entrance side where, as has already been said, much of the late-thirteenth-century masonry was retained, though even here the inner face of the doorway itself was remodelled. The principal focus of the chapter house is on its north side, looking back towards the entrance, where there were the five seats of the dean and other principal dignitaries. Emphasis was given to these seats by five corbelled-out trifoliate arches, with square-flower decoration to the arches and semi-dogtooth decoration to the hood-moulds, motifs which, like those on the nave gable cornices, evidently took some of their lead from the decorative repertory of the late-thirteenth-century work.

6.15 Elgin Cathedral, a detail of the carved decoration in the remodelled chapter house (© Richard Fawcett)

Above the stone bench which runs around the interior, the lower walls of the chamber may still represent the later-thirteenth-century wall-face, and there are filleted wall shafts flanked by quadrant hollows within the angles between the faces. At the level of the window sills these shafts support a widely projecting string course which is richly decorated with an extraordinary variety of foliage and figurative carving in an idiom related to that employed for the reworked west front of the cathedral (Illus 6.15). Above this string course the wall is advanced forward between the windows. It should perhaps be conceded that the inter-relationships

6.16 Elgin Cathedral, the chapter house pier capital (© Richard Fawcett)

between the two planes of the walls and the window embrasures is not fully resolved in all respects, possibly because of the difficulties of adapting the retained masonry to the new design.

At the centre of the chapter house is the pier supporting the vault, which has eight shafts directed towards the angles of the chamber; the shafts are separated by quadrant hollows (Illus 6.16). The pier rises from an octagonal sub-base, above which are individual bases with multiple mouldings below each shaft. A stone lectern is embodied at the north-west angle of the pier, the desk of which is carried by a pair of weather-eroded angels. The capital of the pier has an octagonal abacus, with its alignment corresponding to that of the sub-base. The bell of the capital has oak leaf decoration, the leaves being set on each side of a horizontal stem, with a series of shields above the hollows of the pier. These shields depict:

- the royal arms of Scotland below a crown, the upper part of the tressure being omitted[438]
- the Arma Christi, showing fifteen instruments of the Passion
- the arms of Bishop Andrew Stewart below a mitre[439]
- the Arma Christi, showing the five wounds, the cross and the crown of thorns
- St Andrew crucified

- the royal arms (with the complete tressure)
- the arms of Stewart
- the Arma Christi with the five wounds

The vault of the chapter house has sixteen ribs springing from the central pier, which arch up to an octagonal ridge rib that is equidistant between the pier and the walls of the chamber (Illus 6.17). From the ridge rib eight of the ribs are met by ribs from the angles of the chamber, while the other eight continue horizontally as radiating ridge ribs, meeting the wall at the apices of the wall ribs above the windows. Seven ribs rise from each of the vault springings at the angles of the chamber: apart from the wall ribs and the transverse ribs which go directly across to the central pier, there are two diagonal ribs which meet the octagonal ridge rib at the junction with the radiating ridge ribs, and there are two tierceron ribs which meet the radiating ridge ribs halfway along their length.

The pattern of ribs is in some respects a reduced version of that devised for the decagonal chapter house at Lincoln, where the chamber is said to have been completed by 1235, although its vault could be a little later.[440] There are, however, two significant differences at Lincoln: there, the angles of the main ridge rib alternate with those of the corners of the chamber, and the radiating ridge ribs go no further than the junction with the tierceron ribs. There are also similarities

6.17 Elgin Cathedral, the chapter house vault (Historic Scotland © Crown Copyright)

with the vault over the octagonal chapter house at York Minster, which was possibly finished by the later 1280s,[441] except that at York in the course of construction it was decided to omit the central pier and to construct the vault of timber rather than of stone, so that the centre of the vault is slightly domical rather than being a descending cone of ribs. The similarities with those thirteenth-century vaults raise the possibility that the final vault at Elgin was of a similar type to what had originally been constructed as part of the post-1270 operations.

Minor excavations in 1999 suggested that much of the existing floor paving within the chapter house could be medieval, if not necessarily of the post-1390 campaign.[442]

The Later-Medieval Liturgical Furnishings

A great deal of the internal visual impact of the cathedral in its final late-medieval state would have been created by the fixtures and furnishings that were provided to enhance the setting of the liturgy, and on which it is likely that almost as much was spent as on the structure of the building. Unfortunately, however, except where these were of stone, or where their location had some physical impact on the fabric, we know nothing of them. In the former category are items such as the later-thirteenth-century sedilia and some piscinae, which were retained and have already been

touched upon. A number of new liturgical furnishings were inserted within the south nave aisle during the later-medieval remodelling, indicating the location of a number of altars. In the third bay from the east, recesses with moulded three-centred arches were provided as aumbries. In the fourth bay from the east a piscina with a three-centred arch below a gablet was inserted, apparently within an earlier arched opening.

We shall see shortly that some of the bishops' tombs may also have been designed and located with the aim of attracting prayers for their occupants through having supplementary liturgical functions. As far as furnishings that have left an impact on the building are concerned, it has been suggested above that it was the provision of a bishop's throne that necessitated cutting back the south respond between the presbytery and choir, while it was presumably the fierce burning of the timber choir stalls that caused such damage to the north wall of the choir.

The only item of lost furnishing that has left no physical trace, but for which we have a description as some compensation, was the painted panel above the screen that separated the canons' choir from the nave, and which is assumed to have been set on the east side of the crossing. Towards the nave it had a depiction of the crucifixion, while towards the choir there was the last judgement. This survived until 28 December 1640 when it was pulled down and burnt by the minister of Elgin, Mr Gilbert Ross, acting together with the lairds of Innes and Brodie.[443] A description of this painting records that:

'On the wast syde wes painted in excellent cullouris illuminat with starris of bright gold the crucefixing of our blessed Saueour Jesus Christ. This peice was so excellentlie done, that the cullouris nor starris never faidit nor evanishit bot keipit haill and sound, as they were at the begining notwithstanding this colledge or channonrie kirk wantit the rooff sen the reformatioun, and no haill wyndo thairintill to saif the same from storme, snaw, sleit or weit, quhilk myself saw, and mervallous to considder. On the vther syde of this wall, touardis the eist, wes drawin the day of judgement.'

This description does not make clear how the painted panel related either to the screen or to the crossing arch within which it was presumably set. The only comparable painting surviving in Scotland is at the small collegiate church of Fowlis Easter, where parts of the depiction of the crucifixion from above the screen have survived, and where we can see that the panel must have filled the space between the screen and the ceiling.[444] But Elgin was a much taller building than Fowlis Easter, and it is perhaps more likely that the painted panelling either formed a tympanum within the bowed triangle of the crossing arch, or that it was placed directly above the screen.

7.1   Elgin Cathedral, the tomb within the arch at the entrance to the presbytery from the north aisle (© Richard Fawcett)

7 THE MEDIEVAL TOMBS

Elgin has the largest group of medieval memorials of any Scottish cathedral, and it is nowhere more clear that a cathedral might be the preferred burial place for the nobility of the diocese as well as for its bishops and senior clergy. Yet, for all that such a large number of tombs survives, it seems certain that even more have been lost. Keith's catalogue of bishops claims that of the eighteen bishops whose remains were deposited in the cathedral, seven of them found their last resting place within the choir,[445] by which he presumably meant the central vessel of the eastern limb. There are only two medieval canopied tombs that could be said to be within that space, though several of the burials must have had no more than ledger slabs or brasses over them, and a number of the former are still to be seen around the cathedral. Nevertheless, few bishops were notable for the modesty of their sepulchral monuments, and there seems little doubt that we have lost as many canopied tombs as we have retained.

7.2   Reconstruction sketch of the tomb within the arch at the entrance to the presbytery from the north aisle of Elgin Cathedral (© Richard Fawcett)

The earliest surviving tomb is presumably that in the shallow third bay from the east on the north side of the presbytery, which is an integral part of the design of the east limb (Illus 7.1, 7.2). It has a cinquefoiled arched head carried on jambs with filleted shafts on each side of a band of dogtooth, and the whole is embraced within a steeply pointed gable with a blind trifoliate arch at its head. Thirteenth-century tombs are a relatively rare survival in Scotland, and one of the few partial parallels for the design of this example is a less elaborately embellished tomb in the south nave aisle of Kirkwall Cathedral, Orkney, which similarly has an arched recess below a steeply pitched gable. The Kirkwall tomb bears the arms of the Paplay family in its gable and is usually dated to the fourteenth century, but, since its arch mouldings show some relationship with the mid-thirteenth-century eastern bays of Kirkwall Cathedral, it may be earlier. The Elgin tomb recess was presumably provided for himself by Bishop Archibald (1253–1298), who must have carried out much of the rebuilding of the cathedral after the fire of 1270, and who is recorded as having been buried in the choir of his cathedral.[446] In its provision of an arch and gable over a mural recess, the tomb shows some formal similarities with that in Rochester Cathedral of Bishop Bradfield, who died in 1283, and since Bradfield's tomb has been described as 'the earliest high-quality example of . . . the ciborium tomb',[447] this provides a reminder that at least some of the work at Elgin was fully in step with the most advanced current ideas (Illus 7.3). In the later Middle Ages one of the reasons that the north side of the presbytery became the favourite position for the tomb of the founder or rebuilder of a church was because in this position its occupant might gain added spiritual advantages through his tomb being used as an Easter Sepulchre. This was where the consecrated host, believed to be the very body of Christ, was ritually enclosed between Good Friday and Easter Sunday to symbolise Christ's entombment.[448] The earliest examples of the use of Easter Sepulchres appear to be of the thirteenth century,[449] though it is only at a later date that it became common for those planning their place of burial to specify that their tomb should also be used as a sepulchre.[450]

Thus, while Bishop Archibald's tomb might be an early example of such usage, it may simply be that he was seeking a last resting place as close as possible to where the holy mystery of the mass was celebrated. It is attractive to suspect that a fine but badly damaged episcopal effigy excavated in 1936 originated in this tomb (see page 161).

In the bay to the west of the presumed Archibald tomb is a tomb which also served as a screen at the entrance to the presbytery from the north aisle and which, although badly damaged, must have been one of the most ingeniously designed in the cathedral. It can be seen to have been capped by three arches surmounted by three gablets; the two eastern arches and gablets were suspended over the tomb chest, which is now gone, while the western arch and gablet were over the doorway from the aisle into the presbytery. A particularly attractive feature of this tomb would have been the way in which the two eastern arches had no intermediate support, but were suspended from the voussoirs of the three-centred vault-like arch over the tomb itself. We cannot know for certain whose tomb this was; however, bearing in mind that Keith appears to indicate

that Bishop Andrew Stewart, who died in 1501, was the first bishop to have been buried in the choir since William Spynie in 1406,[451] and that the tomb is directly opposite the entrance to the chapter house that Stewart repaired, he must be regarded as a likely candidate for its occupancy. Tombs that also served as screens in this way are to be found in a number of churches, though there are no other certain examples in Scotland and it is best to look to England to understand how such combined tombs and screens would have appeared when complete.[452] Amongst examples which might be cited are the Cheney monument in the nave at Edington Church in Wiltshire, of about 1400,[453] or the screen that opens into the chantry founded by Bishop Fleming in 1425 at Lincoln Cathedral.[454]

The only other memorial within the central vessel of the eastern limb is a ledger slab in front of the lowest step of the presbytery, directly opposite the arch opening from the south choir aisle. It appears to be of Tournai marble, or some similar dark-coloured stone, and has an indent for a large rectangular sheet of brass or other metal. This is perhaps the memorial of 'blue marble' that Keith says commemorated Bishop Andrew de Moravia,[455] though it is likely that a slab of this type is of a considerably later date than Moravia's death in 1242.

The largest grouping of medieval tombs is in the aisle and chapel running along the south side of the presbytery and choir, suggesting that this was a favoured spot for

7.3 Rochester Cathedral, the tomb of Bishop John of Bradfield (1278–1283) (W. H. St John Hope, *The Architectural History of the Cathedral Church and Monastery of St Andrew at Rochester*)

7.4 The tomb of Bishop John Winchester in the south presbytery chapel of Elgin Cathedral (© Richard Fawcett)

7.5 Elgin Cathedral, the effigy of Bishop John Winchester (© Richard Fawcett)

important burials. In the north wall of the chapel is the tomb which bears an inscription showing it was that of Bishop John Winchester, who died in 1460; since he is said by Keith to have been buried in St Mary's aisle we can assume that this chapel was dedicated to the Virgin and that those buried within it were deemed to be under her particular protection (Illus 7.4). The chest of his tomb is decorated with a blind arcade of ten cusped arches with crockets and finials. It is set within a recess framed by an ogee-arched canopy with cusped cusping along its intrados, square flower within the continuous mouldings, and with lavishly carved crockets and a finial; there possibly used to be smaller finials at the ends of the cusping. On each side of the arch, and rising from the same plinth as the chest, is a small buttress capped by a pinnacle; each buttress has a shield in front of a pastoral staff at arch springing level. The effigy of the bishop is depicted in mass vestments, his mitred head resting on a pillow and his feet on a lion; he holds a pastoral staff in the crook of his left arm, which is joined in prayer with the right arm (Illus 7.5).

Along the front chamfered edge of the tomb chest slab is the inscription: '*hic jacet recolende memo^e johanes Winnechestair dns epus moravien: q obiit xxii die me Apl Ano dni M^occcclx'.*[456] Despite the high-quality workmanship of the tomb, it is worth noting that much of the stonework that might have been expected to be carved, such as the

7.6 Traces of painted decoration on the tomb arch of Bishop John Winchester in Elgin Cathedral (© Richard Fawcett)

shields on the buttresses and any orphreys on the chasuble, is left plain, as if the intention was that that the detail should be provided by modelled gesso and paint. We know, of course, that colour was always very important in the final appearance of tombs, but very little painted decoration has come down to us in Scotland, and it is therefore particularly fortunate that some of the under-drawing for painting on this tomb remains on the soffit of the main arch, where the outlines of a number of angels are to be seen, censing the effigy of the dead bishop (Illus 7.6).

As has been seen (see page 44), his name indicates that Bishop Winchester was of English origin, and it is likely that he initially came to Scotland in the train of James I and his queen, Joan Beaufort, when that king returned from English captivity in 1424. Indeed, his name could suggest that he had been a protégé of the queen's uncle, Cardinal Henry Beaufort of Winchester. The design of his tomb appears to be most closely related to a number found in England, such as that of Sir William and Lady Wilcote at North Leigh in Oxfordshire of around 1442; under the circumstances, it must be seen as a real possibility that Winchester had brought up a mason from England to design it. In its turn the design of the Winchester tomb was to be of considerable influence, being copied soon afterwards in a monument in the south transept at Elgin itself, which will be discussed below, and possibly also in another in the north transept.

It is not surprising that one high-quality monument should be an inspiration to other patrons within the

7.7   Fordyce Church, the tomb of James Ogilvy of Deskford
       (© Richard Fawcett)

same building, but it is clear that the Winchester tomb exercised an even wider influence, since a very similar design was adopted for the tomb at Fordyce of Sir James Ogilvy of Deskford, an ancestor of the earls of Seafield, the similarities extending even to the use of related mouldings to the arch (Illus 7.7). Since Sir James died in 1509,[457] it is unlikely that it was the work of the same mason who made Bishop Winchester's tomb, however, and we must simply conclude that a particularly prestigious tomb could be a major influence for several years after its creation. It seems that members of the Ogilvy family were particularly drawn to the design of this tomb, since there is another at Fordyce in a slightly simplified form for an unnamed member of the same family. Perhaps even more remarkably, the tomb was also taken as a model for the monument at Cullen Collegiate Church to Alexander Ogilvy, who died in 1554, though in that case the design was only the starting point for a very much more lavish composition.[458]

Two bays west of the Winchester tomb is another tomb recess, set within the low wall inserted into the arcade behind the choir stalls (Illus 7.8). The arch is of four-centred form, an almost unique Scottish example of a form that is far more common south of the Border, raising the possibility that, like Winchester's tomb, it was the work of an English mason. It has had large-scale cusped cusping on the soffit of the arch, and in the spandrels of the arch are bowed triangles, which are repeated on a smaller scale within the major cusps, while the lesser cusps have rounded trefoils. The arch is enclosed by a rectangular frame of moulding with a small buttress on each side. If this was a bishop's tomb, it may have been that of William Tulloch, who died in 1482 and who is said by Keith to have been buried in St Mary's aisle. But the effigy it now contains clearly does not belong within it, and is equally clearly of an earlier date than Tulloch. This effigy is in full mass vestments and mitre, and is set within a recumbent tabernacle with an arched canopy and shaft supports, beneath which is a lion supporter (Illus 7.9). Regrettably the head of the effigy and the canopy have both been badly damaged, although it is still possible to see that the arms of the kingdom of Scotland are carved on one side of the canopy and the arms of Moray on the other. There is no way of knowing who is represented, though the low profile of the mitre suggests a date before the end of the fourteenth century. It has been suggested that the effigy could be that of Bishop John Pilmuir (1326–1362) since Pilmuir's seal, like this effigy, displayed the arms of both Scotland and Moray,[459] and this is certainly a possibility on stylistic grounds, albeit one that is not open to proof.

7.8   Elgin Cathedral, the tomb within the south choir arcade (© Richard Fawcett)

7.9   Elgin Cathedral, the effigy reset in the tomb within the south choir arcade (© Richard Fawcett)

7.10   Elgin Cathedral, the effigy of the earl of Huntly in the south choir aisle (© Richard Fawcett)

Within the body of the aisle is the free-standing tomb of the first earl of Huntly, who died in 1470 (Illus 7.10). Since 1924 it has been on a line with the entrance to the presbytery, but apparently it had earlier been moved to the site of the altar.[460] The chest is plain apart from the earl's arms which are carved on the south side, and around the slab on which the effigy rests is the inscription: '*hic jacet nobilis et potens dñs allexāder gordone primus comes de huntlie dns de gordone et badzenoth qui obiit apud huntlie 15 iulii anno dñe 1470*'.[461] This inscription is notable for its early use of Arabic numerals, but the effigy, which is now headless, is even more remarkable for showing the earl in secular dress rather than in armour. Amongst the few other Scottish late-medieval magnates who chose to be shown in secular dress on their tombs were the fifth earl of Douglas, who died in 1439 and whose tomb is at Douglas, and the first earl of Morton, who died in 1493 and is buried at Dalkeith.

Also in the centre of the south aisle, but in the third bay from the east, is the tomb of William de la Hay of Lochloy, who died in 1422 (Illus 7.11). However, this tomb was only brought into the shelter of the aisle in the early years of this century, and views of the cathedral in 1826 suggest that it was then in the open to the west of the enclosed area of the south aisle. The effigy rests on a made-up tomb chest with arcading along parts of its two long sides, and is in full armour with the arms of Hay carved in relief on the jupon.

The inscription along the south edge of the slab below the effigy reads: '*hic jacet wills de la hay quōdā dns de lochloy qui obiit viii die mēse decebris ano dni mccccxxii āte piciet*'.[462] Immediately to the south of this tomb is a matrix stone with provision for a rectangular brass, which appears to be of Tournai marble. Set within the floor of the aisle are also a number of inscribed ledger slabs commemorating some early-sixteenth-century clergy or officials associated with the cathedral.[463]

Moving on to the south transept, there are two arched tombs against its south wall (Illus 7.12). The eastern of the two has a depressed three-centred-arched canopy with an ogee flip at its apex. There are the remains of elaborate dropped cusping along its soffit and of crocketing along its extrados; foliage trails further enrich the arch mouldings. Flanking the arch and the tomb chest, which has an arcaded front, is a pair of small buttresses, each with a shield at arch springing level: the western shield bears the arms of Stewart in front of a pastoral staff,[464] while the eastern shield is said to have borne the arms of Stewart quartering Mar.[465] This heraldry presumably refers to Bishop James Stewart (1460–1462), who is said by Keith to have been buried in the aisle of St Peter and St Paul, though Keith was mistaken in saying that aisle was the north rather than the south transept. The tomb now contains the effigy of a knight instead of a bishop, who bears the arms of Innes on its jupon,[466] and since Shaw

7.11 Elgin Cathedral, the effigy of William de la Hay of Lochloy in the south choir aisle (© Richard Fawcett)

states that the south transept was the family burial place of the family of Innes of Invermarkie we must assume that one of their effigies has been reset here.

The western of the two tombs in the south transept is of a related design to that of Bishop Winchester in the south choir chapel aisle, albeit with some coarsening of detail. It has a tomb chest with an arcaded front, an ogee-arched canopy with cusped cusping and highly enriched crocketing, and flanking buttresses with shields at arch springing level. At the back of the recess is the inscription 'memēto finis'.[467] The shield on the eastern buttress bears the arms of Stewart,[468] while the arms on the western shield have not been identified.[469] Bishop James Stewart was succeeded as bishop by his brother David (1462–1476) and Keith says that the two brothers were buried in the same aisle,[470] in view of which it is possible that this tomb was Bishop David's. The tomb now houses the effigy of an unidentified knight.

Like the south transept, the north transept has two tombs against the inside of its gable wall, though the collapse of the upper parts of the wall has left them in a far less complete condition (Illus 7.13). Running along the lower part of the wall is a bench, much of which is carried on a blind-arcaded dado made up of discarded tomb chest panels reset here in the early nineteenth century. The western tomb recess, which is almost on the central axis of the transept, seems to have had a canopy with continuous mouldings on the slight

evidence of the two or three surviving courses of stone with moulded jambs. It contains a much defaced figure in a richly flowing costume which falls over the feet. The eastern recess, which extends up to the junction of the north and east walls, was of a more complex design, with flanking buttresses and moulded jambs that show some similarities with those of the Winchester tomb in the south choir chapel. It contains the effigy of a knight with the arms of Dunbar on its jupon,[471] which has been seen as supporting a probably mistaken tradition that a chapel of the Dunbar family in this transept was dedicated to St Thomas Becket.[472] Arcaded tomb chest fronts have also been reset along the base of the west wall of the transept, and at the north end of that wall is the jamb and arch springing of what appears to have been another inserted tomb canopy. The wall at the back of the recess has been disturbed on more than one occasion, and there is now a memorial plaque set on the inner face where the arch apex would have been; this commemorates John Dunbar of Bennetfield and his family, the last of whom died in 1648.[473] Despite this disturbance, the ghosting of part of the southern arc of the tomb canopy is still discernible about 2.5 metres south of the northern arch springing.

Reset against the east wall of the south-eastern nave chapel, between the figures of the bishop and knight said to have come from the central tower, which have been described above, is the kneeling figure of a bishop which has

7.12 Elgin Cathedral, the tombs in the south wall of the south transept (© Richard Fawcett)

7.13 One of the effigies in the north transept of Elgin Cathedral (© Richard Fawcett)

lost its head and shoulders. This figure is generally assumed to be from the tomb of Bishop John Innes (1407–1414), which Keith says was at the foot of the north-west pier of the central tower,[474] the inscription of which has been referred to above (Illus 7.14). The figure wears a processional cope and holds the staff of a crozier between his praying hands; he is kneeling on a cushion which is itself on top of a draped kneeler. If this figure was indeed from the tomb of Bishop Innes, it is uncertain how it would have related to that tomb. During the period of the Renaissance, kneeling figures were to become relatively common within mainland Europe as the principal representation of the deceased, as is seen on Roullant le Roux's tomb of the d'Amboise cardinals of 1522 at Rouen Cathedral.[475] In the Middle Ages, however, the rare examples of kneeling figures on sepulchral monuments were usually relegated to secondary roles, such as that of 1375–80 on the tomb of Edward Lord Despenser at Tewkesbury, which is placed in the canopied superstructure, where it is shown praying towards the high altar.[476] On a more elaborate scale the occupant of a tomb might be represented in a whole range of attitudes, as at Avignon Cathedral on the destroyed tomb of Cardinal de Lagrange of Amiens, who died in 1402, on which he was shown in a range of scenes as a decaying corpse, as a living person, and as a kneeling figure.[477] It is very unlikely that Bishop Innes' tomb was as complex as any of those, though, if Scottish parallels are to be sought, it has been suggested that the markedly vertical tomb recess of Bishop James Kennedy of St Andrews could have had a kneeling figure.[478]

Set within the wall of the second bay from the east of the outer south nave aisle is a stone coffin, and there are the remains of an arch in the wall at its west end, which is likely to have been part of the canopy of a tomb. The mouldings of this arch are similar to those of the aumbry in the bay to the west, and were perhaps part of a late-medieval unified scheme to fit out what had been the south-east nave chapel as a chapel of an individual or family. As suggested above (see page 100), this could have been the tomb of Bishop Columba Dunbar, who died in 1435, in which case this would have been the chapel dedicated to St Thomas of Canterbury.

Several of the memorials in the cathedral would have relied on inset brasses as their most prominent element, and two that were clearly intended to receive such insets have already been mentioned. None of the brasses has survived, though a rubbing of one that is thought to have come from the cathedral was published in 1906 (Illus 7.15).[479] Below a male figure in secular dress was the inscription: 'Of yoᶜ charite pᵃy for the soulles of Johñ younge Johñ Thomᵃs Elyn and susan his children whoˢ soullˢ ihū pdō'.

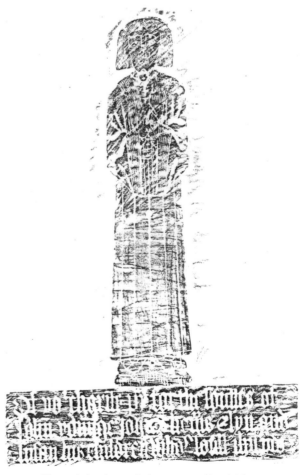

7.14 The kneeling figure of a prelate, said to be from the tomb of Bishop John Innes in Elgin Cathedral (© Richard Fawcett)

7.15 Rubbing of a lost brass of John Young and his children (*Transactions of the Scottish Ecclesiological Society*, 1905–6)

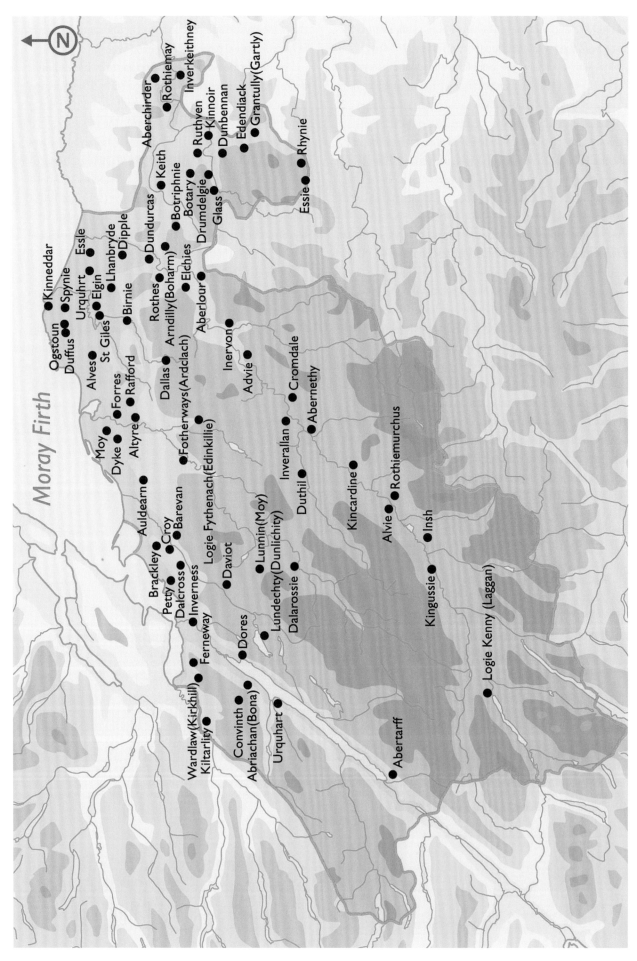

8.1 A map of the Diocese of Moray (drawn by Arka Cartographics, Historic Scotland © Crown Copyright)

8 PARISHES AND PREBENDS

In this chapter we explore the evidence for the structures which supported the diocese and the cathedral at its heart, chiefly the parishes, which formed the most local institutions of Church government in western Christendom (Illus 8.1). Here, rather than providing a history of the parishes themselves, however, the focus will be on how they were used to provide financial support for the bishops, their cathedral and its chapter. When looking at a building on the scale of the cathedral at Elgin and talking in general terms about the numbers of clerics who were based within it, there is a danger of failing to understand the intimate relationship between this central organism and the wider parish network which lay behind it. It is an obvious statement to make, but it must be remembered that without the parish system and the host of ordinary men and women who lived within it, the great cathedral which rose within the chanonry at Elgin would never have existed.

The fundamental building-block of Christian religious life for most of the Middle Ages was the parish. This was the territory – of hugely varying extent – whose population received certain key spiritual services from the church at its core and from which revenues were drawn to support the priest serving in that church. There could be other churches and chapels within a parish, but only one had the right to dispense certain sacraments – baptism especially – so possession of a font usually distinguished the *parish* church from these other buildings. A network of parishes had emerged in much of southern England before the end of the tenth century, but provision became patchier through northern England and into Scotland, a situation which arose from a number of factors, including lower levels of population and different systems of social organisation. A more fragmentary pattern, however, does not mean that there was no means of people in the localities receiving even basic levels of spiritual service and across large parts of northern Britain we can identify a number of important churches which appear to have served wide areas. Some of these churches were perhaps still monastic in the eleventh and early twelfth centuries, like Old Deer in northern Aberdeenshire or Brechin in Angus, but others were more akin to what in parts of England were described as minsters, churches where a number of secular priests as opposed to monks lived in a community. The church at Jedburgh, mentioned in the 1080s,[480] and that at Stobo, both in the Borders, appear to have been minsters of this type and possessed outlying chapels to serve the population more locally in parts of the wide hinterland dependent upon them as the 'mother-church'. Elsewhere, however, there is no firm evidence for the nature of any local system of religious organisation; in the remoter and more thinly populated parts of Scotland there may have been no regular provision of spiritual services.

In southern England by the end of the tenth century, and more widely across most of Western Europe by the mid-eleventh century, Church lay authorities were enforcing the payment of a portion of the produce of the parish district for the support of the priest. This system of tithe payment – teinds in Scotland – assigned one-tenth of the annual yield of the land to the Church. As collection of these tithes became more rigorously enforced and regularly gathered, priests became keen to safeguard their interests and to maintain control of the often extensive parishes which they nominally served. In Scotland, there is no evidence for the regular collection of teind before the second quarter of the twelfth century, but it is probable that in areas close to the better-organised and politically influential minster-type churches in the south and east of the country some revenues were being gathered at an earlier date. The step change appears to have come with King David I (1124–1153), who was credited by his successors with issuing a decree which instructed payment of teind to the Church;[481] the result was the crystallising of a parish network as territories contributing to specific parish churches then needed to be defined. By the end of the thirteenth century the pattern of parishes which served the religious needs of the people of Scotland down to the Reformation in the mid-sixteenth century, and which provided the basic structure of local government until 1974, had come into being.

A national network of parishes did not simply spring into existence overnight.[482] In parts of Scotland it was a long-drawn-out process which provoked conflict between priests locally, larger ecclesiastical institutions like minsters and monasteries, and lay lords, as each felt that they possessed the best claim to the teinds of an area; they might not want another church within 'their' territory to gain parish status and take away part of the teind income for its support. Against that view was the opposing desire of bishops to increase the number of churches locally and so develop both their own influence and, more importantly, ensure the better care of the spiritual welfare of the people. To meet their spiritual obligation to secure the salvation of the souls of their human flock, bishops strove to construct the mechanism which would deliver religious services locally. As the population of the country grew and settlement became more widespread, bishops attempted to provide an adequate level of service to new communities.

One further question which complicated the full development of the parish network was: to whom did the churches belong? While some were ancient and had long histories as independent institutions, others were clearly more recent creations and had been built at the expense of local lords who had also endowed them with property from their own resources to support the priests in future. These so-called proprietary churches (built and paid for by a layman and regarded as part of his property) were intended to serve both the owner's family and household and the population living on his estate. In effect, they came to function as the churches of parishes which were coterminous with the secular unit. This development was generally welcomed by bishops, but towards the end of the eleventh century when a tide of reform was sweeping through the Church they also had mounting qualms over the control that these laymen continued to hold over the churches they had founded. Of gravest concern was their possession of the right to appoint the parish priest, which in an atmosphere of growing demands for the ending of lay interference in clerical appointments and lay control of Church property was regarded as a sinful corruption. Understandably, however, lay lords who had heavily invested in the building and endowment of a church were reluctant to part with a right which added a significant item to their reserves of patronage from which they could reward loyal servants or provide for members of their family. The process of formation of such churches and the granting away of the right to patronage can be seen in various parts of Scotland in the early twelfth century. Perhaps the best-known example is at Ednam in the Borders where the lord, Thor the Long, had with King Edgar's encouragement built a church dedicated to St Cuthbert on the lands which the king had given to him. In c 1105, Thor granted the right to present the parish priest to the monks of Durham priory, renouncing his rights

as patron.[483] Over time, the patronage of more and more parish churches was granted by lay lords to various religious institutions, from the bishop in whose diocese the parish lay to monasteries to whose monks the lords wished to show favour. Even on the eve of the Scottish Reformation in the sixteenth century, however, there remained some parishes over which laymen had retained the right of patronage.

In Moray, where no documentation survives for the process of parish development before the mid-twelfth century, we can nevertheless trace similar processes of parish origins in proprietary churches (built and controlled by a lay patron to serve the needs of his estate) and a gradual granting of their patronage to religious bodies. A number of churches, for example, first appear in the king's gift in the second half of the twelfth century, the most important of which were the churches which came to serve the burghs which David I and his successors established through Moray from Elgin to Inverness.[484] The Crown, however, also had the patronage of several other churches, like Urquhart east of Elgin which appears to have been given by David I to the priory of Benedictine monks which he established there in the 1130s.[485] Some of these may have been new churches developed by the Crown on estates which they had seized from the old ruling family of Moray in the 1130s, but others are likely to have been more ancient foundations which Earl Angus and his predecessors might have endowed. A larger number first appear in the hands of the bishops of Moray in the second half of the twelfth century and, while some may recently have come into their possession, others had probably been developed by them on episcopal estates. Several of these in the south and west of the diocese appear to be ancient possessions of the bishops and served the populations of extensive upland parishes.

Others, however, were clearly proprietary churches, controlled by laymen and probably built by them on lordships which were being created by Crown grant from the middle of the twelfth century onwards. One of the most important of these was Duffus, where the mid-twelfth-century colonist Freskin appears to have founded a church to serve his dependants on the new land which was being won from the marshes of the Spynie lagoon which formed the greater part of his estate. His successors retained control of the church until the 1220s, when its revenues were used to endow a new canonry and prebend in the cathedral at Elgin, but even then they continued to hold the patronage of the prebend until 1294.[486] Laymen like Freskin and his heirs, who from their initial foothold at Duffus acquired extensive estates throughout Moray, or the earls of Fife who held a major lordship in central Speyside and Stratha'an, appear to have been responsible for founding, building and endowing churches on those properties and their descendants were reluctant to yield up their interests in them until cajoled or coerced by the bishops. Some of the parishes created by lay lords in this way may have been unviable long-term as independent entities, yielding too limited a level of revenue to sustain church and priest. This over-optimistic creation and resulting poverty may lie behind annexations such as that of Kilravock to Dalcross, which had happened before 1274, with the former parish church of Kilravock remaining as a simple dependent chapel of its larger neighbour.[487]

As Bishop Brice sought to reorganise his see and to construct a sound financial basis for both its proper administration and the adequate discharge of spiritual functions through its parishes, he was drawn into conflict with laymen who themselves claimed to have property interests in various parish churches. At Aberchirder, now known as Marnoch, he became involved in a three-cornered dispute over the patronage of the church with King William and Gillechriosd, earl of Mar. Although the conflict was resolved by what was euphemistically termed an 'amicable' agreement, it seems that the king's will prevailed, for the right of patronage was granted to the abbey which William had founded at Arbroath.[488] Brice may have intended to appropriate the parish revenues of Aberchirder for one of his planned prebends in his new cathedral at Spynie but any such notion was stymied by the king's alternative plan (Illus 8.2). Shortly after Brice's death in 1222, his successor, Bishop Andrew, appropriated the parsonage revenues to Arbroath Abbey.[489] The process of parish formalisation throughout the diocese also continued in tandem with the development of the cathedral and its complement of canons. In 1226, what appears to have been a long-running dispute between the bishop and James son of Morgrund, earl of Mar, over various lands and revenues within the lordship of Abernethy was finally resolved in a legal composition whereby James renounced all of his rights to the disputed property, agreed to pay the bishop an annual render of one mark of silver, and promised to build a suitable manse for the parson close to the parish church.[490]

Gaining control of the patronage of parish churches was seen as being of great importance in the process of reforming Church structures and of freeing what was God's special domain from the interference of lay powers. Control of patronage also enabled the new ecclesiastical patrons to ensure the appointment of suitable candidates to serve as parish priests and in turn they would work to raise the quality of religious life for their parishioners. There was, however, an associated risk that the ecclesiastical patron might see the exercise of their right to appoint a parish priest as an opportunity to make some kind of financial gain for themselves or their institution, or at the very least possibly to use their right as patron to favour an individual whom they wished to reward. From control of the right to appoint the

8.2   The site of Spynie church, from the south-east (© Richard Oram)

parish priest there was also another possible step; the use of that right to appoint either yourself or one of your fellows if it was a religious community who held the patronage to the church in question. It was by that route that the process known as appropriation began to gather momentum in the Scottish Church.

Appropriation is the process whereby the revenues of one institution were diverted to the uses of another. In the case of parish churches, when the controller of the right of patronage was a large religious corporation – a cathedral chapter or a monastery – the usual outcome was that the corporation first secured the right to appoint one of their members to the parsonage of the parish church in question. The revenues of the church then in theory went to that member, although generally in reality to the common funds of the appropriating community. This was a matter of grave concern for bishops since, if all of the revenues were diverted into the hands of an appropriator with no obligation on them to be resident and provide proper spiritual services, the outcome was likely to be contrary to what they were striving to achieve by way of reform of spiritual practice. Nevertheless, in many cases they confirmed the appropriators' actions, ratifying the process through charters which permitted the patrons to take the revenues 'in proprios usus' (for their own use). In most cases, the intention was for the revenues that were specifically tied to the parsonage of the parish – principally the so-called garbal revenues, which comprised the main teind offerings to the church – to pass to the appropriator; the remainder, the so-called vicarage which was made up mainly of all other offerings at the church's altar and payments for other religious services, would be used to sustain a properly instituted and suitably qualified priest – the vicar. In too many cases, however, the appropriators sought full annexation of both parsonage and vicarage revenues, leaving a pittance for the support of a curate who looked after the cure of souls of the parishioners. By the early 1200s, bishops were struggling to ensure that appropriation did not mean a collapse in the level of spiritual provision for the lay population at parish level.

Following the decrees of the Fourth Lateran Council of 1215 concerning proper provision for priests serving the cure of souls in parish churches, bishops were empowered to enforce adequate vicarage settlements in appropriated parishes. In both Scotland and England this decree triggered a rash of new vicarage settlements between bishops and appropriators, confirmed by new charters which gave the bishop or his official the power to accept or reject the appropriator's nominee as vicar following an examination of his merits, and rights to impose an adequate allocation of stipend as a reserved portion of the vicarage revenues. The majority of portionary or pensionary vicarages – those

where only part of the revenues attached to the vicarage were left for the incumbent – which are identifiable in both kingdoms, date from this episode, and the see of Moray was no exception to this process. As bishops Brice and Andrew Murray set in place the college of canons to serve in their new cathedral, they worked conscientiously to ensure that a proper balance was achieved between their desire to have a well-staffed and adequately resourced cathedral and their duty to ensure that the souls of their flock across the diocese were being suitably cared for. In the following sections, how that balance was or was not achieved is explored.

Mensal Churches

The parish churches appropriated to the Church of Moray fall into two distinct groups. The first are the mensal churches, that is, those whose revenues were assigned to the bishop's *mensa* or table for the support of him and his household. The second are the prebendal churches, those whose revenues were assigned to the support of an endowed canonry in the cathedral church, some of which were held by the principal dignitaries responsible for the administration of the cathedral and the wider diocese.

The route by which some of the mensal churches came into the hands of the bishops of Moray is unknown, possibly indicating that they had been associated with the bishop, or the churches where he made his see, from some early date, and had passed into episcopal control as the see became better organised in the later twelfth century. Others came by direct grant of them to the bishop. When King William invested Richard of Lincoln in the temporalities of his see in 1187, he made additional grants to the bishop of churches in which he still had the right of patronage; Elgin itself with its dependent chapels of St Andrew and Manbeen; and Auldearn with its dependent chapels at Nairn, Rait and Moyness (Illus 8.3).[491] Possession, however, was not immediate, for the two parishes were then held by the king's clerk of the provend, Richard *de prebenda*, who in 1203 became bishop of Dunkeld, with Elgin held of him by his own clerk Walter. By the terms of the king's charter, neither church was to pass into Bishop Richard's hands until the deaths of both Richard *de prebenda* and Walter. When the king confirmed Bishop Brice Douglas in the bishopric in c1205 he likewise confirmed the gift of the churches of Elgin and Auldearn.[492] The grant, however, was still inoperative, for although Richard *de prebenda* had apparently given up his interest in the churches on his election to Dunkeld, the clerk Walter still held a life interest in Elgin. His interest was eventually ended in December 1207 when he was elected to the bishopric of Glasgow.

As the long process which was required before the various churches granted to Bishop Richard came into episcopal

8.3 The chancel of Auldearn church from the north-east (© Richard Oram)

possession reveals, the assembly of the portfolio of mensal churches was a protracted process, with some being granted and obtained at later dates whilst others were alienated or assigned to other purposes. For most of the Middle Ages the bishops of Moray controlled fifteen parish churches that could in some way be regarded as mensal. The revenues of most were assigned specifically for the support of the bishop and his wider household, but a significant number were assigned to provide money from which the cathedral building and the lights of the church could be funded. The bishops controlled that latter group, but their revenues were not drawn upon in the same way as the mensal churches proper. The churches assigned to support the fabric and lighting funds are examined separately later (see page 133). The nine mensal churches proper for most of the pre-Reformation period were Birnie, Drumdelgie, Dyke, Elgin, Gartly, Keith, Ogstoun, Rothiemay and Wardlaw.[493] In most of these churches, only the parsonage teinds were attached to the episcopal *mensa*, the vicarages remaining unappropriated as perpetual vicarages, but in a few cases calls were also made on the revenues of the vicar. At Elgin, for example, part of the vicarage income was assigned by Bishop Andrew Murray to sustain one of the prebends of his new cathedral, but this proved inadequate and the entire vicarage was subsequently annexed to the prebend.[494] There were also other efforts made to use the mensal churches as items of ecclesiastical patronage. This was attempted at

Birnie, where Bishop Brice wished to grant it to Kelso Abbey, but the former episcopal see at Birnie continued as one of the bishops' mensal churches down to 1331, when Bishop Pilmuir awarded it as a common church for the support of the cathedral chaplains.[495] While some mensal churches passed out of the bishops' hands, others, like Ogstoun, may have been created out of dependent chapels in larger parishes, the parsonage of whose mother church may have been used by the bishops to fund a prebend in the cathedral.[496] Ogstoun was still a chapel in the time of Bishop Andrew, presumably attached to Kinneddar parish, but it appears as a separate vicarage by the mid-fourteenth century, with its parsonage annexed to the episcopal *mensa*.[497]

The effort on the part of bishops to ensure adequate provision was made for vicars under the terms of the Fourth Lateran Council does not mean that they were not themselves guiltless of over-milking parish revenues; the vicarages of some of the mensal parishes were amongst those with the poorest provision. At Wardlaw – or Dulbatelauch as it was originally known – and Conveth in the Aird west of Inverness, rights of advowson in the churches and to teind from specific lands in their parishes, which the king had assigned to the Church of Moray before he had given the lordship of the Aird to John Bisset, were disputed between Bishop Brice and Bisset (Illus 8.4). To settle the dispute, Bisset resigned all rights in the church of

Dulbatelauch and to all ecclesiastical revenues from the nine davochs attached to it in favour of Brice and the Church of Moray. In return Brice quitclaimed in favour of Bisset and his heirs his rights in the advowson of Conveth and the eleven davochs associated with it. In addition, Brice resigned all claim to the teind of the royal properties, reserving only twenty shillings from the £10 annually which Bisset paid to the king as the annual ferme of the royal lands in the Aird. Bisset also gave, for the souls of his parents, himself and his descendants, seven acres of land as a site for a new church for the parish of Dalbatelauch at Wardlaw in the davoch of Fingask.[498] This settlement was confirmed, probably in 1221, by the papal legate to Scotland, who confirmed also the annexation of Wardlaw to the episcopal *mensa* in the settlement which confirmed the annexations of Keith and Edindivach.[499] The settlement was confirmed by Pope Honorius III in 1222 to Andrew, bishop-elect of Moray, as part of a general confirmation of the mensal properties of the bishopric.[500] The parsonage revenues only were appropriated to the episcopal *mensa*, a vicarage being set up at some point between 1222 and 1274 to serve the cure of souls, but its resources were so slender that it was united with the vicarage of Conveth c 1330 and remained so into the fifteenth century. The vicarage thereafter seems to have been pensionary, receiving only a set component of the vicarage revenues, the remainder of the income being taken by the bishops.[501]

Arrangements like that used at Wardlaw to ensure adequate income for the vicar were probably common in the bishops' management of the mensal churches. It is probable that their right to appoint the vicars perpetual or portioner in those churches was employed by them as a source of patronage from which to sustain the young clerks and ambitious chaplains who formed a part of his immediate household. We can see this process in the manner in which Bishop Brice used his control of the patronage of other churches within his see to provide for clerks who may have been in some way connected to his Lanarkshire-based kindred. Between 1203 and 1210, for example, he gave the church of Kingussie and its dependent chapel in Glen Banchor, with everything pertaining to them, to Gilbert of Cathcart.[502] Elsewhere, revenues could be brought together to make better provision for a particularly favoured individual, then disjoined once he had secured a better benefice elsewhere. By the later Middle Ages, practices like that emphasise how the mensal churches had become little more than items in a portfolio of properties and rights which the bishops deployed as necessary to sustain the increasingly complex apparatus of Church government that was necessary for the running of the diocese.

8.4　Wardlaw (Kirkhill) church from the south (© Richard Oram)

Prebendal Churches

The histories of the churches attached to the various prebends in the cathedral are inseparable from the histories of the diocesan officials and individual canons who occupied them. These were the sources of the wealth which sustained the senior dignitaries, coveted by ambitious and rising clerks who, by the later Middle Ages, were more often than not absentees who either held more senior offices in other dioceses or who were deeply involved in royal government or in the service of great lay or ecclesiastical magnates. An exploration of the men who held these offices would require a far longer study than is possible here and would take us far from consideration of the Church of Moray. In this section, therefore, the discussion concentrates simply on the process of creation of the prebends rather than on either the men who held them or the parishes affected.

As Bishop Brice began to organise the clergy of his new cathedral at Spynie into a college of eight canons between 1205 and 1215, he assigned the revenues from twelve parish churches and various parcels of landed property as prebends for the support of the four principal dignitaries and four simple canonries who were to serve as the chapter, setting out the arrangements in a comprehensive new constitution modelled on the example of the English see of Lincoln.[503] The chapter was headed by the dean, for whose support was assigned the whole revenues of the parish

church of Auldearn and its dependent chapel at Nairn. In 1226, the altarage revenues of Auldearn, excluding those of the chapel, were detached from the dean and assigned as part of the prebend of the new office of subdean in Bishop Andrew Murray's enlarged cathedral chapter, a small portion being reserved for the stipend of a pensionary vicar to serve the cure in the parish.[504] The full revenues of the parish churches of Alves and Lhanbryde, plus a davoch of land in the latter parish, were appropriated as the prebend of the second canon, the chanter, who was responsible for the music of services in the cathedral choir. Brice intended that the church of Rothes should also be annexed to this prebend, but his assignment of its revenues to the chanter failed to be put into effect.[505] The third canon, the treasurer, received the teinds of the churches of Essil and Kinneddar. The chancellor was assigned the fourth canonry, which was supported on income from various parcels of land rather than on the appropriated teinds of parish churches. Amongst these lands were Lunan and Coldoich, which in the 1170s had been granted for life to John the hermit by Bishop Simon de Toeni.[506] The remaining four canonries held no specific office but were equally generously provided for under the terms of the constitution. For the support of the fifth canonry the teinds of the churches of St Peter at Inveravon and its chapels, plus a davoch of land, and of Urquhart on Loch Ness were annexed.[507] Forres and the

8.5   The interior of Barevan church, looking east (© Richard Oram)

church of Edinkillie were annexed to the sixth canonry, which was also assigned in perpetuity for the support of the principal diocesan cleric after the bishop, the archdeacon.[508] The seventh canonry was supported on the parochial teinds of Spynie itself, while the eighth had the revenues of the churches of Ruthven and Dipple.[509]

In May 1226, perhaps in an indication that work was as yet inadequately far advanced on the new cathedral church of the Holy Trinity of Elgin, Bishop Andrew held his diocesan synod in the parish church of St Giles in Elgin. Amongst the chief business of that gathering was a revision and expansion of the college of canons which Bishop Brice had instituted for his cathedral at Spynie, with new prebends and dignitaries being added to the original eight canonries and some of the original appropriations of revenues reallocated to the new creations.[510] The first change was the assignment of the formerly 'simple' prebend known as Strathavon for the support of the chancellor, who under Brice's constitution had drawn income from various properties. The second change rectified an omission in Brice's constitution, which had provided no place in the chapter of the cathedral for the bishop himself; from 1226 bishops of Moray were to sit in chapter as holders of the simple canonry and prebend of Fotheruays. In addition to these significant changes to revenues and roles, Bishop Andrew added nine new churches to fund six new prebends: Rhynie, Dunbennan (which had already been added to the canonries in 1222), together with Kinnoir, Inverkeithny, Elchies and Botary, Moy, and finally Cromdale and Advie.[511] Andrew created a further prebend funded on a pension of 100 shillings annually drawn from the vicarage of St Giles' church in Elgin.[512] This rather slenderly funded prebend continued on this basis into the episcopate of Bishop David Murray who annexed the rest of the vicarage revenues to the prebend with the exception of certain specified items, including the teind of the salmon fishery of the port of Speymouth and the rents of a croft called Vicarshaugh.[513]

Bishop Andrew also sought to augment his canons' resources through establishment of a common fund, and on 30 December 1239 he drew up a deed which appropriated to it the revenues of nine parish churches: Abernethy, Altyre, Arndilly, Barevan, Birnie, Bona, Farnua, Kincardine and Laggan (Illus 8.5, 8.6, 8.7).[514] At neither Birnie nor Bona was this annexation effective, for Birnie was evidently still one of the bishops' mensal churches in 1331, when Bishop John Pilmuir assigned its revenues to support the chaplains of the cathedral and Bona remained an independent parsonage in the gift of the bishops.[515] At Abernethy, where the bishop had only in 1226 finally settled a dispute over church lands and teinds with the local lord, both the parsonage and vicarage teinds were appropriated to the common fund,

the sprawling parish which stretched into the heart of the Cairngorms being served thereafter by only stipendiary curates. Here, he also retained a half-davoch that had been assigned within the parish as part of the demesne of the bishops of Moray. Similar retentions of a half-davoch occurred at six of the remaining eight parishes[516] – Birnie and Farnua having no such provision made – but in all cases the parsonage and vicarage teinds were appropriated fully to the common fund. At Arndilly, which had been given to the Church of Moray by William Murray, lord of Boharm, everything which William had granted additionally to the parish church for its support, excepting the chapel serving his castle of Boharm, was annexed. Almost a century later, in 1331, Bishop John Pilmuir detached the church of Altyre from the common fund and assigned its revenues instead for the support of the cathedral chaplains.[517]

The constitution of the chapter as established by Bishop Andrew should not be thought of as fixing the number of canons at a maximum of twenty-three. On occasion supernumerary canonries were created, including one by Andrew himself. This extra canonry was erected out of the revenues of the church of Gartly, which had been annexed to the episcopal *mensa* in the time of Bishop Richard (1187–1203) but which Richard had granted for life to one of his clerks. Sometime after 1226, Bishop Andrew apparently made the clerk a canon of the cathedral but on the clear understanding that this *ad hoc* prebend would end on the death of the incumbent and the fruits revert to his own hands.[518] Changes could also be made, usually temporarily, to the offices attached to particular prebends. In 1469, for example, the prebend of Kinnoir and Dunbennan was mentioned as being attached to the office of sacristan in the cathedral, but this link appears at no earlier or later date.[519] Another temporary prebend appears to have been created by 1539 for one Thomas Gaderar using the revenues of the bishop's mensal church of Dalarossie, which reverted to the bishop on the incumbent's death.[520] There were, however, cases where a temporary prebend might achieve permanence, as occurred in respect of the church of Kincardine in Strathspey. It had been one of the group of churches whose fruits had been assigned by Bishop Andrew in 1239 to the common funds of the canons, but in 1328 it was recorded as being held singly by one of the cathedral canons, albeit not as his prebend but as an additional free parsonage in his hands.[521] This separation from the common fund continued thereafter, but before 1537 it had been erected into a separate prebend and remained as such down to the Reformation.[522] In 1542, a further permanent canonry was added to the chapter by the erection of the chaplainry of the Virgin Mary in Duffus Castle into a new prebend of Unthank.[523] These two new prebends brought the final

8.6   Birnie church chancel arch (© Richard Oram)

8.7   Birnie church from the south-east (© Richard Oram)

complement of permanent canonries in the cathedral to twenty-five by the eve of the Reformation.

A final complement of twenty-five does not mean that all of the prebends were permanently or even regularly in residence at Elgin. Absentees were meant to ensure that there was a suitable representative for them to take their place during the services in the cathedral – a vicar or even a simple staller (literally a clerk who would fill their place in the choir stalls) – but it seems that by the later fifteenth century many of the prebendaries were failing to meet that requirement. In May 1489, Bishop Andrew Stewart held a convocation of the canons of the cathedral which passed a raft of reforming legislation intended to reaffirm the founding principles of the prebends and other beneficed clerical positions in the cathedral and to increase the level of residence amongst the clergy.[524] It was, for example, agreed that the seventh part of the annual income of an absent prebendary would be assigned to be divided equally amongst the residents and that otherwise all prebendaries should be resident in the chanonry, eating and sleeping there and participating in the daytime and night services. Failure to do so would see their deprivation of any share in the common funds of the canons. The prebendaries, moreover, were required to agree to the level of stipend to be paid to their vicars, stallers and choristers, thereby encouraging these deputies to properly fulfil their roles as effective place-fillers for the beneficed clergy and to ensure a suitably full presence of clergy in the choir for the major services in the cathedral.[525] It is in the enactments of this meeting that first reference occurs to the cathedral's clock (horologium) which was in the keepership of the treasurer.[526] The purpose of the clock was to ensure equal division of the daytime and night-time hours for the proper conducting of holy offices in the cathedral. How effective Bishop Andrew Stewart's provisions were is not recorded, but, given that his successors as bishops were themselves regularly absentee from not just the cathedral, but also from the diocese, there is a strong likelihood that this reforming effort failed to bring about any lasting change. While the full body of clergy attached to the cathedral – prebendaries, supernumerary canons, vicars, stallers, chaplains and choristers – probably numbered nearly one hundred on the eve of the Reformation, it is likely that less than half that number was ever present on other than the greatest occasions.

Other Appropriators

The prebends of the cathedral were not the only institutions to acquire interests in the parishes of Moray diocese. By the middle of the twelfth century, control first of the advowsons of churches and then of appropriated revenues from them was passing into the possession of religious corporations

elsewhere in the kingdom, some even having their revenues appropriated for the support of prebends in other dioceses. Some attempts to grant parishes in this way failed, as in the case of the former cathedral at Birnie which Bishop Brice had gifted to the monks of Kelso Abbey in the Scottish Borders, who even secured a confirmation of possession from Pope Innocent IV at some stage between 1243 and 1254.[527] By that date, however, the monks had already lost possession, for Bishop Andrew had annexed it instead to the common fund of the canons of his new cathedral.[528]

Amongst the earliest of such appropriations may have been those of Urquhart, at the east end of the Laich of Moray, and Bellie, east of the River Spey in the Enzie. At Urquhart, any parochial rights had presumably been annexed from the outset in the 1130s to David I's Benedictine foundation there, and the church was confirmed to the priory's mother-house, Dunfermline, in 1182.[529] It is clear that the entire revenues of the parish were annexed and the parochial cure was either served by one of the monks of the priory or by a curate.[530] At Bellie, the church was fully appropriated to the priory of Pluscarden at the time of the Reformation, but there is no clear evidence for when that annexation had occurred. As there is no early reference to the church from before the foundation of Pluscarden in the early 1230s, it is suggested that it may have been attached originally to the priory at Urquhart, which united with Pluscarden in the mid-fifteenth century. It is possible that it had been a dependency of Urquhart since the priory's foundation, and that the monks had secured its establishment as a full parish, but with its revenues appropriated in full to their convent.[531] At the other end of the see, at Dalcross, the parsonage was also annexed to Urquhart Priory from an early date, the church appearing only as a vicarage in the roll of the papal tax-collector Boiamund di Vitia known as Bagimond's Roll.[532] Control of the parsonage passed to Pluscarden on the union of the two priories in the 1450s, but the cure continued as a perpetual vicarage down to the Reformation.[533]

Probably at some time in the early 1190s, King William granted the church of St Mary at Inverness to the monks of the abbey he had founded in 1178 at Arbroath in Angus. Confirmation of that grant and the appropriation of the parsonage revenues to the uses of the monks was soon conceded by Bishop Richard – William's former clerk of the provend and chaplain – and reconfirmed by Bishop Andrew, both grants, however, stipulating that a vicarage perpetual be instituted in the cure.[534] Despite that repeated reservation, the monks made several attempts – and were temporarily successful – in annexing also the vicarage, but by the mid-fifteenth century the vicarage had regained and retained thereafter its independence.[535] As the burgh church of one of the wealthiest urban communities in the

8.8   Dundurcus church from the south-west (© Richard Oram)

8.9   A general view of Kiltarlity church from the south-east (© Richard Oram)

north of Scotland, to which the townsfolk made numerous gifts to endow chaplainries and to enlarge the building, this was a rich prize for the abbey. The loss of its revenues to a community outside the diocese must have been a disappointment to Bishop Richard's successors as they sought to fund the prebends in their cathedral appropriately, but, given the king's involvement as patron of both the parish and the abbey, it was unlikely that the decision would be reversed in their favour. The three-way dispute over Aberchirder or Marnoch in the deanery of Strathbogie in the early thirteenth century had been finally won by King William, who wished to endow Arbroath with the patronage of the church.[536] Bishop Brice had conceded that right to the monks, but his successor, Bishop Andrew Murray, extended their possession by appropriating the parsonage to the abbey. The remaining resources were used to establish a vicarage perpetual to serve the cure of souls, an arrangement which remained in force at the Reformation.[537]

As new lords in possession of significant landed resources who were determined to make their indelible mark on the region as well as to give expression to their piety, the Bisset family in the 1220s and 1230s were generous in the distribution of their religious patronage. Their first foundation was a leper hospital at Rathven in Banffshire,[538] which lay within the diocese of Aberdeen. Probably at the time of its foundation c 1224–6, the hospital had received the grant of the parsonage of the church of Dundurcus on the west of the Spey in the diocese of Moray (Illus 8.8).[539] Probably around the same time, John Bisset granted the hospital the church of Kiltarlity, west of Inverness, confirming the grant in 1226 (Illus 8.9).[540] At almost the same time, an agreement between the bishops of Moray and Ross, who had been in dispute over whether the churches of Kiltarlity and Ardersier belonged to their respective dioceses, placed Kiltarlity in Moray.[541] In respect of both Dundurcus and Kiltarlity, the cure appears to have been a vicarage perpetual and to have remained unannexed at the Reformation. The parsonages, however, shared a different fate, for in 1445 all of the resources of the hospital at Rathven were annexed to a new prebend founded in the cathedral at Aberdeen.[542] The prebend, however, was served by a staller in the cathedral with funds being reserved for six bedesmen at the hospital, which had become an almshouse rather than a leper hospital.

Others in the family had grander ambitions and sought to demonstrate their arrival as magnates through the foundation of substantial monastic communities. When Walter Bisset founded the Valliscaulian priory of Beauly, amongst the resources in his control which he assigned for its support was the church of Abertarff of Kilchuimin at the south end of Loch Ness, possession of the parsonage

being confirmed to the monks by Bishop Andrew Murray c 1230–2.[543] The vicarage appears to have remained unappropriated,[544] but it can be found in the fifteenth century being served by a monk of another Valliscaulian priory, Ardchattan in Argyll.[545] How that connection had been established, and if it was a permanent arrangement, is unknown. A second church annexed to Beauly was Conveth, where Bishop Brice and John Bisset had been involved in a dispute over possession of the patronage. This dispute was resolved in Bisset's favour, but he made over possession of the patronage of the church to the monks soon after Beauly's foundation.[546] It appears that the parsonage was annexed around the time of this grant, for in Bagimond's Roll of 1274 the church is listed only as a vicarage.[547]

In much the same way as his father had used his reserves of ecclesiastical patronage in Moray to endow his monastic foundation, so too did King Alexander II with his. It is likely that a pre-existing parish church at Pluscarden was annexed to the Valliscaulian priory which he founded in the parish in 1231; certainly Pope Urban IV believed this to be the case when he confirmed the priory's possessions in 1263.[548] There is no indication of there ever having been a vicarage settlement, which suggests that the entire revenues of the parish had been annexed to the priory at its foundation, with parish services presumably being provided either by one of the monks or by a curate. Shortly after the foundation of Pluscarden, Alexander requested that Bishop Andrew should annexe the parsonage of the church of Dores on the east side of Loch Ness to the priory.[549] Until that time, the king had controlled the patronage of the church but was now using its revenues to support the convent of Valliscaulians which represented his largest single act of religious patronage during his reign. At the time of its grant to the monks in 1233, a vicarage perpetual had been instituted to serve the cure, and that provision remained in place at the Reformation.[550]

Unappropriated Vicarages

Several vicarages also remained unappropriated through the later Middle Ages. At Aberlour, although the parsonage teinds had been assigned in 1224 towards the prebend of Aberlour and Botriphnie, the vicarage revenues remained intact and were established for the support of the vicarage perpetual which served the cure of the parish down to the Reformation.[551] Similar provision for a perpetual vicarage was set in place at Dallas and Ardclach in 1226 when their parsonage revenues were assigned to support prebends in the cathedral.[552] Botriphnie, too, remained as a vicarage perpetual, although there it seems that it was united with the neighbouring parish of Botarie – where the parsonage had been annexed with that of Elchies to fund a prebend – to form a single vicarage at some late stage.[553] The unification of vicarages in this way may have been a result of a process of rationalisation and economy, rather than being driven by avarice on the part of an incumbent or possible would-be appropriator. It is likely that in some cases the vicarage revenues which remained after the appropriation of the parsonage teinds were inadequate to sustain a vicar. At Brachlie and Petty, where the parsonages of both parishes had been annexed in c 1224 by Bishop Andrew to fund a prebend, at some point after that annexation the two vicarages had been united to form a single cure.[554] A similar approach was apparently taken with the annexed episcopal mensal churches of Drumdelgie and Gartly, where the vicarages perpetual were united into a single cure.[555]

Similar conditions occurred where parsonage revenues were being appropriated to certain of the common funds within the cathedral. At Arndilly in Strathbogie, the church was granted during the time of Bishop Brice to the common fund of the canons, with only the granter's chapel at Boharm excluded from the gift, an arrangement confirmed in 1239 by Bishop Andrew. From that time, the parsonage remained annexed to the common fund whilst the cure was a vicarage perpetual.[556] Bishop Andrew made an identical arrangement in respect of Barevan, the medieval predecessor of the parish of Cawdor, where the cure remained a vicarage perpetual after the annexation of the parsonage to the common fund.[557] Despite the relatively late date of the annexation of the parsonage teinds of Alvie in Strathspey for the support of the cathedral chaplains – 1331, by Thomas Randolph, earl of Moray – the vicarage remained unappropriated and the cure was still served by a vicar perpetual at the Reformation.[558] Few of the parishes where the parsonage had been appropriated to a religious corporation other than the cathedral at Elgin appear to have seen similar appropriation of the vicarages. At Dores where the parsonage was annexed to Pluscarden, or Conveth, for example, where although the parsonage was annexed to Beauly Priory in the mid-thirteenth century and the resulting vicarage perpetual appears to have been united for a time in the late fourteenth and early fifteenth centuries with neighbouring Wardlaw parish, the vicarage regained its independent existence thereafter and remained unappropriated at the Reformation.[559]

Free Parsonages

Only six parishes in the diocese remained independent throughout the Middle Ages, and in two cases their survival may have been a deliberate policy decision by the bishops, possibly as a way of providing themselves with a small reserve of benefices to use as patronage for some of their closest clerical servants or chaplains. Boleskine on the east side of Loch Lomond was one, but it may have been a late creation.[560] The fact that the bishops of Moray had an interest in a half-

davoch there in the early thirteenth century is not in itself an indication of the existence of a parish and church, but in the mid-fourteenth century Abertarff and Boleskine were noted together as a unit paying the highest tax in the deanery of Inverness: three shillings as opposed to two shillings offered by all the other units.[561] This link and higher charge could indicate that Boleskine was at that time a dependency of Abertarff and was only erected into an independent parish at a much later date. It only finally appears as a fully independent parish in the early sixteenth century, and at the time of the Reformation its patronage lay in the hands of the Bishop of Moray.[562] Abriachan or Bona, the parish on the west side of Loch Ness within which lay an important concentration of episcopal lands, was a second such case. There, despite an early attempt to annexe the revenues to the common funds of the canons, the church had remained an independent parsonage in the patronage of the bishop, although it seems that most of the time he may have diverted its revenues into his own funds and served the cure through a pensionary vicar who received only a small stipend.[563]

A handful of churches remained independent in lay patronage. Dunlichty was one. Control of the patronage of the church had been contested between the earls of Crawford and Moray in the fifteenth century, the latter apparently being successful in his claim to the right. The patronage was still in the hands of his successors in the sixteenth century.[564] A second was Essie in Strathbogie, where control of the patronage had been yielded to the lord of Strathbogie in 1226 as part of a complex settlement of disputes over lands and rights between him and Bishop Andrew.[565] It passed with the Strathbogie interest shortly after 1314 to the Campbell earls of Atholl but was separated from them by c 1319 when Robert I granted Strathbogie to the Gordon family. Control of the patronage of the church remained with the earls of Huntly at the Reformation.[566] Glass in Strathbogie had also been quitclaimed to David of Strathbogie in 1226 and remained independent in lay patronage thereafter.[567] Although it presumably followed the same route through Atholl and Campbell hands into the possession of the Gordons of Huntly, there is no documentary evidence to corroborate that suggestion. On Speyside, the church of Rothes had originally been granted in 1235 by Muriel de Pollock, lady of Rothes, to the hospital of St Nicholas which she had founded at the Bridge of Spey (Boat of Brig).[568] In the late Middle Ages, although the hospital continued to function, it had ceased to be a religious institution and the benefices attached to it seem to have reverted to the successors of the original lay patrons. In the case of Rothes, by the sixteenth century this was the Leslie earls of Rothes, in whose hands it remained at the Reformation.[569]

Chaplainries

Soon after Bishop Andrew had established his new constitution for the cathedral in Elgin the complement of clergy serving there began to be expanded by the foundation of chaplainries to serve at additional altars in the church. The first of these was established in April 1235 when King Alexander II made a grant of three merks annually from the burgh ferme of Elgin to endow a chaplainry to celebrate mass for the soul of his ancestor, King Duncan II, who had been slain near Elgin in 1040 by Macbethad.[570] Payments to the chaplains of this royal foundation continued to be made down to the Reformation and are recorded in the Exchequer Rolls.[571] It is not noted in the original foundation charter of the chaplainry to which altar it was attached, but this may be the chaplainry at the altar of the Blessed Virgin Mary, which in 1469 was noted as receiving eight merks annually from the rents of Pittendreich near Elgin by gift of the royal predecessors of King James III.[572] In 1268, William, earl of Ross confirmed the grant made by Fergus of Ardrossan and confirmed by Freskin Murray, lord of Duffus, of the two davochs of Clon described as near Dingwall in Ross to provide revenue to support two chaplains at Elgin who would celebrate mass in perpetuity for the faithful dead.[573] This was a generous award, but the earl augmented it by freeing the land from all rent burdens due to him and his heirs as superior lords and by promising to perform any service demanded from it by the Crown. These three chaplainries were amongst the four that in 1360 were granted by Bishop John Pilmuir a piece of land outside the chanonry wall on its west side as the site for permanent manses for themselves and their successors.[574]

The next chaplainry to be established in the cathedral was that of St Nicholas, one of two founded in 1286 by the Elgin burgess Hugh Herock, the second being in the parish church of St Giles in the burgh.[575] St Nicholas' chaplainry, too, was a pro anima foundation, made for the salvation of the souls of Hugh and his wife Margaret, their parents and their children, but also for the soul of King Alexander III, who had been killed in March that year. The income for the two chaplains, set at six merks each annually, was provided from Hugh's lands of 'Daldeleyt', which he made over to Bishop Archibald and the canons of the cathedral and their successors. It is unknown where in the cathedral the altar of St Nicholas was located, but it is likely to have been in one of the chapels in the outer aisles of the nave. There is little further reference to the chaplainry after its foundation beyond an inquest of 1398 into the sources and extent of its revenues,[576] but it was still in theoretical existence decades after the Reformation when its revenues were being used to provide bursaries for boys to attend grammar school (see page 132).

Rapid expansion of the number of chaplainries in the cathedral and of the resources allocated for their support was made from the 1320s onwards. One of the largest single developments came in May 1328, when Thomas Randolph, earl of Moray, founded five chaplainries in 'a noble chapel to the adornment of the cathedral church of Moray'. Since the early eighteenth century when Robert Keith first produced his description of the burial places of Scottish bishops in his general history of the Scottish episcopate, in which he located the burial place of Bishop Columba Dunbar in St Thomas's chapel in the north transept, it has been assumed that this new chaplainry served at the northern of the two altars in that transept.[577] Thomas Randolph's foundation charter, however, locates it against the south side of the cathedral: 'in the cemetery of the same church on the south side'.[578] Descriptions of chapel buildings as 'in the cemetery' can mean a free-standing structure adjacent to the main church building, but more often in Scotland referred to projections from the flank of the main building into the surrounding graveyard.[579] They are often represented nowadays by lairds' lofts and burial aisles where their founders' descendants retained possession of them post-Reformation. The location given for the new chapel at Elgin suggests either that the plan was originally to build a wholly new structure, either free-standing or contiguous to the south flank of the cathedral, or that the existing south-eastern chapel on the nave was to be rebuilt or refurnished in a grand manner; the description 'in the cemetery' appears to rule out a location in the north transept of the main church.

Randolph's new chapel was dedicated to St Thomas (of Canterbury), bishop and martyr.[580] Founded with the special licence of Bishop Pilmuir and the dean and chapter, the chaplains were to say masses perpetually for the souls of King Robert, the earl's uncle, his heirs and successors, and for Randolph's own soul and those of his ancestors, heirs, affinity and friends. To sustain the chaplains he allocated annual rents to the value of £23 14s 4d from his income from Elgin, with alternative arrangements for supplements from elsewhere in the earldom should that award prove insufficient. The foundation charter contains particular detail of the services to be conducted in the chapel and the involvement of the chaplains in the choir services of the cathedral at matins, prime, high mass and vespers. In the chapel they were to celebrate privately five masses daily; for St Thomas, the mass of the day, for the Virgin Mary, for the dead, and for St John the Baptist. Payments to the chaplains continued throughout the Middle Ages and are recorded regularly in the Exchequer Rolls when allowance was made for them in the accounts of the sheriff of Elgin and Forres for the annuity due to them.[581]

The existing provision for the chaplains serving in the cathedral was augmented in 1331 when Bishop John Pilmuir established a common fund for their support. In the petition to Pope Clement V which secured papal confirmation of the establishment of the common fund, Pilmuir stated that the pre-existing resources had been inadequate to sustain the seventeen resident perpetual chaplains there should be in the cathedral. His arrangements for a common fund brought together various earlier chaplainry endowments and added a series of new sources of income.[582] This new establishment included recent awards, such as that also made in 1331 of the parsonage teinds of the church of Alvie by Thomas Randolph, earl of Moray,[583] but Pilmuir also made new assignments or transferred resources from previous recipients. Birnie, which in 1331 was one of his own mensal churches, was annexed entirely to the new fund with only a reservation on the parsonage and vicarage income for a portionary vicar to serve the cure. He also removed the fruits of the church of Altyre from the canons' common fund and assigned them instead to the chaplains' fund. Possession of the parsonage fruits of Alvie finally passed to the chaplains in 1333 when the incumbent rector, Aymer de Wenton, resigned the cure and Bishop Pilmuir notified the vicar Cristin that he had invested the procurator of the cathedral chaplains, John de Dichton, with the church.[584] The purpose of the endowment was to ensure the better worship of God in the cathedral, but there was a more particular emphasis within the award on provision of *pro anima* masses with King Robert I, the earl, bishop, and their immediate families named as most immediate beneficiaries, but with all the faithful dead embraced in general terms.

Further chaplainries were endowed in the cathedral by various lay patrons from the 1340s onwards. Elaborate provisions were attached to the first of these, a chaplainry instituted by the Murray family in April 1341, which was provided with income from an annual rent of eight merks drawn from the lands of Alturlie and Croy in the Murrays' lordship of Petty between Nairn and Inverness. This chaplainry was established by John Murray, panetar of Scotland, in memory of his father Andrew Murray, and in May 1353 following John's death it was confirmed by his brother and successor Thomas.[585] At the establishment of the chaplainry it was agreed that six merks would be assigned to a chaplain who would say mass in perpetuity at the altar of the Holy Rude for the soul and memory of Andrew Murray. Ten shillings was reserved to be distributed annually between the chaplains and vicars who performed sung exequies on the anniversary of Andrew's death and to pay for four candles which were to be placed around his tomb at that time. John Murray's charter allocated part of the money additionally for lights for the altars of the Holy Rude and of the Virgin.

Similar elaborate allocation of funds for various services

were set out in July 1341 when Isabel Randolph, countess of Moray, assigned rents to the value of 100 shillings annually to establish a chaplainry in the cathedral in memory of her late husband, Thomas Randolph, first earl of Moray.[586] The bulk of the income came from the ferme of half of the church lands of Aberbrandely (unidentified but probably Knockando in Strathspey),[587] which she had bought from Duncan, earl of Fife, who held them at feu from the bishop of Moray, the residue coming from the rent of properties on the north side of Elgin High Street. The chaplain was to serve mainly at the altar of the chapel of St Thomas the Martyr in the cathedral church, but twice weekly he was to perform mass at the altar of St John the Baptist in the chapel of St Mary in Elgin Castle, for which a portion of his income was reserved for providing bread, wine, wax and ornaments for St John's altar. Countess Isabel also provided within her grant for payment to all the canons, vicars, chaplains and choir members of the church to celebrate mass on the future anniversary of her death, and to furnish the bread, wine, wax and altar ornaments for her chaplain in St Thomas's chapel.

Alexander Menzies, lord of Lhanbryde, acting in concert with John of Inverness, chancellor of the Church of Moray, added a further chaplainry in August 1350, where masses would be said for the souls of Alexander, John, and Alexander's mother Eleanor. This was supported on an annual rent of eight merks paid from the ferme of the lands of 'Mayn' in Lhanbryde, but with additional provision for alternative payment should that source prove inadequate.[588] Alexander also introduced a penalty clause whereby he or his successors would be bound to pay £100 towards the fabric of the cathedral if they reneged on the foundation of the chaplainry. In the fifteenth century, when Lhanbryde had returned to the Crown's direct lordship, the annuity of eight merks continued to be paid to the chaplain from the receipts of the king's sheriff of Elgin and Forres.[589]

Robert Lauder, lord of Quarrelwood, added a further chaplainry in May 1362, founded at St Peter's altar in the cathedral church for the souls of himself, his ancestors and successors, but especially for the soul 'of the noble man my lord Sir Hugh late earl of Ross', and for all the faithful dead.[590] The chaplainry was sustained on 100 shillings paid annually from the rents of his lands of Brightmony and Kinsteary, and from the mill and brewhouse of Auldearn. This grant secured a royal confirmation by David II when he was in Elgin in May 1367.[591] A second chaplainry at this altar, endowed out of the rents of the lands of Pitcassie in Stratha'an, Banffshire, was recorded in 1549 as lying in the patronage of George Gordon, earl of Huntly.[592] There is no record of when that second chaplainry was founded, but its advowson had probably been in the hands of the Gordons since they acquired Stratha'an in the mid-fifteenth century.

New chaplainries continued to be endowed by local families through the fifteenth and well into the sixteenth century, adding still further to the collegiate establishment in the cathedral. Royal concern in the later Middle Ages over the volume of lands and rents continuing to be assigned to the Church in alms had led to greater control being exercised through regulation of these so-called 'mortifications' and the requirement that each one should receive a royal confirmation. Thus, in February 1469, royal confirmation was given to James Douglas's endowment of a chaplainry at the altar of the Blessed Virgin Mary in the cathedral with an annual rent of ten merks from the lands of Pittendreich south-west of Elgin.[593] Likewise, in February 1502, a confirmation of the mortification of an annual rent of £10 from lands near Innes given by Bishop Andrew Stewart in his will to endow a chaplainry at St Martin's altar in the cathedral for the souls of his father, brothers and close colleagues was issued to Master John Spens, subchanter of the cathedral, who was the bishop's executor.[594] In September 1529, royal confirmation was given to a charter of Gavin Dunbar, bishop of Aberdeen, which gave an annuity of fifty merks from the rents of Quarrelwood and Lidgait – which he had acquired earlier that year specifically for this purpose – to chaplains serving at the altars of St Columba and St Thomas the Martyr. The grant was made for the souls of Sir Alexander Dunbar of Westfield, his father, Lady Elizabeth Sutherland, his mother, Sir Robert Wells, late archdeacon of St Andrews, Gavin Waich, late dean of Moray, Master James Lindsay and Master James Broun, archdeacon and dean of Aberdeen. Bishop Dunbar was to make the first presentation, but after his death the presentation of both would pertain to the dean of Moray.[595]

The sources of income upon which chaplainries were founded were many and varied. On 5 October 1551, for example, Bishop Robert Reid of Orkney, formerly abbot of Kinloss near Forres, granted twelve merks derived from certain lands which had been adjudged to him within the diocese of Caithness to fund two chaplains at the altar of St Michael in the cathedral at Elgin.[596]

Some attempts to found or further endow chaplainries in the cathedral were unsuccessful due to the would-be founders' failure to secure royal consent and a confirmation of the mortification. For example, in October 1556, the queen made a grant to an Elgin burgess, John Annand, of a piece of property known as 'Boyllis-orcheart' (Boyle's Orchard) at the east end of the burgh close to the Franciscan friary which Sir Tiberius Winchester, a chaplain at the altar of the Blessed Virgin Mary in the cathedral, had attempted to grant to that altar.[597] Since Winchester had failed to secure the proper permission, the land had been seized in the queen's name and was at her disposal. On occasion it is likely that the Crown would have made a re-grant of the property to the intended beneficiary, especially when it was for spiritual purposes, but in the highly charged political climate of the 1550s it is likely that such a windfall was redeployed as a piece of patronage directed towards an individual whom the Crown wished to keep loyal.

In addition to the permanently endowed chaplainries, payment could be made for masses for the souls of specific individuals to be offered up additionally by one of the already established chaplains in the cathedral. In 1456 and 1458, for example, payment was recorded of £8 from royal receipts in Elgin made to Sir Adam Forres, chaplain, for masses said in the cathedral for the soul of the late John Liddale.[598] These appear to have been one-off payments, possibly in commemoration of a royal servant, and did not become a regular component in the round of *pro anima* masses said in the cathedral.

After the Reformation the chaplainries continued to exist in form if not in function, most being used as a source of what could be regarded as bursaries for boys to attend grammar school. In April 1581, for example, James Terras, described as 'sone to schir James Terras, chaplaine in Elgin', and of 'convenient aige to enter in the studie of grammer and is apt and diposit thairfoir', was gifted the revenues for seven years of the chaplainry of the Holy Rude in the cathedral amounting to £5 6s 8d.[599] Young James was unable to take up the grant, for there was a rival incumbent, William Douglas, who had received a lifetime grant of the revenues from Bishop Patrick Hepburn, but in May 1583 a seven-year grant of the Holy Rude revenues was also made to John Mowat, son of Magnus Mowat of Cowie, with the note that the chaplainry was vacant by expiry of the previous seven-year gift to Terras.[600] It is only in this period that some chaplainries can be traced either for the first time, or for the first time since their formal institution in the thirteenth or fourteenth century through grants of this type. In January 1582, for example, a chaplainry of 'Stanewallis' in the cathedral passed to a second generation of Innes for their support at grammar school, while in March 1583 the chaplainry of St Nicholas went to a second Douglas brother after the expiry of the first seven-year grant of its revenues to his elder brother, and in May 1583 an altar of St Laurence likewise provided a bursary for the son of a servitor of the nominal bishop of Moray.[601] St Katherine's chaplainry provided a seven-year bursary for James Dunbar, but was also granted to provide for James Terras, who had missed out earlier on the Holy Rude chaplainry.[602] St Giles's altar appears in a charter of November 1582 granting it to one James Stewart, but in February 1584 it was granted for seven years to John Smyth, son of Thomas Smyth, merchant and burgess of Elgin, for his support whilst studying at grammar school in

Elgin.[603] A chaplainry of St John the Baptist in the cathedral together with the chaplainry of Our Lady in the burgh kirk was granted for the support of George Annand, the son of another Elgin burgess.[604]

The Fabric and Lights of the Cathedral

Building a cathedral was an expensive operation, but the expenditure on its structure did not end when the final piece of its external fabric was in place. As with all structures, maintenance of the built fabric became essential almost as soon as the masons and wrights had finished their tasks. The costs of the first construction may have been provided from special financial provisions and impositions on the clergy of the diocese, gifts from great patrons, and pious offerings from all comers, but recurrent maintenance costs needed to be met from a known and dependable source. Thus, amongst the early acts of Bishop Brice when he was instituting his cathedral at Spynie was the grant of the entire revenues of the church of Daviot south of Inverness towards the needs of the cathedral fabric fund. The grant was made at the instance of Brice's uncle, Freskin of Kerdale, in whose hands the patronage presumably had lain, and was to come into effect after the death or resignation of the incumbent priest, Robert.[605] In the interim, Robert the priest was to pay an annual pension to the church of Spynie of either half a pound of incense or sixpence at Pentecost. When the grant was ratified by Bishop Andrew sometime after 1224, Robert was either dead or had resigned his cure, and the whole revenues of the parish were flowing into the fabric fund of the cathedral.[606] No mention is made then or later as to how the cure was served, but it was presumably through a stipendiary curate appointed by the bishop, who appears to have controlled the fabric fund.[607]

Amongst the other most important of the financial provisions made by the bishops for the proper provisioning of their cathedral was the allocation of revenues from annexed parishes to pay for the lights of the church. All altars which had not received some private endowment from which wax for candles could be purchased required money to buy sufficient candles for the altar and any associated candelabra or oil for presence lamps. Bishop Andrew, who took great care to provide adequately for the needs of his church in the constitution which he implemented at the time of the relocation of the see from Spynie to Elgin, appears to have been the first bishop to make proper provision for the illumination of the church. Amongst the more famous of his grants was a reservation of the entire funds of the church of Rothiemurchus towards the cost of the cathedral's lights, represented in the late fourteenth century by the £8 per annum rent due from Alexander Stewart, lord of Badenoch.[608] Bishop Andrew also made a

second grant, but this time of the entire funds of a church, Dalarossie in Strathnairn, towards the lights.[609] Sometime in the episcopate of Bishop Bur one of the cathedral chaplains, Adam de Sores, bequeathed two perches of land which he had acquired on the north side of the burgh of Elgin to provide for the lights of the Holy Rude in the cathedral. This property was leased to Andrew Robertson, burgess of Elgin, for an annual rent of 6s 8d or one stone of good beeswax for candles.[610]

The Portable Treasures of the Cathedral

At some other cathedrals and major pre-Reformation churches in Scotland we are fortunate to have quite lengthy inventories of the fixtures and fittings and portable treasures with which they were furnished, even though most of those items have themselves long been lost. Inventories from the cathedral at Aberdeen or the major shrine church of St Duthac at Tain provide us with glimpses of the material richness of churches which are now little more than truncated, stripped-down shells that give little impression of the glittering displays which they once presented to the clergy and people who participated in the religious ceremonies.[611] At Elgin we have a few snatches of information embedded in the documentary record to shed some light on the lost treasures with which the devout enriched the church. One of the most detailed is a list of items associated with the altar of St Duthac in the cathedral, which was possibly located in one of the chapels which lined the outer aisles of the nave. It was drawn up in December 1460 at a convocation of the canons of the cathedral summoned by Bishop James Stewart, and comprises equipment and altar vestments provided by the dean, precentor, archdeacon and succentor.[612] The list begins with a chalice of gilded silver, a missal or mass book, and a vestment made entirely of a silken cloth known as *burdalexande*r. Next come two candelabras, a silver spoon, two altar-cloths with two frontals, two tinned (*stannee*) stoles, one pendant, and one hanging bell. These were followed by a candelabrum of iron to be hung over the altar. Finally came two or three corporal cloths (a napkin on which the chalice was placed), one made of linen and the others of broadcloth. Given that St Duthac's altar appears to have been one of the more poorly endowed of the at least sixteen altars in the cathedral by that date, this list provides us with some impression of the quantities of religious artefacts, mass vestments, altar cloths, service books and light-fittings with which the cathedral was furnished.

Books were amongst the single most valuable items in the cathedral, for even after William Caxton's mid-fifteenth-century development of the first printing press, most books were still manuscript productions, copied – and often illuminated – painstakingly by highly skilled scribes. It was only in the early 1500s that King James IV licensed the establishment of the first printing press in Scotland, in Edinburgh. The value of the cathedral's manuscript books therefore explains why amongst the many provisions of Bishop Andrew Stewart's lengthy enactments of May 1489 designed to improve the quality of religious life at Elgin there was a prohibition on any chaplain, staller, or chorister removing any of the books from the choir of the cathedral to their chambers, under penalty of a fine of one pound of wax.[613] The cathedral continued to provide itself with new mass books and texts into the 1550s, including a Scottish manuscript martyrology dated to c 1550 which survives in Edinburgh University Library.[614]

The Wider Ecclesiastical Establishment at Elgin

The ecclesiastical establishment at Elgin was not simply represented by the cathedral and clerical manses within their walled precinct. Around Elgin, the bishops were also responsible for the founding and growth of a number of other institutions which added to the wider ecclesiastical community and which were intended to contribute to the spiritual and physical welfare of the people of the diocese. Little of the material fabric of that wider ecclesiastical landscape has survived, but the fragmentary documentary record which remains provides us with a glimpse of the wider ecclesiastical landscape around Elgin. This section does not look at the parish church of St Giles which stood at the heart of the adjacent urban community, nor at the Dominican and Franciscan convents founded in the burgh,[615] but briefly explores the Maison Dieu, the Leper Hospital, and the cathedral school, which were associated most closely with the bishops.

The Poor's Hospital or Almshouse of the Maison Dieu

The Maison Dieu or poor's hospital, an almshouse, was founded before c 1235 by Bishop Andrew Murray.[616] It is unfortunate that the foundation charter which would have set out the reasons for the hospital and provided details of the numbers of inmates it was intended to support does not survive, but King Alexander II's charter of confirmation, issued at Aberdeen on 23 February 1235, has come down to us within a reconfirmation by King David II drawn up while he was at Kinloss Abbey on 4 April 1343, and itself confirmed by Bishop John Pilmuir at Spynie eight days later.[617] Alexander II's charter provides us with the dedication of the hospital – the Virgin Mary and St John the Evangelist – establishes its role as an almshouse to receive and maintain within it the poor, and identifies its endowment as the lands

of Manbeen and Kellas which had been attached to the episcopal *mensa* when the church of St Giles of Elgin had been given to Bishop Richard in the 1180s. In 1237, Bishop Andrew and the brothers and sisters of the Maison Dieu reached an amicable agreement over property in dispute between them at Manbeen, which Andrew quitclaimed to them in return for their quitclaim to him of their interests in Kellas.[618] Andrew also gave them a property in Elgin next to the precentor's manse at the chanonry. By 1343, when David II confirmed the 1235 act, the Maison Dieu was described as poor and wasted, its revenues apparently being withheld by its nominal tenants.

Worse was to come, for in June 1390, when Alexander Stewart's men burned Elgin, the Maison Dieu became one of their targets-probably on account of its close association with both Bishop Bur and the Dunbars, for its then master was Alexander, younger son of John, earl of Moray.[619] In October 1391 whilst King Robert II was at Spynie, possibly viewing the damage inflicted on the cathedral and the other religious buildings in Elgin, he ordered an inquest to be conducted into who had the right of patronage of the hospital, for a dispute had arisen between him and Sir John Hay of Lochloy on the one hand and Bishop Bur on the other over the right of presentation.[620] It was as part of this formal process of re-establishing title to such rights following the loss of so many of the diocesan records in the burning of the cathedral the previous year that Bishop Andrew Murray's role as founder of the Maison Dieu and the right of his successors to provide masters to the hospital was attested in formal letters drawn up William Spynie, precentor of Moray, Henry Pluscarden, the chancellor, and William Gerland, subdean, at Aberdeen on 3 November 1391.[621] In a second sworn attestation Sir John Wylgus identified four men whom Bishop John Pilmuir had given the keepership of the hospital, starting with Master Roger of Wedale, followed by his uncle John Pilmuir, a Cistercian monk of Coupar Angus Abbey, then Master Simon of Crail, and finally the bishop's kinsman or cousin Master John Kinnaird.[622]

Master Roger's relationship with Pilmuir is unknown, but he had several connections with north-east Scotland between the Tay and the Spey in the earlier fourteenth century.[623] Master Simon's designation 'of Crail' could suggest a link with the bishop through their common north-east Fife association, and he does seem to have moved from the household of Bishop Lamberton of St Andrews to Moray diocese early in Pilmuir's episcopate.[624] By 1343, Master Simon was holding the subchantership of Moray but had been advanced to the subdeanery by 1350.[625] Although he had received papal confirmation of his promotion to the subdeanery in 1351, Master Simon appears to have failed to make the transfer effective and it was possibly as compensation for the failure that Pilmuir gave him the Maison Dieu. On balance, there is a strong indication that Pilmuir was using the resources of the hospital as a means of supporting kinsmen and clerks who had a close personal bond with him. The inquest also confirmed that the right of presentation had remained with Bishop Bur, who had appointed Sir Adam of Dundurcus 'who still remains with the same'.[626] Reinforced with this evidence, Bur was able to sit in tribunal to determine the rights to the mastership of the hospital claimed by Alexander Dunbar, brother of Thomas second earl of Moray.[627] On 21 September 1393, it was adjudged that Dunbar had no rights in the Maison Dieu but had been 'by violent intrusion' imposed on the hospital by his late father. The bishops of Moray, it was settled, had the right of collation and provision, but the right of presentation pertained to the king. That being settled, Bur quickly restored Adam of Dundurcus to possession, whilst Earl Thomas made restitution to Adam for the losses which he had suffered during the period when his brother had held the hospital.

Adam retained possession for less than a year, for by October 1394 the mastership of the Maison Dieu 'near the walls of Moray' was recorded in a papal petition amongst the various benefices held by William Chambers, a pluralist who was a canon in the cathedrals of Elgin and Glasgow as well as being parson of Turriff in Aberdeen diocese.[628] He was given papal dispensation to retain his Moray and Aberdeen benefices even when advanced to a new canonry and prebend in Glasgow. Under such conditions, it is understandable how the hospital and its affairs were in such a precarious condition by the early fifteenth century.

Questions over the condition of the hospital and its affairs were raised in 1432 when a papal mandate was given to the bishop of Moray to undertake an investigation into its management by the then master, John Chambers, and if found unsatisfactory to deprive Chambers and appoint Thomas Fordyce, one of the deans of Christianity of Moray and vicar of the churches of Abernethy and Inverallian.[629] Fordyce's petition was that Chambers had almost totally destroyed the hospital by taking up its rents and fruits and, despite the admonitions of the bishop and leading townsmen of Elgin, had failed to look after the poor as he should, living instead over thirty miles away from his charge and consuming the revenues for himself. Fordyce, by contrast, was said to be ready and willing to restore the hospital and to run it as it should be. By 1445, the Maison Dieu was again reported to be no longer fulfilling its function as a charitable almshouse, its property and revenues being described as assigned to clerks as a secular benefice rather than being used for the maintenance of poor brothers and sisters.[630] In 1520, Bishop James Hepburn granted the

Maison Dieu to the convent of the Dominicans in Elgin, possibly to ensure that its resources were used for their intended purpose rather than simply used to augment clerical incomes. It remained in the hands of the Dominicans at the time of the Reformation, but reference during this same period to payments made to three bedesmen suggest that the friars had been fulfilling their proper duties in respect of the hospital.[631]

The Leper Hospital
Amongst the more ephemeral of the religious establishments which clustered in the shadow of the cathedral was the possible leper hospital, described in 1391 as 'the houses of the lepers in Elgin'.[632] It was said to lie adjacent to the land known as 'Spetalflat' (Hospitalflat) described as between the high road and the Tayock Burn, on which the Maison Dieu stood. This description makes it clear that the reference in 1360 to a plot of land outside the chanonry wall on its west side – possibly in what is now Cooper Park – which was owned by the Lazarites who often ran such hospitals, was not the site of the Leper Hospital.[633]

The Cathedral Schools
A cathedral song school was finally instituted in 1489 at Elgin by the chapter as part of a broad raft of reforms passed by a convocation presided over by Bishop Andrew Stewart.[634] It was the duty of the precentor of the cathedral to instruct the boys of the cathedral choir in singing and to oversee their discipline. He was instructed to hold a song school within the chanonry and to place over it a suitable man to govern and rule it and to provide instruction in music and reading. This song school has often been conflated with the 'general school' which was also instituted in 1489.[635] It, however, was erected in the burgh, not within the chanonry, and was placed under the oversight of the chancellor of Moray who was to appoint a suitable schoolmaster to provide instruction in grammar.[636]

Episcopal Residences
Of the medieval residences of the bishops of Moray, only Spynie has left us with substantial upstanding stone remains of a major residential complex. At Birnie there is nothing left that can be attributed with confidence to any possible twelfth-century or later palace complex, and the fact that it continued to serve as a meeting place for one of the bishop's law courts throughout the Middle Ages should not be taken as evidence that it gathered in an episcopal residence there. At Spynie there is not much more that can be said with any confidence to belong to the later-twelfth- and thirteenth-century castle, although a short section of stonework in the northern boundary wall of the cemetery is pointed out

locally as the last vestige of the bishops' residence. Here, however, geophysical survey in the mid-1990s did provide some indication of the presence of the apparently robbed-out walls of a large complex of buildings north and east of the churchyard;[637] these results have not been tested by archaeology. Unlike Birnie, however, there are a number of documentary references which provide us with evidence for Kinneddar as a functioning episcopal power centre and offer glimpses of activities within parts of the complex. Under Bishop Archibald, Kinneddar was clearly the main residence of the bishops of Moray. In 1294, for example, it was there that he presided over the gathering which resolved various issues surrounding kirklands associated with the church of Duffus.[638] Nevertheless, there are indications that Spynie was not altogether unimportant at this time, for in 1280 it was 'at Spynie' (in what venue is not otherwise specified) that Archibald issued his letters denouncing William de Fenton in the course of their dispute over the church of Kiltarlity (Illus 8.9).[639] Bishop David Murray also had Kinneddar as his principal residential seat with his personal chaplain attached to the chapel there (Illus 8.10).[640]

The location of the principal residence of the bishops of Moray gravitated towards Spynie in the fourteenth century, but Kinneddar remained important certainly into the middle of the century. In 1328, for example, Bishop Pilmuir presided over a tribunal assembled 'in the chapel of his manor of Kinneddar'.[641] Forty years later, record was made of the arrest by Bishop Bur in the water of Lossie of a small ship, which he had discovered whilst crossing from 'his castle of Kinneddar' towards the church of Urquhart.[642] One of the last references to Kinneddar's former importance as an episcopal palace occurs in 1569 when Bishop Patrick Hepburn was granting away much of the bishop's temporal possessions in the Laigh of Moray at feuferme to James Stewart, earl of Moray. In the feu-charter, amongst the properties alienated by him was the 'ruined palace' (*palatium dirutum*) at Kinneddar, along with its rabbit warren, meadow, garden and harbour.[643]

In 1368, when almost the last evidence for Kinneddar's continued function as a working residence occurs, Bur is also recorded as receiving the homage of Alexander Chisholm in his chamber at Spynie, with a 'multitude of canons and chaplains and others invited there to dine'.[644] From that point onwards, Spynie appears to have replaced Kinneddar as the principal residence of the bishops of Moray. The magnificent remains of the fourteenth- to seventeenth-century palace are in the guardianship of Historic Scotland and have been the subject of detailed archaeological and architectural history analysis in recent years.[645] They are not, therefore, discussed here.

8.10   The site of Kinneddar church (© Richard Oram)

The Manses

The stone wall which enclosed the chanonry is on record by the middle of the fourteenth century when in 1360 Bishop John Pilmuir made a grant of land outside it on the west side.[646] In its developed late-medieval form the wall averaged 2 metres in thickness and 3.7 metres in height – ample to deter all but the most determined of assailants – and ran for some 823 metres around the full perimeter of the chanonry.[647] Details of the enclosure emerge late in the fifteenth century, when Bishop Andrew Stewart arranged for the repair of a stone gateway at the east end of the precinct, the cost of the work to be covered by a seventh of incomes deducted from non-resident prebendaries.[648] A new stone gateway was to be erected 'near the manse of Botary', and the gate leading towards the town was also to be repaired. The repaired gate at the east of the precinct is the surviving but much-modified gateway known as Pan's Port. Suitable janitors were to be appointed to keep the gates. It emerges also from Bishop Stewart's enactments that various of the prebendaries had broken little gateways through the precinct wall at the rears of their manses; these were to be closed up within three months following written warning to the canons and, if they failed to do so themselves, they would be fined ten shillings from their annual income to cover the costs of having the work undertaken on their behalf. A second aspect of new delineation within the precinct was the marking out of the bounds of the cemetery attached to the cathedral and notification of the boundaries to all of the canons.[649] The concern over this provision might indicate that some clergy had been allowing burials to take place anywhere within the precinct, possibly because each burial attracted payments to the officiant. Although the landholding inside the chanonry enclosure was quickly feued out in the decades after the Reformation, the enclosing wall remained a demarcation feature. In 1577, for example, the 'stone wall which enclosed the college of the cathedral church' formed one of the boundaries of a property feued out by the holder of the prebend of Unthank.[650]

The boundary enclosure may have been one of the first features of the college establishment to be completed at Elgin, providing the seclusion and separation from the world which was demanded by this ecclesiastical enclave. How rapidly the other structures within it were erected, with the exception of the cathedral itself, is less clear. It is likely that the senior dignitaries and canons involved most closely in the construction of the cathedral and the organisation of the diocese would have moved swiftly to provide themselves with a fixed residence commensurate with their status, but there are signs that not all may have felt that such a rapid move was necessary, especially where the manse of their parish church lay within easy travelling distance of the cathedral. This may explain why it appears only to have been in the early 1290s that the prebendary of Duffus provided himself with a manse within the chanonry. The prebendary, John Spalding, stated that he had constructed the manse, which was built on a site which he had bought from the heirs of William Utrear, with the consent of Bishop Archibald and the dean and chapter. Spalding went through a formal investment and induction into the site at the hands of the bishop, and agreed that all of his successors should pay an annual rent of twenty shillings for the manse, which would be distributed between all of the canons, vicars and other ministers of the cathedral who were present and offering divine service on the anniversary of Spalding's death.[651] In addition to the manse which each canon was expected to pass to his successor, each was also expected to leave the residence furnished with a series of specific items.[652] In the hall of the manse there was to be a table of appropriate size with trestles, a basin and ewer for washing, a tablecloth and towel. The kitchen was to be provided with a pot and a pan, a tripod or chain 'which is called *ketylcrok*', and a mortar and pestle. The brewhouse was to have a lead (vat) with a cup 'which is called *masse fatte* [mash-vat]', and a water container 'commonly called the *trowch* [trough]', one vat, one 'sa' (bucket carried on a pole between two people) and one barrel.

The 1458 Exchequer Rolls contain a detailed account of expenses associated with a period of royal residence in Elgin, during James II's visit to the former Douglas lands in the earldom of Moray which had been annexed to the Crown in 1456 following the overthrow of that family,[653] when the king or at least a part of his household had taken over the manse of Duffus in the chanonry.[654] Expenses included payment for timber for building a kitchen, the following entry noting the costs of fish and peas, and various barrels and other wooden vessels described as 'burnt' in the manse, possibly indicating that the previous kitchen had burned down during the king's occupation. The substantial quantities of salt – fine and coarse – beef-marts and barrelled salmon brought to the king's larder at the manse gives some indication of the storage capacity for bulk household commodities within these large residences.

While the prebendary of Duffus may have received back a refurbished manse following its royal occupation in 1457, there are indications by the end of the century that many of his fellows were failing to maintain adequately their residences in the college. In 1489, Bishop Andrew Stewart was forced to legislate to require thirteen of the prebendaries including the archdeacon and succentor to build for themselves suitable manses within the chanonry.[655] The language of the statute implies that some of the prebendaries' manses were semi-ruinous but others seem to have been completely lacking in suitable accommodation. It is unlikely that this had always been the case – certainly it is improbable that Bishop Andrew Murray and his immediate successors would have tolerated such a situation – but it is possible that increase in tenure of the canonries and senior offices in the cathedral by pluralists and career civil servants in the later fourteenth century had resulted in a failure to replace or repair the eighteen manses burned in 1390 or 1402. There are indications, too, that non-resident canons had been letting their manses and crofts to unsuitable tenants, possibly non-clerics; Bishop Andrew prohibited their lease to anyone apart from other resident canons.[656]

The first reference to manses for specific perpetual chaplains attached to the cathedral occurs in a *pro anima* grant of Bishop John Pilmuir made in 1360.[657] This grant gave a piece of land to the west of the chanonry, outside the wall, to be divided equally between four of the chaplains for them to build manses for themselves and their successors. The chaplainries were those of the king (founded by King Alexander for the soul of King Duncan II), that founded by the lady of Duffus, and the two paid for from the revenues of Ross.

By the early 1570s it seems that properties in the chanonry were being broken up and alienated by the holders of the various prebends, vicarages-choral and chaplainries. Reference in 1574 and 1575 to Patrick Cockburn, 'indweller in the college of Elgin', indicates that a lay population of householders was becoming resident within the formerly ecclesiastical precinct.[658] The 1570s also witnessed the disposal of large blocks of agricultural land around Elgin which pertained as crofts to the prebends' manses. In November 1574, Gavin Dunbar, archdeacon of Moray, feued the crofts which pertained to his manse lying outside the eastern wall of the chanonry to one of his fellow canons, John Gibson, rector of Unthank, and his son William Gibson, 'for a great sum of money paid to him for the repair of the churches of Forres and Edinkillie'.[659] Similarly, in 1577, Master Thomas Austean, holder of the prebend of Advie and Cromdale, disposed of its croftland in the same area to William Douglas, vicar of Elgin, but on this occasion there was no dressing-up of the transaction as anything other than a straightforward disposal of property for a money-rent.[660] In June 1592, parliament ratified the grant made to King James's usher, Alexander Young, of a broad raft of properties including 'the tenements of land, crofts and annuals which pertained to the canons and chaplains of the cathedral kirk of Elgin'.[661]

9.1 Spynie Palace was for five centuries the residence of the bishops of Moray. During that time, the palace stood on the edge of Spynie Loch, a sea-loch giving safe anchorage for fishing boats and merchant vessels. A thriving settlement developed about it. Today, nothing remains of either the sea-loch or the medieval town. (Historic Scotland © Crown Copyright)

9 LANDED PROPERTY

It was not only from teinds and church revenues that the wealth of the bishops of Moray was drawn. In addition to being great spiritual lords, princes of the Church, they were also temporal lords,[662] possessors of extensive landed estates and lords of the men who dwelt on them. This temporal power gave them tremendous influence throughout their diocese; it gave the bishops immense political importance in the consolidation of Scottish royal authority in the central Highlands and along the southern shore of the Moray Firth, but was later to attract the attention of lay lords who coveted that power and authority for themselves. How that temporal power was built up in the twelfth and thirteenth centuries can only be glimpsed and guessed at, for most of the parchment record which charted the growth of the territorial lordship of Moray's bishops was lost in the burning of the cathedral in 1390. Fragments, however, remain, which permit us to see how kings and magnates directed a flow of gifts to the Church that provided the platform upon which the lordships of the bishops of Moray were built.

One of the most important records which enables us to grasp a sense of the physical extent of the episcopal estate is a charter of King James II given in 1451 to Bishop John Winchester, by which the lands of the Church of Moray were erected into a legal entity known as the barony of Spynie.[663] The purpose of the charter was to give the bishops what is known as a jurisdictional franchise over the exercise of justice within their territories. In effect, they were being given authority to hold private – baronial or in this case regality – law courts to hear cases involving most general kinds of crimes committed upon the lands which fell within the territorial limits of the franchise. A regality jurisdiction such as was granted to Winchester by the king gave the bishops' courts competence to hear even business that was usually reserved to the royal courts, and it was a privilege which the bishops of Moray had striven to secure for around a century. To avoid disputes with neighbouring lords who held similar jurisdictions or with the king's own legal officers, the territory embraced by the privilege had to be listed, and this provides us with a clear vision of the scope of the episcopal estate in the middle of the fifteenth century.

King James's charter first identifies a series of smaller baronies brought under the superior lordship of Spynie: Kinneddar, Birnie, Rothenot or Rafford, Ferness and Keith. These smaller units were themselves made up of a series of further fractions of land, some of which are discussed later. In addition to these were a number of other portions of land referred to in the royal charter as comprising simply all the lands and tenancies, glebes, acres and crofts pertaining to any of the clergy of the diocese within its bounds, and also those lying within the sheriffdoms of Inverness and Banff. These are grouped into a series that can be followed west to east but ranging in a north-south zig-zag across the territory of the diocese. It starts around Inverness and Loch Ness, commencing with the two Kinmylies west of Inverness, the two Abriachans on Loch Ness side, Abertarff at the south end of Loch Ness, Boleskine on the east side of the loch, and 'Forthir' (possibly Farr in upper Strathnairn). The next group lay in the middle and upper reaches of the valley of the River Spey, beginning with the lands of the marsh of Strathspey, the lands of Rothiemurchus, the davoch of the Inch, and the very important davoch of Laggankenny which was spread around Loch Laggan in the extreme south-west of the bishopric, straddling the Lochaber border. With the davoch came the lochs and the associated fisheries, with the administrative centre of this valuable property based in the tower which stood on what is nowadays known as King Fergus's Isle in Loch Laggan.[664] The next group lay in the central portion of the Spey's valley north and east of modern Aviemore, beginning with the half-davoch centred on Coulnakyle at Nethy Bridge, Achmony and Kirkmichael (apparently out of place in the list, Achmony being in Glen Urquhart west of Loch Ness), Kinchurdy and Kincardine. After this the list moves to deal specifically with lands attached to parish churches, beginning with a group of parishes in Braemoray; it begins with the kirktons of Dallas (Meikle), Essil, Dipple, and ends at Rothes. The list then jumps west to Kilmorack in Strathconon, or Altre as it was then known, together with the Ord of Altre 'commonly known as Bishop's Ord', Kinnoir, and then progresses eastwards with brief detours south into Strathspey. In amongst this were listed the port and fishery of the Lossie, and a fishery of the River Beauly. All told, it is a wide-ranging listing of properties, but it is only when individual components were the subject of legal disputes or grants that more detail of exactly what in real terms constituted the lands and associated rights emerges.

Despite the seemingly great scale of the properties named in the 1452 charter, it must be stressed that the bishops retained very little of this land as demesne, that is estates that were managed directly by them or their servants and the produce of which was consumed by their households. A surviving group of recorded acts of homage by various major episcopal tenants, made either on the succession of a new bishop or on the entry of an heir into the lands which were held of the bishop as lord, reveals the efforts gone to by bishops to affirm their rights as temporal lords over lands which had effectively been granted away in perpetuity, all dating from the politically troubled years of the mid- and later fourteenth century.[665] Important properties, however, were kept for the direct maintenance of the bishops and the significance of that demesne can be seen in the 1380s in Bishop Bur's dispute with John Dunbar, earl of Moray, when the bishop's principal concern was to establish that certain properties pertained to the bishopric and especially to the bishop's *mensa* 'beyond memory of man'. Chief amongst these lands were Spynie, Kinneddar and 'the land of the island'.[666] This block of territory extending over the high ground north of Elgin between the River Lossie and the marshes around Spynie Loch and continuing on the north side of the marshes in the vicinity of Kinneddar clearly formed a core of lands retained in the bishops' hands to sustain their household and dependants at the palaces of Spynie (Illus 9.1) or Kinneddar. Associated with these properties was the port of Lossie or Spynie and 'the place of fishing', which were also under dispute but which Bur claimed lay within the bounds and limits and within the extent of the plots of land of the country dwellers on his properties of Spynie, Kinneddar and the island. Together, the land and the adjoining aquatic resources provided the bishops' household with a broad range of foodstuffs and other commodities to feed, heat and shelter it.

Throughout the records of the bishopric, hints embedded in charter and other record types give some idea of the range and significance of these other commodities and rights, and their enduring significance in the provisioning of the bishops' household. In the late 1180s, King William gave the bishops of Moray and their men the right in perpetuity to take at will what building timber and fuel they needed for their own use from any of the woods in his hunting forests around the burghs of Elgin, Forres and Inverness.[667] In a region where access to both building materials and fuel was to become increasingly difficult as

these commodities grew scarcer in the later Middle Ages, these privileges gave the bishops more security than many of the local population. Linked to this issue of declining woodland resources, it should be remembered, was also the rights to wood pasture, one of the most important forms of grazing for cattle and pigs practised in the medieval period in Scotland. Amongst other rights granted by King William to Bishop Richard around 1189 were two important concessions in respect of the bishops' cattle and pig herds. The first granted the bishops' men the right of pannage – freedom to graze their pigs on fallen acorns – in the woods on the king's hunting land and around Elgin, Forres and Inverness, while the second gave them rights of wood pasture for their cattle in the same woodland.[668] These grazing areas were tiny when compared with the great expanses of upland pasture which the bishops controlled in the hinterland of Moray and around the headwaters of the Spey and its tributaries, but they were of tremendous importance as a resource close to the economic heart of the diocese where they had their household base and greatest concentration of dependants.

Around Elgin, land which had perhaps been attached to the bishopric since the twelfth century included an arable estate extending to four ploughgates (approximately 480 acres) at Inverlochty on the south side of the great loop of the River Lossie as it turns first east from Aldroughty then south into the hills. By the end of the thirteenth century this had been in the hands of several generations of a family who had acquired the territorial designation 'of Inverlochty' and who paid what was known as a blenchferme rent of a pair of white Parisian hawking gloves or three silver pennies for the land, performing military service appropriate to a holding of that size, being bound to have their grain ground at the bishops' mill of Inverlochty, and performing what was known as 'suit of court' at the bishops' court.[669]

A similar portion of land known as 'Medilhalch' (Middle Haugh), north of the Lossie, estimated as comprising a half-davoch, was granted in March 1309 by Bishop David Murray to the Elgin burgess William son of Adam son of Stephen.[670] For this substantial landed property and all right pertaining to it, William paid to the bishop and his successors an annual rent of four shillings, performed appropriate levels of military service, and was bound to have his grain ground at the bishops' mill of 'Malathy' on the Lossie. William was clearly a prosperous individual with aspirations as a landholder, for at the same time he entered into a second lease which exchanged the bishops' lands of Whiteford, Inverlochty and the mill of Inverlochty, and Milton (probably Miltonduff), for the episcopal property of Auchterspynie north-west of Elgin, from which he excluded the site of Sheriffmill.[671] For this he also paid quite literally a peppercorn rent in the form of a pound of pepper annually, providing also the labour of twelve men for one day of harvesting, appropriate military service for the land, and having his grain ground at the bishops' mill of 'Malathy'.

A third large block of tenanted land was possessed by the bishops at Aldroughty, north of the Lossie west of Elgin. Here, too, the terms of its lease are recorded in the 1390s when an inquest was held following the death of its tenant Robert Sibbald, prior to the entry into it of his son John Sibbald.[672] This inquest reported that the land had formerly been valued at forty shillings annually, but, following the wars, plague and general environmental deterioration of the mid-fourteenth century, was by then valued at only twenty shillings, with a rent due to the bishop of half a mark. Sibbald was to provide three days of plough service – double that in the year of his inheritance – and three days of carriage service, and further service at harvest time.

Outside Inverness the bishops possessed a large landed estate at Kinmylies on the western side of the River Ness. By the 1390s this property was divided into two chief portions – Upper and Lower Kinmylies – with a valuable fishery attached to the latter. Amongst the many legal actions which the energetic Bishop William Spynie pursued in his efforts to restore the lands and rights of the Church of Moray to the control of him and his clergy was an action begun in November 1398 over his rights in Kinmylies.[673] The citation for this action stated that the bishop's rights of lordship there had been usurped by 'that magnificent and powerful man' Alexander (MacDonald) of the Isles, lord of Lochaber. Alexander, the bishop asserted, had given Upper Kinmylies to one Ranald MacAlasdair (Raynald MacAlyschandir), Lower Kinmylies to John Chisholm of the Aird, and the yair or fish-trap of Lower Kinmylies to a certain John White, burgess of Inverness. Alexander's actions here mirrored the earlier efforts of Alexander Stewart, lord of Badenoch and earl of Buchan, to acquire portions of episcopal property and use it as a source of patronage to reward good service or secure the loyalty of potential allies. This latest dispute reflected the spread of MacDonald power north up the Great Glen from Lochaber into the western end of the Moray Firth coastlands and signalled the beginning of a new conflict for lordship locally. At Kinmylies, Alexander was intruding one of his own vassals – MacAlasdair – but also winning influential local friends in the form of Chisholm in the Aird district and White within the burgh. Bishop William's resistance to this usurpation of his rights marked the start of a contest for power that ultimately would see MacDonald lead his men on a raid against Elgin itself.

A large block of hill country in the lordship of Ferness south of Nairn pertained to the bishopric. In March 1421/2, Bishop Henry Lichton granted a portion of this, known as Urchany Beg, in perpetual feuferme for an annual rent of one mark to Donald of Cawdor, the thane of Cawdor.[674] Although once again this was effectively a permanent alienation of church property, it was being used both to secure a source of money rent and also to confirm the loyalty of the thane of Cawdor to the bishop. Donald of Cawdor's loyalty was of critical importance at this time, for his lands and local influence extended south into the moors around Lochindorb and the upper reaches of the Findhorn, territory through which caterans were moving on raids into the farmland of the Laich. Granting possession of a block of land to a reliable protector was seen as a worthwhile and intelligent use of resources where the alienation of a small portion of property helped to safeguard the more valuable districts to their north and east.

It was during the long series of disputes with Alexander Stewart, lord of Badenoch and earl of Buchan, that we can identify for the first time a series of landed properties in the central reaches of the Spey valley in Badenoch which pertained to the bishops' estate. In 1383, whilst trying to mollify Stewart, Bishop Bur had set his lands of Rothiemurchus in feuferme to him for the lifetime of Stewart and two of his legitimate heirs.[675] This was a major estate which encompassed the lands of six davochs extending south and east into the Cairngorm Mountains, and for this Stewart was to pay an annual rent of £16. By 1386 Alexander was already in arrears of rent for Rothiemurchus and also for the lands of Coulnakyle in the barony of Abernethy which he had added to his portfolio.[676] Although arrangements were made on that occasion which covered the outstanding amount owed, the constant battle to extract the full rents due contributed significantly to the growing friction between the bishop and his tenant. One of the issues which contributed to the spectacular outburst of violence against the cathedral in 1390 had been the formal legal process against Alexander Stewart in October 1389 whereby he had been obliged to quitclaim formally to Bishop Bur all rights to a number of properties which he had been detaining and occupying.[677] These included the lands of Laggankenny at the north-east end of Loch Laggan, Ardinch, Raits and Dunachton near Kingussie.

The relationship between Bishop Bur and Alexander Stewart arose ultimately from the long-established need for the bishops to attract the service of influential laymen who could act on their behalf in matters that were regarded as incompatible with the bishops' status as priests or who were able to offer them support and protection. Portions of the episcopal estate were regularly made over to such men, sometimes for short terms, sometimes for life and on occasion to pass hereditarily to the beneficiaries' heirs. One of the more important concentrations of episcopal estates lay around the north and north-west ends of Loch Ness at Abriachan and Bona and it was from this land that some of these grants made in respect of past, current or future service were made. In 1334, Bishop Pilmuir granted for his service to Sir Robert Lauder – probably the same man who held Quarrelwood west of Elgin in the mid-fourteenth century – the half-davoch of episcopal land at Abriachan lying between the baronies of Bona and Urquhart on Loch Ness, and his lands of Achmony (just west of Drumnadrochit) lying between the lands of Drumbuie on the east and Gartally on the west.[678] For these large properties, Lauder was obliged to pay the bishop and his successors four merks of silver annually, for which he and his heirs would be free and quit of all other service demand and burden on that property, and for which they would give the bishops of Moray their fealty and homage. By the 1380s the lands of Abriachan and Achmony were in the hands of another episcopal tenant who had received them as fee for services, Sir Robert Chisholm, but he was prevailed upon in 1386/7 to surrender them to Bishop Bur who needed them to offer as a further inducement to Alexander Stewart.[679] Whereas previous tenants had held the land for fixed terms of lives, the award to Stewart in February 1387 was in perpetuity but for the same annual rent of four merks that his predecessors had paid. The outcome of this deal has already been explored above in the outline of Bishop Bur's career.

From the early 1400s onwards the amount of landed property retained in the hands of the bishop or his direct representatives began to contract sharply as more and more was granted out on leases and under feuferme grants. Rental income rather than the produce of their estates became the chief source of revenue demanded by the bishops. This trend probably accelerated after 1501 under the largely absentee bishops, for whom the diocese was principally a source of a salary to fund them as they pursued their careers as senior royal servants. That trend towards leasing increased sharply in the 1530s when King James V began to tax clerical incomes, for senior clerics needed access to ready cash to pay the king. Although he can be rightly accused of having plundered the resources of the diocese to support his family, friends and profligate lifestyle, Bishop Patrick Hepburn was also required to push ahead with this process of alienation to meet the demands of first of all royal government and then, after 1560, to buy off the acquisitive lay lords who circled the institutions of the old Church hierarchy like vultures around a dying animal. By the time of his death in 1573 Hepburn had alienated the bulk of the landed resources of his see, much of it through a series of forced grants to James, earl of Moray. The four-centuries-long process of assembling this once rich resource had come full circle in the final dissolution of the episcopal estate.

9.2 The coats of arms of Bishop William Tulloch, Bishop David Stewart and Bishop Patrick Hepburn above the first-floor window of the great tower at Spynie Palace (Historic Scotland © Crown Copyright)

The Mills

Land was not the only source of revenue for the bishops of Moray. In a culture where even the majority of urban dwellers were directly involved in the production of their own primary foodstuffs, control of the means to bulk-process those foodstuffs was an important source of income. Where tenants on land were obliged legally to have their grain processed at their lords' mills – and to pay for the work – that importance increased even more. It is thus no surprise that amongst the first items of non-ecclesiastical or landed property endowment which the bishops received in the twelfth century were grain mills.

Between 1189 and 1195 King William granted leave to Bishop Richard for him to build a mill on the River Lossie 'on my land above the cruives (fish-traps) on the Lossie below the castle of Elgin'.[680] This mill has been believed to have become Bishopmill, from which the bridge-end settlement north of Elgin subsequently took its name, but it seems from later references to the mill below the castle as Sheriffmill that the bishop may not have acted upon his option to construct on the site offered by the king in the twelfth century and instead leased the land back to the

Crown and its representatives. It was there that a mill was later established for the uses of the royal tenants in the district, passed into the hands of the earls of Moray and then reverted to the Crown following the forfeiture of the Douglases in 1455, but, since it was founded on land which had previously been given to the Church of Moray, the king or earls were obliged to pay rent. This mill was referred to by the fifteenth century as Sheriffmill.[681] At the end of the thirteenth century, reference survives to a mill on the bishops' lands at Inverlochty on the south side of the Lossie, south-west of Elgin.[682] In 1309, a further mill was named at 'Malathy' on the Lossie, north of Elgin, possibly being the establishment from which Bishopmill took its name.[683]

Fishing

Sea and river fishing rights were amongst the most valuable of the properties held by the bishopric throughout the Middle Ages and by the sixteenth century exports of barrelled fish probably constituted the single most important source of income for the bishops of Moray. Fish-traps, referred to as cruives, are mentioned on the River Lossie by Elgin in King William's charter to Bishop Richard in the 1190s, but these were apparently either royal property or the property of the burgesses.[684] Later charters, however, imply that as the bishops built up their landholding around Kinneddar and Spynie they also acquired rights in the waters adjacent to those lands and had a number of tenants working primarily as fishermen in the shallow inshore waters on the lagoons between the mainland and the almost-island which extends from Lossiemouth west to Burghead, and in the deeper waters of the Moray Firth beyond. Traps, however, emerge as important elements within the episcopal property portfolio across the Middle Ages. For example, a yair or fixed trap for catching fish, usually salmon, is mentioned in 1398 as one of the features associated with the episcopal lands of Lower Kinmylies on the west side of the River Ness opposite Inverness.[685] It is unclear whether the yair was in the Ness or in the shallow tidal waters of the Beauly Firth, where a number of early fish-trap sites have been identified archaeologically. The Kinmylies yair was in dispute in 1398, Bishop William Spynie pursuing an action against Alexander MacDonald, lord of Lochaber, whom he claimed had usurped rights to the fishery and given its keeping to one John White, burgess of Inverness.

Disputes such as that concerning Kinmylies are an indication of how significant the fisheries were as components of the episcopal property portfolio. Amongst the long list of complaints levelled by Bishop Bur against John Dunbar, earl of Moray, was his interference with the bishop's fishing interests. Attached to his lands of Spynie, Kinneddar and the island and extending for the full length

of the areas worked by his rural tenants were, he stated, fishing-places. Bur further asserted that the bishops had been accustomed to have fishers of sea fish dwelling in the toun of Spynie with their wives and families and that they sailed from Spynie to the sea and returned to Spynie with their catch.[686] He also asserted that the bishop's fishermen had used cobles and boats for catching salmon, grilse and *pectines* and other types of fish with nets and with single and multiple hooks in the places which they worked without any previous hindrance or impediment. Bur went on to state that his predecessor, intending to improve and deepen the channel of the port of Spynie, had diverted the course of the water from its old channel by sinking boats within it. He and his predecessors, together with their men, had long exercised unchallenged the right to sail with their boats to and from the sea to the port of Spynie, to throw nets or lines, and to take fish singly or by the load.

The riverine salmon fisheries of Moray and the involvement of the bishops and the major ecclesiastical landlords of the region in their exploitation is a vast topic which cannot be dealt with in this present study. It is, however, important to emphasise that it was not just from the coastal and estuarine fisheries that the bishops were able to draw significant income. Almost every body of fresh water – rivers or lochs – contained within the bounds of the diocese was either exploited directly by the bishop as lord or indirectly in the form of teinds of the catches made within it. In the mid-fifteenth century, for example, we see the fishery of Loch Laggan and other lochs within the davoch of Laggankenny emerge in the record as an important economic resource in the hands of the bishops.[687] It is unlikely that this was a new development; fishing had probably been conducted in the lochs for centuries if not millennia. What was new, however, may have been the scale of the exploitation and the potential for revenue generation which it represented to bishops who were eager to maximise their incomes. By the time of the Reformation, the freshwater fishing of the hinterland of Moray was being exploited as intensively and effectively as the marine and maritime fisheries of the coastal districts and river-mouths.

As a coda to this brief discussion of the bishops' fisheries, there was another associated industry which would have been required to enable the bishops and their tenants to maximise the productive value of their fishing and livestock operations. Salt was the only bulk preservative available in northern Europe in the medieval period, needed for pickling of fish, prolonging the storage life of meat, cheese and butter, and necessary in the processing of skins and the hardening of leather and canvas. There is little evidence for a salt production industry along the Moray coast, but a few documentary and place names records show that the bishops also possessed saltworks on the margins of the lagoon south of Kinneddar where the modern place name Salterhill is suggestive of an earlier industrial activity. The land of 'Saltcotis' is mentioned in 1456 as paying an annual rent to the bishop.[688] In 1566, reference is made to 'Spyne-pannis' as pertaining to the lands of the regality of Spynie, the name preserving the actual process of salt production through the boiling of brine in large metal pans.[689] The actual process of production in saltpans is mentioned in the time of Bishop Brice on the south side of the lagoon between Duffus and the area stretching from Kintrae towards Spynie, but these pans appear to have belonged to the Murray lords of Duffus rather than to the Church of Moray.[690] Their presence, however, confirms that salt manufacture to supply the needs of both the lordly estates of the neighbourhood and their local agricultural populations was being undertaken by the early thirteenth century. Although they are otherwise largely invisible in the documentary record, it is likely that the numbers of saltpans only increased as fishing activity and agricultural output increased in Moray down to the mid-fourteenth century, then as specialised fishing activity – mainly for salmon – increased in the fifteenth and sixteenth centuries.

This brief survey of the lands and economic resources which were enjoyed by the bishops of Moray in the Middle Ages offers only a glimpse of the sources of wealth and scale of the revenues which they commanded. A full analysis of the changing nature of the income of the bishops and its sources over the centuries is a study yet to be undertaken; the outline above provides some idea of the scale of the task ahead. Brief though this overview has been, however, it reminds us that the bishops of Moray were truly 'princes of the church', lords of land and men as well as wielders of spiritual authority. It was that wealth and power as much as piety and devotion, or the search for spiritual salvation, which built and paid for the cathedral of Moray and the treasures with which it was filled.

The east front of Elgin Cathedral with the River Lossie in the foreground (Historic Scotland © Crown Copyright)

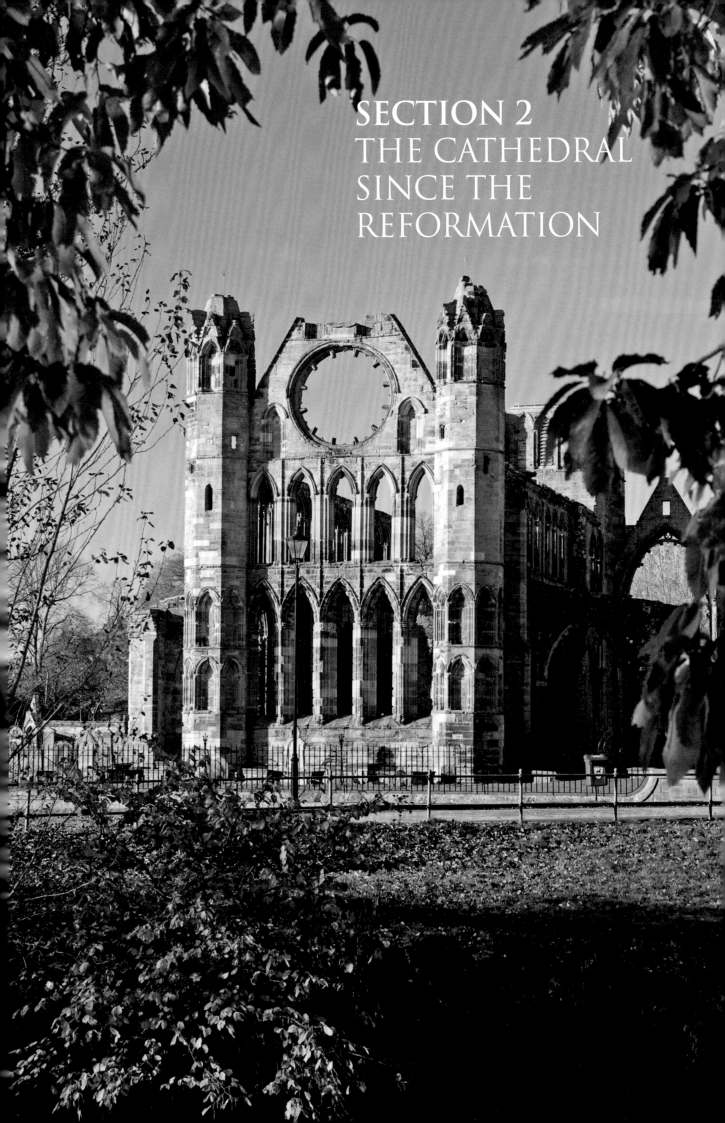

SECTION 2
THE CATHEDRAL
SINCE THE
REFORMATION

10.1   David's Tower at Spynie Palace, named after Bishop David Stewart (Historic Scotland © Crown Copyright).

10 THE POST-REFORMATION BISHOPS OF MORAY

Services within the cathedral had, at least in theory, ended in the 1560s as the Protestant lords who controlled the parliament in Edinburgh pushed through a raft of legislation to abolish the forms of Roman Catholic worship. Long before Bishop Hepburn's death, the cathedral had ceased to possess any useful function as a centre for religious devotions, or at least for those sanctioned by the Reformed Church. Since it was not the parish church for Elgin it had no routine function to serve and, consequently, no one wished to take any responsibility for its upkeep. The men appointed as bishops in the Protestant see of Moray chose not to have the cathedral as their church, adopting instead the large parish church of St Giles in the adjacent burgh(Illus 10.4).

George Douglas, 1573–1589

The younger son of Archibald, sixth earl of Douglas, George Douglas was elected by the remaining members of the cathedral chapter on 22 December 1573.[691] Douglas was no shrinking cleric; in November 1581, John Carnegie of that ilk brought charges against the bishop, claiming that in 1570 Douglas and a band of accomplices had forcibly ejected him from his house at Seton and plundered the house of its contents.[692] A political figure and closely involved in the turbulent affairs of the minority of King James VI, he was little more than titular bishop and spent most of his time in Edinburgh. It was there that he died on 28 December 1589 and, according to Keith writing in

10.2   The ruins of Holyrood Abbey from the north-east. Bishop George Douglas was buried in the church at Holyrood. (Historic Scotland © Crown Copyright)

the early eighteenth century, was buried in the church of Holyrood in Edinburgh (Illus 10.2).[693]

Alexander Douglas, 1602–1623

Having been minister of Elgin for some seventeen years, he was promoted to the bishopric when James VI again formally instituted an Episcopalian regime in the Scottish Church. Alexander died, according to Keith, at Elgin in May 1623 and was buried in the south aisle of the church of St Giles which was serving as his cathedral (Illus 10.3).[694]

John Guthrie, 1623–1638

Guthrie, a member of the Angus family of that name, had been minister successively at Perth and Edinburgh before being provided to the see of Moray on the death of Alexander Douglas. On the outbreak of the Civil War in 1638, he was deprived of his see by the General Assembly which was meeting at Glasgow and which declared the abolition of episcopacy in the Scottish Church. Although deprived of his bishopric and its possessions, he continued to live at Spynie until 1640 when he was ejected by a Covenanter army. He retired to his family lands in Angus and lived there until his death in 1649.[695]

Murdo Mackenzie, 1662–1676

A younger son of a cadet line of the Mackenzie earls of Seaforth, he spent much of his early adulthood as a chaplain serving in Germany in the armies of the Swedish king Gustavus Adolphus. On his return to Scotland he became first parson of Contin on his family's Ross-shire estates, then served at Inverness and finally at Elgin. On the restoration of episcopacy in Scotland following the return of King Charles II from Continental exile, the already elderly Mackenzie was provided to the bishopric of Moray, which he held until his translation to the see of Orkney in 1676.[696]

James Aitken, 1676–1680

Nominated to Moray on 9 September 1676 but not formally provided until 7 May 1677, Aitken held the see only until February 1680 when he was transferred to Galloway.[697]

Colin Falconer, 1680–1686

According to his contemporary, Robert Keith, Falconer died at Spynie on 11 November 1686 aged sixty-three and was buried in the church of St Giles in Elgin in a tomb in the south aisle, at the bottom of the tower on its east side.[698]

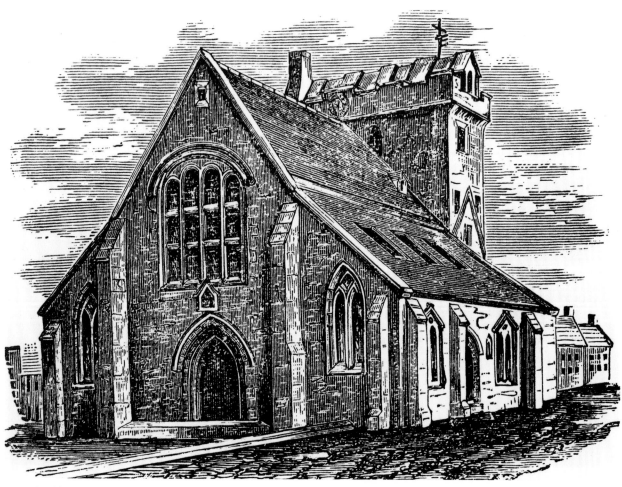

10.3   The old church of St Giles, Elgin, which served as the cathedral of Bishop Alexander Douglas. Douglas was buried in the south aisle of the church.

Alexander Rose, 1686–1687

After a distinguished career as a university academic at Glasgow and St Andrews, he was nominated to the see of Moray on 17 December 1686. He was consecrated on 1 May but served as bishop for only seven months before he was translated from Moray to Edinburgh.[699]

William Hay, 1687–1707

The last of the episcopal succession at Moray, Hay was nominated to succeed Rose on 3 December 1687 and was consecrated on 11 March 1688. When the English political revolution against King James VII and II led to the coup in Scotland which placed control of the government in the hands of a Presbyterian-inclined group within the nobility, the episcopalian Church regime in Scotland was speedily abolished. Deprived of his office, Hay lived on in his former diocesan territory, eventually dying in 1707 near Inverness.[700]

Prospectus Oppidi ELGINÆ. The Prospect of the Town of ELGINE.

10.4 Detail from John Slezer's 'Prospect of the Town of Elgin' (1693) showing the cathedral and chanonry.

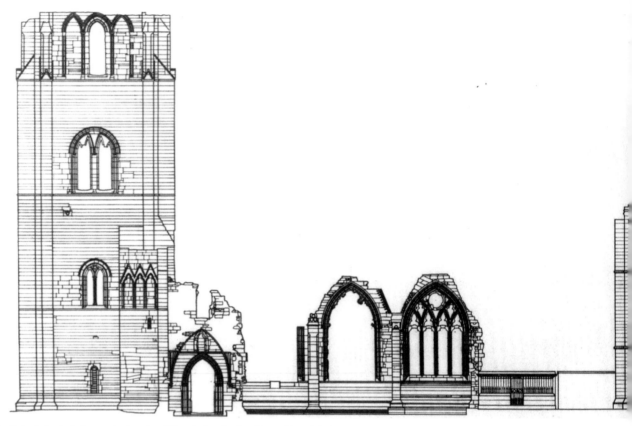

11.1 Elgin Cathedral, the south elevation (Historic Scotland © Crown Copyright)

11 THE FATE OF THE BUILDING SINCE THE REFORMATION

Although many cathedrals survived the Reformation in whole or in part because they also served as parish churches and continued to be needed for the worship of layfolk, at Elgin there was the parish church of St Giles at the heart of the burgh that was enough both for the spiritual needs of the parishioners and for the reduced dignity of Moray's bishops. The physical impact of the Reformation on the cathedral during the later years of the episcopate of Patrick Hepburn (1538–1573) has already been touched upon (see page 49). The cathedral was probably 'cleansed' of most of the accessible fixtures and furnishings associated with the medieval forms of worship as early as about 1561, when Lord James Stewart was purging considerable numbers of churches in the northern part of the kingdom.[701] In 1567–8 orders were given by the Regent Moray's Privy Council to remove the lead roofing from both Elgin and Aberdeen Cathedrals,[702] though it seems that the ship which was to carry it for sale in Holland was so overladen that it sank in Aberdeen harbour.[703] There was evidently a change of heart towards the cathedral soon afterwards, and in 1569 orders were given to have the roof re-covered,[704] with Bishop Patrick Hepburn offering to contribute, though it is doubtful

if anything was done to put this into effect.

If reliance can be placed upon the depiction of the cathedral on the map of the area by Timothy Pont, despite the loss of protection from the elements resulting from the removal of lead, by as late as around 1595 the building was still essentially structurally complete, with spires rising over its western towers.[705] This accords with the description given by Taylor, the 'Water Poet', in 1615 of 'a faire and beautifull church with three steeples, the walls of it and the steeples all yet standing; but the roofes, windowes and many marble monuments and tombes of honourable and worthie personages all broken and defaced'.[706] Services and private worship are known to have taken place within the building on many occasions, both by those adhering to the old and to the new religious ways. Because of this, in December 1614, it had been ordered that no one was to frequent the cathedral 'during thir superstitious dayis' until the following February, suggesting that the weeks around Christmas were a particular problem period for those who hankered after the old ways.[707] In the following year, orders were given that private prayers in the cathedral were to be prohibited,[708] though these orders had to be repeated many times and

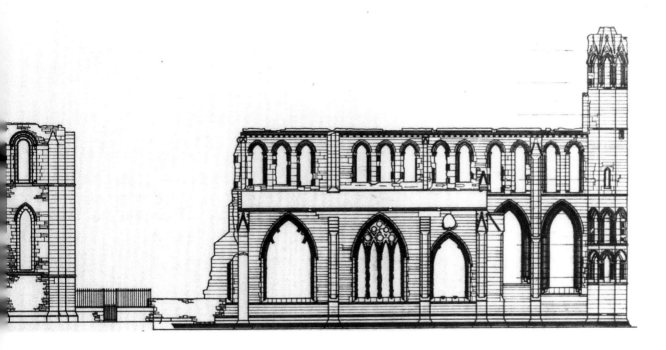

to little apparent effect, since many offenders compeared before the Kirk Session. Parts of the cathedral were more popular than others, and it was said that up to about 1640 areas in the towers and choir that still retained their painted decoration were being used for Catholic worship.[709]

Yet the process of decay was gathering momentum, and the roof of the eastern limb blew down in a gale of 4 December 1637.[710] Despite even this, at least some of the more inaccessible furnishings that had escaped earlier attempts at cleansing remained in place and may have been a continuing focus for the illicit worship of those who found the reformed practices of the parish minister unsatisfying. As we have seen, the most important recorded survivor was the rood screen, and on 28 December 1640 the minister, Mr Gilbert Ross, along with the lairds of Innes and Brodie, pulled it down and chopped it up for firewood, though it was remarked by those who saw significance in such things that the wood refused to burn.[711]

Taking all of this into account, it is clear that there must have been considerable ambivalence of feeling towards the cathedral, with some continuing to be drawn to it as a focus of piety and others fearing its continued hold over unreformed imaginations. Yet by this stage there may also have been those who were beginning to be fascinated by it as a fine old building at the heart of what had become the burgh's main burial ground, and it is perhaps significant that, when the Town Council announced it was about to repair

the boundary wall of the churchyard in 1685, it was ordered that the stones of the cathedral itself should not be used for this purpose.[712] The state of the cathedral some decades after this was carefully depicted in views of the north and south flanks by John Slezer. The former was published in his *Theatrum Scotiae* of 1693 (Illus 11.2), while the latter (Illus 11.3) is amongst the Gough papers in the Bodleian Library in Oxford.[713] Those views show the building without roofs or spires, but substantially complete apart from the northern aisles of the nave. Despite the accelerating state of decay, parts of the building remained in occasional use and roofed over, with the chapter house providing a meeting room for the Incorporated Trades from 1671 to 1676 and again from 1701 to about 1731.[714] Another part to remain in use was the south choir aisle, which was walled in to serve as a burial place for the family of the dukes of Gordon;[715] the stone vaulting was thus preserved, while views by John Campbell of 1747(Illus 11.4)[716] and Edward Dayes of 1792[717] show that the window arches of the south choir aisle were by then largely walled up, leaving only small openings.

Yet, despite such uses, there was little incentive to carry out the works that might have forestalled a major catastrophe, and the greatest single disaster in the progressive collapse of the building was the fall of the central tower on Easter Sunday 1711,[718] which brought down with it much of the adjacent masonry of the four limbs of the cathedral. The later stages of structural collapse are more

11.2   The north flank of Elgin Cathedral in 1693 (John Slezer, *Theatrum Scotiae*)

11.3   The south flank of Elgin Cathedral in the late seventeenth century by John Slezer (The Bodleian Libraries, University of Oxford, Gough Maps 38, fol 24r, drawing top left)

difficult to document, and the principal source of evidence is the growing number of views that were made of the cathedral as awareness of the picturesque potential of the great buildings of the Middle Ages increased. Significantly, by the second half of the eighteenth century interest in Elgin Cathedral was becoming sufficiently widespread for information to be prepared for those who wished to learn about it. Samuel Johnson could record of his visit in 1773 that 'a paper was put into our hands, which deduced from sufficient authorities the history of this venerable ruin'.[719]

The value of early views is usefully demonstrated when we try to determine at what stage the gable over the south wall of the south transept collapsed. The drawings by John Slezer of the later seventeenth century and by John Campbell of 1747 both show the gable complete, with what appears to be a three-light traceried window as its main feature. A view in the National Gallery of Scotland, said to be by one of the Sandbys,[720] also shows the gable relatively complete, and if the attribution to the Sandbys has any basis, this view is most likely to have been drawn by Paul Sandby

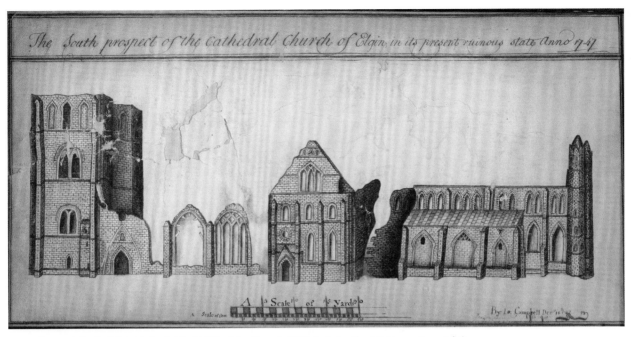

11.4 The south flank of Elgin Cathedral in 1747 by John Campbell (Historic Scotland © Crown Copyright)

before he left Scotland in 1752. P Mazell's view for Thomas Pennant, published in 1769 (Illus 11.5), shows a similar state, as does an undated drawing in the collections of General Hutton.[721] The view engraved for Francis Grose by S Hooper, however, which is dated 1791, shows the gable much as we now see it, with only a stump of the western side (Illus 11.6), and the view by Edward Dayes of 1792 shows a similar state. This suggests that much of the gable must have collapsed at a date between 1769 and 1791, though the tendency of some artists to copy the work of predecessors rather than to draw what was there at the time means that a note of caution should be sounded on what might seem to be a straightforward sequence of evidence.

Following the final removal of bishops from the national Church in 1689 their revenues had passed to the Crown, a process that eventually came to be deemed to have made the Crown the technical owner of the cathedrals. This was of little real significance until interest in the cathedrals, both as works of architecture and as illustrations of an aspect of Scottish history, began to gather strength from the later eighteenth century onwards. It was usually the local community who first showed any concern for their medieval church, and who then attempted to persuade the Crown to become financially involved as the momentum for action grew. At Elgin, in 1809, the Town Council rebuilt the perimeter wall around the cathedral graveyard.[722] At that time the need was still perhaps more to protect the graves and to shut out the brewery that had been built directly to the east (Illus 11.7) rather than to enhance the setting of the cathedral. Nevertheless, it was around this time that active measures began to be taken to stabilise what remained of the historic structure. A plan by William Duff of 1815,

now in the Hutton Collection,[723] shows that the original layout of the cathedral was then only partly understood, and that there was no suspicion that the nave had double aisles or a south porch, and this reminds us that collapsed masonry must have obscured much evidence. It appears that around this time a Mr Gillespie, Architect – presumably James Gillespie Graham – was engaged to carry out works on the cathedral 'by which the remaining walls and roof were cleared';[724] this was perhaps in the same years that he was at work on Dr Gray's Hospital in Elgin, which was between 1815 and 1819.[725] Certainly we know that what was described as a new roof was being built over the chapter house in 1816, although it was soon afterwards damaged by visitors and later accounts suggest this may have been no more than a protective covering to the extrados of the vault. Following a petition from the provost of Elgin, the King's Remembrancer stated in August 1824 that £121 had been issued to Robert Reid for a new roof.[726] Reid was a particularly important figure in the earlier stages of the development of a conservation philosophy for ancient buildings. Having held the honorary title of 'King's Architect and Surveyor in Scotland' since 1808, in 1824 he secured the succession to the titular Mastership of Works, and in 1827 a short-lived separate Scottish Office of Works was set up under his leadership.[727] As part of his new duties he became active in reporting on those ruined buildings that were deemed to be Crown property,[728] and it is significant that we find him becoming involved in the work at Elgin. It was probably at this stage that a number of masonry buttresses were built to support the most alarmingly broken and overhanging ends of the choir and transept walls, since some of those buttresses appear in views published in 1826.[729]

11.5   View of Elgin Cathedral from the south-east in 1769 (Thomas Pennant, *A Tour in Scotland*)

11.6   View of Elgin Cathedral from the south-east in 1791 (Francis Grose, *The Antiquities in Scotland*)

The greatest single contribution to the welfare of the cathedral was made by a shoemaker of Elgin, John Shanks, acting under the guidance of a local gentleman, Isaac Forsyth. Shanks developed an almost obsessive love for the building and by 1826 it was said that he had 'removed about 2853 cubic yards of Rubbish from the Area and parts adjacent . . . consisting of large masses of grouted building stones and earth; separated the stones from the earth,

and built them up in convenient places; and levelled the Area and other places, where necessary, with the earth'.[730] In 1826, possibly at the behest of Robert Reid, Shanks was appointed Keeper and Watchman with an annual salary of £5 from the Collector of Bishop's Rents,[731] and by January 1827 it was said that his clearance of collapsed masonry had left only a small number of gravestones elevated two or three feet above the later ground levels.[732] He had probably started

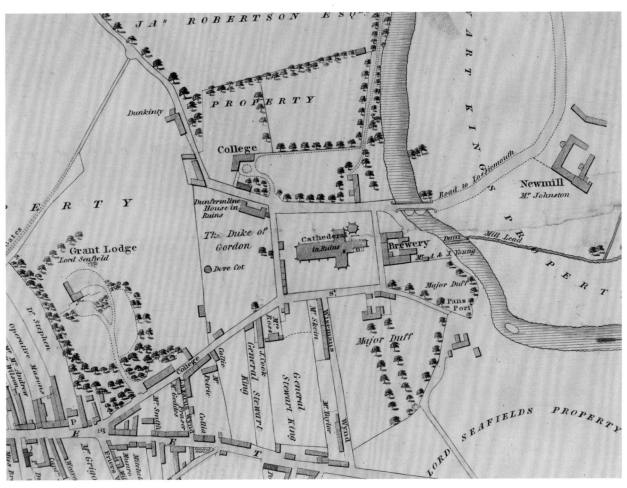

11.7 Map of the area around Elgin Cathedral in 1828 by John Wood (Historic Scotland © Crown Copyright)

his work as early as 1824, because at his death on 14 April 1841, the inscription on his memorial, which was composed by no less an admirer than Lord Cockburn,[733] recorded that:

'For 17 years he was the keeper and the shower of this Cathedral and while not even the Crown was doing any thing for its preservation he, with his own hands, cleared it of many thousand cubic yards of rubbish disclosing the bases of the pillars, collecting the carved fragments, and introducing some order and propriety.'

Shanks' achievement caught the public imagination and was commemorated in a number of ways. Most attractive of these was a series of views prepared by W Clark in 1826 (Illus 11.8, 11.9),[734] while a small leaflet on his work was printed by R Johnston in 1830.[735] Shanks' work was also referred to in the text accompanying Robert William Billings' exquisite engravings of the recently cleared cathedral, published in 1845–52.[736] The most eccentric manifestation of the interest in his work, however, was a book apparently written by Shanks himself and eventually published in 1866, which is mainly given over to musings on the religious significance of the cathedral 'evoked by the resident spirit of the ruins'.[737] Shanks' achievement was extraordinary and with few contemporary parallels. But, without detracting from his achievement, we can now understand that

much architectural and archaeological evidence for our understanding of the cathedral must have been lost in the course of an operation that, by modern standards, was very invasive. No record was kept of where stones were found, and those stones that were retained appear to have been set out around the cathedral with an eye to artistic impact rather than with any wish to link them with their possible original location, while those regarded as uninteresting were dumped in a pond known as the Order Pot.[738] Nevertheless, for its time it was a highly enlightened campaign of work and, from brief accounts of subsequent work carried out in the 1920s and 1930s, it seems that the clearance may not have extended down through medieval floor levels,[739] so that the disturbance was probably largely limited to collapsed masonry in the post-medieval overburden.

Other works known to have been carried out in the early nineteenth century included the re-erection within the chapter house of a number of memorials from the old parish church of St Giles, which was demolished in 1826 in advance of rebuilding to the designs of Archibald Simpson, while in 1834 Robert Reid recommended works of consolidation costed at £131.10s.[740] These included yet further attempts to make the chapter house vault waterproof, making wall-heads watertight with Roman cement, underbuilding

11.8   The interior of Elgin Cathedral from the west in 1826 (W Clark, *A Series of Views of the Ruins of Elgin Cathedral*)

11.9   View of Elgin Cathedral from the south-east in 1826 (W Clark, *A Series of Views of the Ruins of Elgin Cathedral*)

overhanging masonry, flagging the mural passage in the west front, flagging over window arches in the towers, and relocating the west wall of a burial enclosure on the east side of the chapter house so as to leave it clear of the chapter house itself. By this time the Crown's responsibility for the cathedral was accepted without serious question and Reid's interest in Elgin was continued by his official successors, working in co-operation with the Town Council. In 1847–8, some old houses were removed from the west side of the cathedral and the boundary wall was extended across the gap created.[741] By the early twentieth century, however, it was coming to be felt that the high wall which had been built around the churchyard in 1809 did not allow it to be seen to best advantage, and that active measures should be taken to improve the cathedral's setting. From 1912 onwards there were proposals to remove the brewery on the east side and to lower the boundary wall. After a long series of exchanges, in 1915 it was agreed that the graveyard should be extended by sixty feet over the site of the by then demolished brewery, with the east boundary wall being replaced by a sunken ha-ha. This had been carried out by 1921. Further work to replace the rest of the high wall by a fence, so far as the existence of burial enclosures would allow, followed a bequest of £3,000 in that same year, and this campaign was nearing completion in 1934.[742]

Within the cathedral itself the state was carrying out major campaigns of structural stabilisation and improvement of amenity from the early years of the twentieth century, though it has to be said that the records of that work are very incomplete. Our knowledge of what was done has to be pieced together from information found in official files, dated record drawings, photographs, brief published references and the evidence of the fabric itself. According to dates inscribed in the masonry, there was work on the east gable rose window in 1904, and at the same time the missing form pieces and mullions of the window tracery in the north-east face of the chapter house were reinstated.[743] According to a report of 1913 there was by then an ongoing programme of works, which appears to have consisted chiefly of repointing the walls and further waterproofing of the wall-heads, and there were also proposals to support the crumbling tracery of two windows with gun metal armatures;[744] according to later correspondence some stained glass fragments were found in the south nave aisle at this time.[745] By 1924 work to complete the lowering of ground levels was in progress, starting with the aisle along the south side of the eastern limb; in the process, the tomb of the earl of Huntly was relocated away from the site of the altar, having been placed there in the seventeenth century.[746]

Work continued through the 1930s, and in 1935 the

early-nineteenth-century buttress supporting overhanging masonry at the west end of the north choir wall was partly dismantled. In the same year the lower parts of the nave arcade piers were tentatively reconstructed with fragments that had been found, with further work being carried out on them in 1939.[747] One find which appears to have been made in 1936, on the west side of the chapter house, was the damaged effigy of a thirteenth-century bishop that it has been suggested above might possibly be of Archibald, in whose time the cathedral was enlarged after the fire of 1270 (Illus 11.10).[748] It may also have been in 1936 that parts of a rose window were found in the course of works on the vault of the south choir aisle (Illus 11.11) (see page 74),[749] and in 1937 it was proposed that the roof over that vault should be renewed and the buttresses at the end of the south choir wall reduced, though this latter may not have been carried out until 1939.[750] By 1939 there are also references to the repointing of the north transept. But the main ongoing problem was to be the friability of the cathedral's masonry, almost certainly exacerbated by the discharges that had

11.10 The late-thirteenth-century effigy of a bishop excavated at Elgin Cathedral in 1936 (Historic Scotland © Crown Copyright)

come over many years from the brewery to the east, and this has called for a number of major interventions. Amongst the more recent of these may be included:[751]

1957	general consolidation[752]
1961	repairs and stone indentation in the clearstoreys of the eastern limb
1972–86	progressive replacement of the chapter house window tracery, following the recommendation of the Ancient Monuments Board in 1962;[753] the east window was completed in 1972; the west window in 1973; the south-east window in 1974; the north window in 1981; the north-west window in 1983; the south-west window in 1985
1976–88	stabilisation and stone indentation of the east gable and the east limb clearstoreys, with some minor works continuing until 1992
1977	stone indentation in the south-west tower windows
1980	partial replacement of the upper mouldings of the tomb recess in the south choir aisle
1987–9	construction of a new chapter house roof
1988–98	stone indentation, reroofing, insertion of floors and glazing in the south-west tower
1998–2000	stone indentation, reroofing, insertion of floors and glazing in the north-west tower

11.11 The fragments of a rose window from Elgin Cathedral (© Mike Pendery)

NOTES

Abbreviations used for Primary Sources, Journals and Institutions Frequently Cited in the Notes

Aberdeen Registrum   *Registrum Episcopatus Aberdonensis,* ed C Innes (Maitland Club, 1845).

Arbroath Liber   *Liber S Thome de Aberbrothoc,* ed C Innes and P Chalmers (Bannatyne Club, 1848–56).

Barrow, *David I Charters*   G W S Barrow ed, *Charters of David I* (Woodbridge, 1999).

CDS   *Calendar of Documents relating to Scotland,* ed J Bain *et al* (Edinburgh, 1881–).

Chron Holyrood   *A Scottish Chronicle known as the Chronicle of Holyrood,* ed M O Anderson (Scottish History Society, 1938).

Chron Melrose   *Chronica de Mailros,* ed J Stevenson (Bannatyne Club, 1835).

CPL   *Calendar of Entries in the Papal Registers relating to Great Britain and Ireland. Papal Letters,* ed W H Bliss *et al* (London, 1893–).

CPL Benedict XIII   *Calendar of Papal Letters to Scotland of Benedict XIII of Avignon, 1394–1419,* ed F McGurk (Scottish History Society, 1976).

CPP   *Calendar of Entries in the Papal Registers relating to Great Britain and Ireland: Petitions to the Pope,* ed W H Bliss (London, 1896–).

ER   *The Exchequer Rolls of Scotland,* ed J Stuart *et al* (Edinburgh, 1878–1908).

Glasgow Registrum   *Registrum Episcopatus Glasguensis,* ed C Innes (Bannatyne and Maitland Clubs, 1843).

James IV Letters   *The Letters of James the Fourth 1505–1513,* ed R K Hannay (Scottish History Society, 1953).

James V Letters   *The Letters of James V,* ed R K Hannay and D Hay (Edinburgh, 1954).

Keith, *Bishops*   *An Historical Catalogue of the Scottish Bishops down to the year 1688 by the Right Rev. Robert Keith,* new edition, ed M Russel (Edinburgh and London, 1824).

Kelso Liber   *Liber S Marie de Calchou,* ed C Innes (Bannatyne Club, 1846).

Moray Registrum   *Registrum Episcopatus Moraviensis,* ed C Innes (Bannatyne Club, 1837).

NRS   National Records of Scotland (formerly Scottish Record Office and National Archives of Scotland).

Proc Soc Antiq Scot   *Proceedings of the Society of Antiquaries of Scotland.*

RCAHMS   Royal Commission on the Ancient and Historical Monuments of Scotland.

RMS   *Registrum Magni Sigilii Regum Scotorum,* ed J M Thomson *et al* (Edinburgh, 1882–1914).

RPS   *Records of the Parliaments of Scotland* (web resource, www.rps.ac.uk).

RRS, vol i   *Regesta Regum Scottorum,* vol i: *The Acts of Malcom IV,* ed G W S Barrow (Edinburgh, 1960).

RRS, vol ii   *Regesta Regum Scottorum,* vol ii : *The Acts of William I,* ed G W S Barrow (Edinburgh, 1971).

Scotichronicon   *Scotichronicon by Walter Bower,* ed D E R Watt *et al* (Aberdeen or Edinburgh, 1987–98).

1   A Woolf, *From Pictland to Alba 789–1070* (Edinburgh, 2007), 56.

2   P Dransart, 'Saints, Stones and Shrines: The Cults of Sts Moluag and Gerardine in Pictland', in J Cartwright (ed), *Celtic Hagiography and Saints' Cults* (Cardiff, 2003) 232–48.

3   Dransart, 'Cults of Sts Moluag and Gerardine', 241–2; P Dransart, 'Two Shrine Fragments from Kinneddar, Moray', in M Redknap, N Edwards, S Youngs, A Lane and J Knight (eds), *Patterns and Purpose in Insular Art* (Oxford, 2001), 233–40.

4   A Aspinall, N Q Bogdan and P Z Dransart, 'Kinneddar', *Discovery and Excavation Scotland* (1995), 35–6; Dransart, 'Two Shrine Fragments', 233.

5   Dransart, 'Cults of Sts Moluag and Gerardine', 236–8.

6   R D Oram, *Domination and Lordship: Scotland 1070–1230* (Edinburgh, 2011), 75–85.

7   Oram, *Domination and Lordship*, 30.

8   *Anglo-Saxon Chronicle*, trans G N Garmonsway, new edition (London,1972), s.a. 1078.

9   Oram, *Domination and Lordship*, 60–1.

10   Oram, *Domination and Lordship*, 71; *Annals of Ulster*, ed B MacCarthy (Dublin, 1887), s.a. 1130.

11   I B Cowan, 'The Medieval Church in the Diocese of Aberdeen', *Northern Scotland* 1.1 (1972), 21.

12   *Registrum Episcopatus Moraviensis*, ed C Innes (Bannatyne Club, 1837), no. 75.

13   A A M Duncan, *Scotland: The Making of the Kingdom*, revised paperback edition (Edinburgh, 1978), 104.

14   H B Mackintosh and J S Richardson, *Elgin Cathedral: The Cathedral Kirk of Moray*, new edition (Edinburgh, 1980), 32.

15   *Liber Ecclesie de Scon* (Bannatyne and Maitland Clubs, 1843), no. 4.

16   G W S Barrow (ed), *Charters of David I* (Woodbridge, 1999), no. 33.

17   Mackintosh and Richardson, *Elgin Cathedral*, 32.

18   *Moray Registrum*, no. 46.

19   Mackintosh and Richardson, *Elgin Cathedral*, 32.

20   Barrow, *David I Charters*, 33, 157.

21   Barrow, *David I Charters*, nos 62, 129, 212.

22   Barrow, *David I Charters*, nos 214, 215.

23   *RRS* vol i, *The Acts of Malcom IV*, ed G W S Barrow (Edinburgh, 1960) no. 114.

24   *RRS* vol i, nos 118, 119, 131, 135–7, 158–60, 173, 175, 176, 182, 186, 195.

25   *Chronica de Mailros*, ed J Stevenson (Bannatyne Club, 1835), s.a. 1159–60; D E R Watt, *Medieval Church Councils in Scotland* (Edinburgh, 2000), 19–20.

26   *RRS* vol i, 11.

27   P C Ferguson, *Medieval Papal Representatives in Scotland* (Stair Society, 1997), 40–3.

28   *Chron Melrose*, s.a. 1160.

29   *A Scottish Chronicle known as the Chronicle of Holyrood*, ed M O Anderson (Scottish History Society, 1938), s.a. 1162.

30   *Chron Melrose*, s.a. 1161.

31   *Johannis de Fordun, Chronica Gentis Scotorum*, ed W F Skene (Edinburgh, 1872), ii, 251–2.

32   *Chron Holyrood*, 142–3; Duncan, *Making of the Kingdom*, 191.

33   *RRS* vol ii, *The Acts of William I*, ed G W S Barrow (Edinburgh, 1971), no. 116.

34   *Moray Registrum*, no. 277.

35   *Chron Melrose*, s.a. 1171.

36   *Chron Melrose*, s.a. 1172; *RRS* ii, 12; Duncan, *Making of the Kingdom*, 269.

37   *RRS* vol ii, no. 132.

38   *RRS*, vol ii, no. 139.

39   Duncan, *Making of the Kingdom*, 269.

40   *RRS*, vol ii, no. 142; *Moray Registrum*, no. 3. The lands and island of Moy were recovered as pertaining to the bishop and Church of Moray by Bishop John Winchester in 1456: *Exchequer Rolls of Scotland*, ed J Stewart *et al* (Edinburgh, 1878–1908), vol vi, 376.

41   *Scotichronicon by Walter Bower*, ed D E R Watt *et al* (Aberdeen or Edinburgh, 1987–98), vol iv, 349; *An Historical Catalogue of the Bishops of Scotland down to the year 1668 by the Right Rev Robert Keith*, ed M Russel (Edinburgh and London, 1824), 136.

42   *Chron Melrose*, s.a. 1187; *Scotichronicon*, iv, 377. For Richard's service as a clerk in the writing office of King William's chancellor, see *RRS*, vol ii, 32. For the MacWilliam insurrections, see Oram, *Domination and Lordship*, 140–5, 148–9.

43   *RRS*, vol ii, no. 272.

44   Oram, *Domination and Lordship*, 148–9; *RRS*, ii, 12; *Chron Melrose*, s.a. 1187.

45   *RRS*, vol ii, no. 273; *Moray Registrum*, no. 7.

46   *RRS*, vol ii, no. 281; *Moray Registrum*, no. 5.

47   *RRS*, vol ii, nos 394, 395; *Moray Registrum*, nos 8, 9.

48   *RRS*, vol ii, no. 421; *Moray Registrum*, no. 17.

49   *RRS*, vol ii, no. 359; *Moray Registrum*, no. 14.

50   *RRS*, vol ii, no. 393; *Moray Registrum*, no. 15.

51   *RRS*, vol ii, nos 360, 361; *Moray Registrum*, nos 11, 12.

52   *Moray Registrum*, no. 13; *RRS*, ii, no. 362.

53   *RRS*, vol ii, no. 421; *Moray Registrum*, no. 17.

54   Keith, *Bishops*, 137.

55   *Scotichronicon*, iv, 433.

56   Duncan, *Making of the Kingdom*, 279.

57   *RRS*, vol ii, nos 465, 478; *Moray Registrum*, nos 18, 20.

58 *RRS*, vol ii, nos 476, 477; *Moray Registrum*, no. 19; *Liber S Thome de Aberbrothoc*, ed C Innes and P Chalmers (Bannatyne Club, 1848–56), no. 33.

59 *Moray Registrum*, no. 45.

60 *Moray Registrum*, no. 46.

61 The prebends and their holders are discussed on page 123.

62 *Chron Melrose*, s.a. 1215.

63 Oram, *Domination and Lordship*, 175–82.

64 Watt, *Medieval Church Councils*, 37.

65 *Chron Melrose*, s.a. 1218.

66 *Vetera Monumenta Hibernorum et Scotorum Illustrantia*, ed A Theiner (Rome, 1864), no. 14.

67 *Vetera Monumenta*, no. 19.

68 *Moray Registrum*, nos 51, 52.

69 *Chron Melrose*, s.a. 1222.

70 Keith, *Bishops*, 138.

71 D E R Watt, *A Biographical Dictionary of Scottish Graduates to AD 1410* (Oxford, 1977), 407–8.

72 *Moray Registrum*, no. 56.

73 *Moray Registrum*, no. 57.

74 *Moray Registrum*, no. 58.

75 Cowan, *Medieval Church*, 33.

76 See, for example, Mackintosh and Richardson, *Elgin Cathedral*, 34; Watt, *Scottish Graduates*, 408.

77 *Moray Registrum*, no. 26.

78 *Moray Registrum*, no. 28.

79 *Moray Registrum*, no. 29.

80 *Moray Registrum*, no. 30.

81 *Moray Registrum*, no. 69. For discussion of the new constitution see page 123.

82 *Moray Registrum*, nos 81, 82.

83 *Registrum Episcopatus Aberdonensis*, ed C Innes (Maitland Club, 1845), vol i, 16.

84 *Scotichronicon*, vol v, 183, 187; Keith, *Bishops*, 138.

85 R Fawcett, *Elgin Cathedral* (Edinburgh, 2001), 67, 70.

86 *Moray Registrum*, nos 79, 80.

87 *Calendar of Entries in the Papal Registers relating to Great Britain and Ireland. Papal Letters*, ed W H Bliss *et al* (London, 1893–), vol i, 258.

88 *Moray Registrum*, no. 99.

89 *Moray Registrum*, no. 214.

90 *Moray Registrum*, no. 277.

91 Keith, *Bishops*, 139.

92 See discussion in M Ash, 'The Church in the Reign of Alexander III', in N H Reid (ed), *Scotland in the Reign of Alexander III, 1249–1286* (Edinburgh, 1990), 31–52 at 36–41.

93 A Young, 'Noble Families and Political Factions', in N H Reid (ed), *Scotland in the Reign of Alexander III, 1249–1286* (Edinburgh, 1990), 1–30 at 5–7.

94 *CPL*, vol i, 351.

95 *Scotichronicon*, vol v, 379.

96 Fawcett, *Elgin Cathedral*, 16–18.

97 *Moray Registrum*, no. 128.

98 *Moray Registrum*, no. 127.

99 Watt, *Medieval Church Councils*, 98–9.

100 *Vetera Monumenta*, no. 296; *CPL*, vol i, 481.

101 *Moray Registrum*, no. 129.

102 *Records of the Parliaments of Scotland* (web resource, www.rps.ac.uk), 1290/3/2. Date accessed: 1 February 2012.

103 *CPL*, vol i, 534–5.

104 E L G Stones and G G Simpson (eds), *Edward I and the Throne of Scotland* (Oxford, 1978), ii, 150–1; A A M Duncan, *The Kingship of the Scots 842–1292* (Edinburgh, 2002), 296–8.

105 *Calendar of Documents relating to Scotland*, ed J Bain *et al* (Edinburgh, 1881–), vol i, no. 839.

106 *Moray Registrum*, 359; Keith, *Bishops*, 139; Fawcett, *Elgin Cathedral*, 43, 67.

107 Fawcett, *Elgin Cathedral*, 12–13 and fig 9.

108 G W S Barrow, *Robert Bruce and the Community of the Realm of Scotland*, 3rd edition (Edinburgh, 1988), 116.

109 *CDS*, vol ii, 212; Francis Palgrave (ed), *Documents and Records Illustrating the History of Scotland* (London, 1837), 330.

110 *CDS*, vol ii, no. 1396.

111 Barrow, *Robert Bruce*, 177.

112 *CDS*, vol iv, 480.

113 Barrow, *Robert Bruce*, 151, 263.

114 *CDS*, vol ii, no. 1820.

115 *CDS*, vol ii, no. 1827.

116 *CDS*, vol ii, no. 1907; Barrow, *Robert Bruce*, 163, 168.

117 *CDS*, vol ii, no. 1907; *CDS*, iv, 400.

118 *CDS*, vol iv, 400 and no. 1837.

119 Barrow, *Robert Bruce*, 175.

120 *RPS*, 1308/1. Date accessed: 1 February 2012.

121 *Foedera, Conventiones, Litterae et Cuiuscunque Generis Acta Publica*, ed T Rymer (London, 1816–69), vol ii, 363–4.

122 *CPL*, vol ii, 191.

123 *CPL*, vol ii, 199.

124 Keith, *Bishops*, 140.

125 Barrow, *Robert Bruce*, 266–7.

126 *CDS*, vol iii, no. 718; Barrow, *Robert Bruce*, 381, note 45.

127 Barrow, *Robert Bruce*, 258.

128 *ER*, vol i, 211.

129 *Scotichronicon*, vol vii, 119.

130 *Moray Registrum*, no. 114.

131 *Moray Registrum*, no. 117.

132 *RPS*, A1357/9/1. Date accessed: 1 February 2012.

133 *Moray Registrum*, no. 236.

134 I B Cowan and D E Easson, *Medieval Religious Houses, Scotland, 2nd edition* (London and New York, 1976), 178.

135 *Scotichronicon*, vol vii, 323; *Moray Registrum*, 360.

136 Fawcett, *Elgin Cathedral*, 71.

137 R Oram, 'Alexander Bur, Bishop of Moray (1362–1397)', in B E Crawford (ed), *Church, Chronicle and Learning in Medieval and Early Renaissance Scotland* (Edinburgh, 1999), 195–213, at 197 and notes.

138 *Registrum Magni Sigilii Regum Scotorum*, ed J M Thomson et al (Edinburgh, 1882–1914), vol i, no. 117.

139 S Boardman, *The Early Stewart Kings, Robert II and Robert III, 1371–1406* (East Linton, 1996), 11.

140 Oram, 'Alexander Bur', 195–7.

141 *Scotichronicon*, vol vii, 323 and notes; *Vetera Monumenta*, no. 653; *Calendar of Entries in the Papal Registers Relating to Great Britain and Ireland: Petitions to the Pope*, ed W H Bliss (London, 1896–), vol i, 401; Watt, *Scottish Graduates*, 68.

142 Oram, 'Alexander Bur', 198–200.

143 Oram, 'Alexander Bur', 199; J Dowden, *The Bishops of Scotland* (Glasgow, 1912), 155 and note 1 (where the sums paid by Bur are misquoted); *Moray Registrum*, nos 161–4.

144 *CPP*, vol i, 401.

145 *Scotichronicon*, vol vii, 119.

146 *Moray Registrum*, no. 147; *RRS*, vol vi, no. 348.

147 Oram, 'Alexander Bur', 200.

148 R Oram and P Adderley, 'Lordship and Environmental Change in Central Highland and Scotland, c 1300–c 1400', *Journal of the North Atlantic 1* (2008), 74–84; Oram, 'Alexander Bur', 200.

149 *Moray Registrum*, no. 154.

150 *RMS*, vol i, nos 382, 405.

151 *Moray Registrum*, no. 169; Oram, 'Alexander Bur', 203–4.

152 *Moray Registrum*, no. 162.

153 *Moray Registrum*, no. 283.

154 *Moray Registrum*, no. 167; *RMS*, i, no. 790.

155 *Moray Registrum*, no. 168.

156 Oram, 'Alexander Bur', 204; *Moray Registrum*, no. 169.

157 *Moray Registrum*, no. 271; A Grant, 'The Wolf of Badenoch', in W D H Sellar (ed), *Moray, Province and People* (Edinburgh, 1993), 151; Boardman, *Early Stewart Kings*, 151.

158 *Moray Registrum*, no. 170.

159 Oram, 'Alexander Bur', 204–5. For a traditional interpretation, see R Nicholson, *Scotland, the Later Middle Ages* (Edinburgh, 1974), 204–5; A Grant, *Independence and Nationhood: Scotland 1306–1469* (London, 1984), 208; M Lynch, *Scotland: A New History* (London, 1991), 139.

160 *Moray Registrum*, 381.

161 *Moray Registrum*, nos 114–18 and see page 135.

162 *Moray Registrum*, 381.

163 *Moray Registrum*, no. 65.

164 *Moray Registrum*, no. 303; Boardman, *Early Stewart Kings*, 176.

165 *Moray Registrum*, no. 172.

166 *Moray Registrum*, nos 172, 173; *ER*, iii, 276, 316, 348, 376, 403, 430.

167 *Moray Registrum*, no. 266.

168 On 1 November 1395, Pope Benedict XIII gave a mandate to the bishop of Aberdeen to hold inquests to determine the contents of the books which had held details of the statutes and privileges of the Church of Moray and to make copies where possible. This mandate followed a petition from the bishop, dean and chapter of Moray, narrating how the church and a large part of their living quarters had been burned, together with records relating to the priories of Urquhart and Pluscarden, the Maison Dieu and the Hospital at the Bridge of Spey. *Calendar of Papal Letters to Scotland of Benedict XIII of Avignon, 1394–1419*, ed F McGurk (Scottish History Society, 1976), 51.

169 Oram, 'Alexander Bur', 206–307; S Boardman, 'The Man Who Would Be King: The Lieutenancy and Death of David, Duke of Rothesay, 1378–1402', in R Mason and N MacDougall (eds), *People and Power in Scotland* (Edinburgh, 1992), 1–27 at 8–9; *Moray Registrum*, no. 272.

170 *Moray Registrum*, 204.

171 *Moray Registrum*, 360.

172 Keith, *Bishops*, 142.

173 Watt, *Scottish Graduates*, 503–4.

174 *CPP*, vol i, 386–7.

175 *CPL*, vol iv, 188.

176 Watt, *Scottish Graduates*, 504–5.

177 *Moray Registrum*, no. 252.

178 *Moray Registrum*, 360.

179 *Moray Registrum*, no. 176.

180 *Moray Registrum*, no. 177.

181 *Moray Registrum*, no. 178.

182 *Moray Registrum*, no. 265.

183 Watt, *Scottish Graduates*, 506.

184 *Moray Registrum*, no. 184.

185 *Moray Registrum*, 382–3.

186 *Moray Registrum*, 360; Keith, *Bishops*, 142.

187 Watt, *Scottish Graduates*, 278; Oram, *Domination and Lordship*, 319.

188 *Moray Registrum*, no. 175 and page 202.

189 Watt, *Scottish Graduates*, 278.

190 Watt, *Scottish Graduates*, 279; *Moray Registrum*, nos 251, 252.

191 *Moray Registrum*, 360.

192 *RMS*, vol i, 383–4.

193 R M A Monteith, *Theater of Mortality* (London 1704), 251; *The Warrender Papers*, ed A I Cameron (Scottish History Society, 1931–2), vol i, 275.
194 *Moray Registrum*, no. 187.
195 *Moray Registrum*, 360.
196 Keith, *Bishops*, 142.
197 Fawcett, *Elgin Cathedral*, 75.
198 Watt, *Scottish Graduates*, 360.
199 *CPP*, vol i, 506.
200 *CPP*, vol i, 602, 639.
201 *Moray Registrum*, no. 187.
202 *CPP*, vol i, 602.
203 *Moray Registrum*, 360.
204 Watt, *Scottish Graduates*, 361.
205 He has left few records of his activities in Moray, mainly relatively routine administrative processes, for example *Moray Registrum*, no. 188, but was later remembered as an active diocesan; *Ferrerii Historia Abbatum de Kynlos*, ed W D Wilson (Bannatyne Club, 1839), 29.
206 *Registrum Episcopatus Glasguensis*, ed C Innes (Bannatyne and Maitland Clubs, 1843), vol ii, 307–12.
207 Watt, *Scottish Graduates*, 361.
208 Watt, *Scottish Graduates*, 159–61.
209 *CDS*, vol iv, 131.
210 *CPP*, vol i, 602.
211 *Calendar of Scottish Supplications to Rome, 1418–22*, ed E R Lindsay and A I Cameron (Scottish History Society, 1934), 294.
212 Watt, *Scottish Graduates*, 160; *CPL*, vol vii, 254.
213 Fawcett, *Elgin Cathedral*, 6.
214 *Moray Registrum*, 360; Watt, *Scottish Graduates*, 161.
215 Keith, *Bishops*, 143.
216 Fawcett, *Elgin Cathedral*, 74–5.
217 *Calendar of Scottish Supplications to Rome, 1423–28*, ed A I Dunlop (Scottish History Society, 1956), 23, 43–4, 50, 52, 67; *RMS*, vol ii, nos 84, 138, 140.
218 M Brown, *The Black Douglases* (East Linton, 1998), 239.
219 Watt, *Church Councils*, 153–4.
220 M Brown, *James I* (Edinburgh, 1994), 195.
221 For example, NRS GD198/11, dated 29 September 1434; NRS GD124/1/136, dated 19 March 1435.
222 *RPS*, 1439/0/1. Date accessed: 1 February 2012.
223 Dowden, *Bishops*, 160.
224 Brown, *Black Douglases*, 269.
225 Brown, *Black Douglases*, 269–70.
226 C A McGladdery, *James II* (Edinburgh, 1990), 94–5.
227 *Moray Registrum*, no. 192.
228 *RMS*, vol ii, no. 488.
229 *RMS*, vol ii, no. 489.
230 *Moray Registrum*, no. 193.
231 *ER*, vol vi, 469, 474, 521, 656; McGladdery, *James II*, 104.
232 Keith, *Bishops*, 144.
233 Fawcett, *Elgin Cathedral*, 70–1.
234 *Moray Registrum*, 255–6.
235 Dowden, *Bishops*, 161.
236 Keith, *Bishops*, 144.
237 Fawcett, *Elgin Cathedral*, 72.
238 Dowden, *Bishops*, 161–2.
239 *RMS*, vol ii, nos 800, 803–6.
240 *RMS*, vol ii, no. 984.
241 Dowden, *Bishops*, 162.
242 Dowden, *Bishops*, 162.
243 Keith, *Bishops*, 145.
244 Fawcett, *Elgin Cathedral*, 74.
245 *RMS*, vol ii, no. 1376.
246 N MacDougall, *James III: A Political Study* (Edinburgh, 1982), 77.
247 MacDougall, *James III*, 78.
248 MacDougall, *James III*, 92, 116.
249 MacDougall, *James III*, 91.
250 Keith, *Bishops*, 145; Fawcett, *Elgin Cathedral*, 71–2.
251 MacDougall, *James III*, 165.
252 Nicholson, *Later Middle Ages*, 510–12; MacDougall, *James III*, 128, 166, 172–3, 179, 230.
253 Watt, *Church Councils*, 169.
254 *Moray Registrum*, no. 198; MacDougall, *James III*, 247.
255 MacDougall, *James III*, 251; N MacDougall, *James IV* (Edinburgh, 1989), 32, 37.
256 MacDougall, *James III*, 252, 254.
257 MacDougall, *James III*, 256; MacDougall, *James IV*, 38, 42.
258 *RPS*, 1488/10/49. Date accessed: 1 February 2012.
259 MacDougall, *James IV*, 60–1.
260 *Moray Registrum*, no. 210.
261 MacDougall, *James IV*, 72–3.
262 MacDougall, *James IV*, 129.
263 MacDougall, *James IV*, 137.
264 MacDougall, *James IV*, 213.
265 Keith, *Bishops*, 146.
266 Fawcett, *Elgin Cathedral*, 67, 70.
267 Fawcett, *Elgin Cathedral*, 67.
268 MacDougall, *James IV*, 95, 213.
269 MacDougall, *James IV*, 131, 132.
270 J E Dawson, *Scotland Reformed, 1488–1587* (Edinburgh, 2007), 69. Forman was described as 'postulate' on 8 October 1501: *RMS*, ii, no. 2602.
271 MacDougall, *James IV*, 149; Nicholson, *Later Middle Ages*, 554.
272 MacDougall, *James IV*, 249.
273 *The Letters of James the Fourth 1505–1513*, ed R K Hannay (Scottish History Society, 1953), no. 116.
274 MacDougall, *James IV*, 254–5.
275 Nicholson, *Later Middle Ages*, 594.

276 *James IV Letters*, no. 258.

277 *James IV Letters*, no. 268.

278 MacDougall, *James IV*, 206; *James IV Letters*, nos 332–4.

279 *James IV Letters*, nos 361, 365–6.

280 *James IV Letters*, nos 388–9.

281 MacDougall, *James IV*, 207; *James IV Letters*, nos 403–4, 410, 461.

282 *James IV Letters*, nos 530, 548.

283 Nicholson, *Later Middle Ages*, 597.

284 Nicholson, *Later Middle Ages*, 599; *James IV Letters*, nos 551, 561.

285 Nicholson, *Later Middle Ages*, 559.

286 L J Macfarlane, 'The Primacy of the Scottish Church, 1472–1521', *Innes Review* 20 (1969), 111–29 at 126.

287 MacDougall, *James IV*, 295–7.

288 MacDougall, *James IV*, 297–8.

289 *The Letters of James V*, ed R K Hannay and D Hay (Edinburgh, 1954), 8.

290 *James V Letters*, 16.

291 Dowden, *Bishops*, 167.

292 *James V Letters*, 3, 19.

293 *James V Letters*, 6.

294 *James V Letters*, 13, 16n.

295 Dowden, *Bishops*, 167.

296 *RMS*, vol iii, no. 71.

297 *James V Letters*, 97.

298 Dowden, *Bishops*, 168.

299 *Moray Registrum*, no. 355.

300 Dowden, *Bishops*, 168.

301 Keith, *Bishops*, 148.

302 D E R Watt and N F Shead (eds), *The Heads of Religious Houses in Scotland from the Twelfth to the Sixteenth Centuries* (Edinburgh, 2001), 170.

303 *RMS*, vol iii, nos 9, 19, 54, 75, 92, 97, 98, 101, 102, 104, 105, 107, 108, 110, 112, 114, 117, 153, 191, 192, 203, 204, 206, 271, 272, 274, 275, 276, 280, 281, 283, 285–91, 294.

304 *James V Letters*, 113.

305 *James V Letters*, 116.

306 *RPS*, A1525/7/2. Date accessed: 1 February 2012. The other ambassadors were Gavin Dunbar, archbishop of Glasgow, Archibald Douglas, earl of Angus, George Crichton, abbot of Holyrood, Sir William Scott of Balwearie and Master Adam Otterburn.

307 Dowden, *Bishops*, 169.

308 Keith, *Bishops*, 148

309 *James V Letters*, 145.

310 Dowden, *Bishops*, 169.

311 *James V Letters*, 3, 13.

312 *James V Letters*, 23. Alexander was still attempting to secure possession in 1517 (*James V Letters*, 37–8).

313 *James V Letters*, 36–7.

314 *James V Letters*, 49–50, 64–6, 71, 73, 74–5, 80, 84.

315 *James V Letters*, 138–9.

316 Dowden, *Bishops*, 170.

317 *James V Letters*, 164, 166–7.

318 *RMS*, vol iv, no. 157.

319 *RMS*, vol iv, no. 452.

320 Dowden, *Bishops*, 171.

321 *The Black Book of Taymouth*, ed C Innes (Bannatyne Club, 1855), 121.

322 *RMS*, vol iii, no. 1743.

323 Keith, *Bishops*, 150.

324 Dawson, *Scotland Reformed*, 130.

325 Dowden, *Bishops*, 172.

326 *Heads of Religious Houses*, 191.

327 J Kirk, 'Hepburn, Patrick (c.1487–1573)', *Oxford Dictionary of National Biography* (Oxford, 2004). Date accessed: 10 February 2012.

328 Kirk, 'Hepburn, Patrick'.

329 *James V Letters*, 342–3.

330 *James V Letters*, 348.

331 Watt and Shead, *Heads of Religious Houses*, 191.

332 Kirk, 'Hepburn, Patrick'; *Moray Registrum*, nos 308–14, 316, 318–23, 325–31, 333–8, etc.

333 *RMS*, vol iv, no. 2632.

334 Kirk, 'Hepburn, Patrick'.

335 Dawson, *Scotland Reformed*, 192–3.

336 Dowden, *Bishops*, 172.

337 *RMS*, vol iv, no. 460.

338 *RMS*, vol iv, no. 492.

339 G Donaldson, 'The Scottish Episcopate at the Reformation', *English Historical Review* 60 (1945), 355.

340 W C Dickinson (ed), *John Knox's History of the Reformation in Scotland* (Edinburgh, 1949), vol i, 190.

341 G Donaldson, *Scotland: James V to James VII* (Edinburgh, 1971), 93.

342 Kirk, 'Hepburn, Patrick'.

343 Donaldson, *Scotland: James V to James VII*, 94.

344 Kirk, 'Hepburn, Patrick'.

345 *RMS*, vol iv, no. 2679.

346 D McRoberts, 'The Material Destruction Caused by the Scottish Reformation', *Innes Review* 10.1 (1959), 155.

347 *The Register of the Privy Council of Scotland*, ed J H Burton, vol i (Edinburgh, 1877), 608–10.

348 RPC, vol i, 677–8.

349 *RPS*, A1567/12/47. Date accessed: 1 February 2012.

350 *RPS*, 1585/12/83. Date accessed: 1 February 2012.

351 *RMS*, vol iv, no. 1886.

352 *RMS*, vol iv, no. 1907.

353 *RMS*, vol iv, no. 2463.

354 *RPS*, 1585/12/84. Date accessed: 1 February 2012.

The pension was confirmed in December 1585 to Haliburton's heirs.

355   Keith, *Bishops*, 150.

356   For a discussion of the architecture of Dornoch Cathedral see W D Simpson, 'The Architectural History of the Cathedral', in C D Bentinck, *Dornoch Cathedral and Parish* (Inverness, 1926), 377–412.

357   *Hectoris Boetii Murthlacensium et Aberdonensium Episcoporum Vitae*, ed J Moir (New Spalding Club, 1894), says Aberdeen's two western towers were started by Bishop Alexander Kininmund (1355–1380) (24), and finished by Henry de Lichton (1422–1440). Lichton evidently started the central tower but left it unfinished (34). Bishop William Elphinstone (1483–1514) completed the central tower (97). The spires on the western towers were added by Bishop Gavin Dunbar (1518–1532). As at Elgin, the western towers were over the aisle ends, though they did not project laterally beyond the aisles; also as at Elgin, the towers were walled off from the nave.

358   The central tower of Glasgow was probably first started as a continuation of the general rebuilding of the eastern parts instigated by Bishop William de Bondington in about 1242, but it was rebuilt, after being hit by lightning, by Bishop William Lauder (1408–c 1426) and Bishop John Cameron (1426–1446), on heraldic evidence. The north-western tower was evidently started in the earlier thirteenth century since it was said at the time of its demolition in 1848 that it appeared to have been built after the window at the west end of the north aisle had been built but before it was glazed (Archbishop Eyre, 'The Western Towers', in G Eyre-Todd (ed), *The Book of Glasgow Cathedral* (Glasgow, 1898), 277), though its upper parts and spire were probably not completed for many years. Excavations in 1988 on the site of the south-western tower suggested it had been started no earlier than the fifteenth century (H McBrien, *An Interim Report on Excavations at the West Front of Glasgow Cathedral* (Scottish Urban Archaeological Trust, 1989)). The western towers of Glasgow projected fully from the west wall of the aisles, and, since they were wider than the aisles, they also projected laterally beyond them.

359   The only reason for thinking that western towers may have been planned at St Andrews when it was first set out is that, after the nearly complete west front was blown down in a gale during the episcopate of Bishop William Wishart (1271–1279), the west front was rebuilt on a line which appears to have been further east by about the depth that would have been taken up by towers. This is very uncertain evidence.

360   The main arguments in favour of there having been western towers at Kirkwall are that the ambitious mid-thirteenth-century triplet of doorways was built before the western bays of the nave, as if to make allowance for settlement due to the expectation of a greater weight to be supported, and when those western bays were eventually built without towers the spacing between the piers was greater than for those further east, possibly in order to reallocate space that had been initially provided for large tower piers. This is inadequate evidence.

361   The partial shells of the two western towers of Arbroath stand to almost complete height, but nothing remains of the central tower. Although founded in 1178, the architectural evidence suggests that the main campaign of building the church may not have started until around the later years of the twelfth century (R Fawcett, 'Arbroath Abbey: A Note on its Architecture and Early Conservation History', in G Barrow (ed), *The Declaration of Arbroath* (Society of Antiquaries of Scotland, 2003), 50–85). The western towers opened fully into both the central vessel and the aisles, with the main elevation apparently continuing without break across the inner faces of the towers towards the central vessel. It seems that there were no floors within the towers at gallery or clearstorey levels and that the arches at those levels were thus essentially flying screens.

362   Of the three towers at Dunfermline, the central one fell in 1753 and is completely gone, though a new one was built further east as part of the church built on the site of the choir and transepts in 1817–21. On heraldic evidence the north-western tower was largely rebuilt for Abbot Richard de Bothwell (1446–1482), with possible further reconstruction of the upper parts in the late sixteenth century under the direction of the master of works, William Schaw. What remained of the south-western tower collapsed in 1807, and its meagre replacement was designed by William Stark. From the surviving evidence it seems that the western towers originally opened fully into both the central vessel and aisles. (R Fawcett, 'Dunfermline Abbey Church', in R Fawcett, *Royal Dunfermline* (Society of Antiquaries of Scotland, 2005), 27–63).

363   The early-thirteenth-century western towers at Holyrood, which project for their full depth out from the west front, and which are also so far displaced laterally that they leave much of the aisle ends free, survive up to belfry stage (J P McAleer, 'A Unique Façade in Great Britain: The West Front of Holyrood Abbey', *Proc Soc Antiq Scot* 115 (1985), 263–75). No central

tower is shown on the earliest view of the abbey, the so-called English spy view of 1543–4, but by then the abbey had suffered major English attacks in 1322 and 1385; any remains of it would have been demolished along with the remains of transepts and choir in about 1570 by Bishop Adam Bothwell of Orkney, who was then commendator.

364 The form of the western towers at Kilwinning is discussed in J P McAleer, 'Towards an Architectural History of Kilwinning Abbey', *Proc Soc Antiq Scot* 125 (1995), 813–79. The north-western tower survived until being struck by lightning in 1805; the existing tower dates from 1815. The towers were associated with a full-height laterally-extending space akin to a western transept.

365 The intention to build a pair of western towers at Paisley is indicated by the surviving massive thirteenth-century western nave arcade piers. The central tower occupies the site of its medieval predecessor, but in its present form was built between 1897 and 1928 (R Fawcett, 'Paisley Abbey: The Medieval Architecture', in J Malden (ed), *The Monastery and Abbey of Paisley* (Paisley, 2000), 37-49).

366 *The Original Chronicle of Andrew of Wyntoun*, vol iv, ed F J Amours (Scottish Text Society, 1903–14), 426–7.

367 For discussion of the architectural history of Jedburgh, see R Fawcett, 'The Architectural Development of the Abbey Church', in J Lewis and G Ewart (eds), *Jedburgh Abbey: The Archaeology and Architecture* (Society of Antiquaries of Scotland, 1995), 159–74; M Thurlby, 'Jedburgh Abbey Church: The Romanesque Fabric', *Proc Soc Antiq Scot* 125 (1995), 793–812.

368 Fawcett, 'Arbroath Abbey'.

369 See the plan in RCAHMS, *Inventory for Berwickshire* (Edinburgh, 1915), 133.

370 See the plan in RCAHMS, *Inventory for Fife* (Edinburgh, 1933), 8.

371 See the plans in RCAHMS, *Inventory for the City of Edinburgh* (Edinburgh, 1951), 129, 130.

372 W A Wickham, 'Some Notes on Chapter Houses', *Transactions of the Historical Society of Lancashire and Cheshire* 64 (1912), 143–248.

373 R Fawcett and R Oram, *Melrose Abbey* (Stroud, 2004), 134–64.

374 For plans of Cistercian chapel aisles see A Dimier, *Recueil de Plans d'Eglises Cisterciennes* (Commission d'Histoire de l'Ordre de Citeaux, Paris, 1949).

375 See the plans in RCAHMS, *Edinburgh*, 28, 30.

376 R Willis, *The Architectural History of Chichester Cathedral* (Chichester, 1861), 25–30.

377 J Watson, *British and Foreign Building Stones: A Descriptive*

Catalogue of the Specimens in the Sedgwick Museum, Cambridge (Cambridge, 1911), 114, 155, 268, 300.

378 A A McMillan, *Quarries of Scotland* (Historic Scotland, Technical Conservation, Research and Education Division, Technical Advice Note 12, 1997), 55. See also Andrew A McMillan, R J Gillanders and J A Fairhurst, *Building Stones of Edinburgh*, 2nd edition (Edinburgh, 1999), 62.

379 It is thought that some of the quarry workings along the cliff faces to the east of Hopeman, for example, could be of medieval origin (R Oram, *Moray and Badenoch: A Historical Guide* (Edinburgh, 1996), 152–3).

380 McMillan, *Quarries of Scotland*, 55, 83.

381 For discussion of medieval quarrying and the costs of transport, see L F Salzman, *Building in England down to 1540*, revised edition (Oxford,1967). 119–39. See also D Parsons, 'Review and Prospect: The Stone Industry in Roman, Anglo-Saxon and Medieval England', in D Parsons (ed), *Stone Quarrying and Building in England AD 43–1525* (Chichester, 1990), 1–15.

382 See the comparative plans in R Fawcett, *Scottish Cathedrals* (London, 1997), 118–21. The sacristy range on the south side of Dunblane's eastern limb has something of the appearance of an aisle in plan, though the only opening into the eastern limb was a single doorway.

383 The final plan of the eastern limb of Whithorn Cathedral is uncertain, though it seems likely that it was unaisled; the nave remained aisle-less throughout its history. See R Oram, 'The Buildings', in C Lowe (ed), *'Clothing for the Soul Divine': Burials at the Tomb of St Ninian* (Edinburgh, 2009), 147–56.

384 For brief discussion of the plans of the earlier phases of Glasgow Cathedral see R Fawcett, 'Introduction', in R Fawcett (ed), *Medieval Art and Architecture in the Diocese of Glasgow*, British Archaeological Association Transactions 23 (Leeds, 1998), 1–8.

385 J Bilson, 'The Architecture of the Cistercians, with Special Reference to some of their Earlier Churches in England', *Archaeological Journal* 66 (1909), 230.

386 M Thurlby, 'St Andrews Cathedral-Priory and the Beginnings of Gothic Architecture in Northern Britain', in J Higgitt (ed), *Medieval Art and Architecture in the Diocese of St Andrews*, British Archaeological Association Transactions for the Year 1986 (Leeds, 1994), 47–60.

387 For details of the Rievaulx mouldings see E Sharpe, *Supplement to Architectural Parallels* (London, 1848); see particularly the arcade arches in plate XXXIV.

388 The start of construction of St Andrews Cathedral was ascribed by Wyntoun to Bishop Arnold (1160–1162). The approximate date for the start of work on the

enlarged choir of Glasgow Cathedral is linked with an ordinance for a national collection for the fabric during Lent 1242 (*Glasgow Registrum* vol i, xxviii).

389   For views of the naves of St David's Cathedral and Llanthony Priory see G Webb, *Architecture in Britain: The Middle Ages* (Harmondsworth, 1956), plates 85A and 85B.

390   For discussion of the design of Pershore see C Milburn, 'Pershore Abbey: The Thirteenth-Century Choir', *Journal of the British Archaeological Association* 137 (1984), 130–44.

391   For discussion of the design of Southwell see J McNeill, 'The Chronology of the Choir of Southwell Minster', in J S Alexander (ed), *Southwell and Nottinghamshire: Medieval Art, Architecture and Industry*, British Archaeological Association Conference Transactions 21 (Leeds, 1998), 24–32. For a wider discussion of two-storeyed designs see U Engel, 'Two-storeyed Elevations: The Choir of Southwell Minster and the West Country', in Alexander, *Southwell and Nottinghamshire*, 33–43.

392   P Héliot, 'La Suppression du Triforium au Début de la Période Gothique', *Révue Archéologique* 1 (1964), 131–68; L Grant, *Architecture and Society in Normandy 1120-1270* (New Haven and London, 2005), 167–79.

393   R Fawcett, 'Dunblane Cathedral: Evidence for a Change in the Design of the Nave', *Proc Soc Antiq Scot* 112 (1982), 576–8.

394   R Fawcett, 'The Priory Church', in F McCormick *et al*, 'Excavations at Pluscarden Priory, Moray', *Proc Soc Antiq Scot* 124 (1994), 396–403.

395   In Glasgow Cathedral nave the upper storeys are interlinked by a pair of embracing arches in each bay, with the gallery arches set back on a recessed plane, thus giving a sense of unity to those upper storeys.

396   At Paisley Abbey the upper parts of the internal elevations of the nave were largely rebuilt by Abbot Thomas Tarvas (1445–1459) ('The Auchinleck Chronicle', in W A Craigie (ed), *The Asloan Manuscript*, i, (Scottish Text Society, 1923), f113v.). Against the retained thirteenth-century west front at gallery level, however, are fragments of substantial shafts which appear to have been intended to rise up into the clearstorey level, and which could therefore be interpreted as having belonged to arches embracing the two upper storeys.

397   For a discussion of certain pier types see L Hoey, 'Pier Design in Early Gothic Architecture in East-Central Scotland, c 1170–1250', in J Higgitt (ed), *Medieval Art and Architecture in the Diocese of St Andrews*, British Archaeological Association Transactions for the Year 1986 (Leeds, 1994), 84–98.

398   For details of the Blackadder Aisle piers see R Fawcett, 'The Blackadder Aisle at Glasgow Cathedral: A Reconsideration of the Architectural Evidence for its Date', *Proc Soc Antiq Scot* 115 (1985), 277–87.

399   For sketches of the Inchmahome piers see D MacGibbon and T Ross, *The Ecclesiastical Architecture of Scotland*, vol ii (Edinburgh, 1896), 116–17.

400   See R Fawcett, 'Scottish Medieval Window Tracery', in D Breeze (ed), *Studies in Scottish Antiquity* (Edinburgh, 1984), 161.

401   S Harrison and P Barker, 'Byland Abbey, North Yorkshire: The West Front and Rose Window Reconstructed', *Journal of the British Archaeological Association* 140 (1987), 134–51; S Harrison, 'Elgin Cathedral: The Western Rose Window Reconstructed', *Journal of the British Archaeological Association* 156 (2003), 138–49.

402   R Fawcett, *The Architecture of the Scottish Medieval Church*, 1100–1560 (New Haven and London, 2011), 17, 37, 63–5, 67–9, 80, 90, 119, 135, 183.

403   For an illustration of this detail at Wells see L S Colchester, *Wells Cathedral* (London, 1987), 60.

404   The interpenetrating mouldings are just visible in National Art Survey of Scotland, vol iv, J Begg and G P H Watson (eds), *Examples of Scottish Architecture from the 12th to the 17th century* (Edinburgh, 1933), plate 26.

405   For a brief account of the introduction of bar tracery to England see P Binski, *Westminster Abbey and the Plantagenets* (New Haven and London, 1995), 36–43.

406   See Fawcett, 'Window Tracery', 151–3, 162–4.

407   Presumably for 'Ancient Monuments'.

408   V Jansen, 'Dying Mouldings, Unarticulated Springing Blocks, and Hollow Chamfers in Thirteenth-Century Architecture', *Journal of the British Archaeological Association* 135 (1982), 35–54.

409   R Fawcett and R Oram, *Dryburgh Abbey* (Stroud, 2005), 75–7.

410   For a discussion of barrel ceilings in Scotland see M Thurlby, 'Glasgow Cathedral and the Wooden Barrel Vault in Twelfth- and Thirteenth-Century Architecture in Scotland', in R Fawcett (ed), Medieval Art and Architecture in the Diocese of Glasgow, British Archaeological Association Transactions 23 (Leeds, 1998), 84–7.

411   The present barrel ceiling over the choir of Glasgow Cathedral was largely replaced in about 1914, but its slightly cusped profile was dictated by the wall rib in the east wall, and its pattern of ribs was based on that shown in early views, such as that by William Brown of 1822.

412   P Frankl, *Gothic Architecture*, 2nd edition, revised Paul Crossley (New Haven and London, 2000), 146.

413 The Fortrose vaults remain in place, but only the springings survive for the St Andrews precinct gateway vault.

414 At Bourges the double aisles were part of the echelon arrangement of volumes in which the double aisles stepped progressively upwards to support the high central vessel. For a discussion of the implications of such designs see J Bony, *French Gothic Architecture of the 12th and 13th Centuries* (Berkeley, 1983), 202–20.

415 I Nairn and N Pevsner, *The Buildings of England*, Sussex (Harmondsworth, 1965), 136.

416 E Lefèvre-Pontalis, 'L'origine des gables', *Bulletin Monumental* 71 (1907), 92–112; R Branner, *St Louis and the Court Style* (London, 1965), 23–4.

417 Rather confusingly, a view of the south flank of the cathedral in the Bodleian Library that was almost certainly drawn by John Slezer shows gables in the three west bays of the outer aisle, that is behind the porch and in the two bays to its east. However, that must be a mistake. (See J Dunbar, 'Two Drawings for John Slezer's *Theatrum Scotiae*? Elgin and Fortrose Cathedrals', *Review of Scottish Culture* 20 (2008), 110–21.)

418 The continuity of base course at Glasgow shows that the chapter house was built along with the choir in the mid-thirteenth century, but the vault of the lower chamber and much of the upper chamber were rebuilt after damage caused by a lightning strike. Heraldry indicates that the rebuilding was started by Bishop John Cameron (1426–1446) and completed by Bishop William Turnbull (1447–1454).

419 The functions of the Dunblane north range are discussed in D McRoberts, 'Dunblane Cathedral under the Chisholms', *Journal of the Society of Friends of Dunblane Cathedral* 11 (1971), 41–2.

420 *Vitae Dunkeldensis Ecclesiae Episcoporum . . . ab Alexandro Myln*, ed T Thomson (Bannatyne Club, 1823), 23.

421 N Stratford, 'Notes on the Norman Chapter House at Worcester', *Medieval Art and Architecture at Worcester Cathedral*, British Archaeological Association Conference Transactions for the Year 1975 (Leeds, 1978), 51–70.

422 For a view of the chapter house entrance at Westminster Abbey see Royal Commission on Historical Monuments (England), *Inventory of London*, vol i (London, 1924), plate 158.

423 For a view of the chapter house entrance at Southwell see P Brieger, *English Art 1216–1307* (Oxford, 1957), plate 72b.

424 For views of Fortrose see R Fawcett, *Beauly Priory and Fortrose Cathedral* (Edinburgh, 1987).

425 For a brief discussion of the links between Elgin, Fortrose and Tain see R Fawcett, 'Reliving Bygone Glories? The Revival of Earlier Architectural Forms in Scottish Late Medieval Church Architecture', *Journal of the British Archaeological Association* 156 (2003), 104–37.

426 According to Monteith, *Theatre of Mortality*, the inscription on the Innes tomb stated 'hoc notabile opus extruxit'.

427 L Shaw, *The History of the Province of Moray*, enlarged by J F S Gordon (Glasgow, 1882), citing 'Hay of Drumboot', 3, 281.

428 The lateral gables of the chapels at Edinburgh St Giles were removed during the restoration of 1829–33, but they are shown on the elevations published in *Registrum Cartarum Ecclesie Sancti Egidii de Edinburgh*, ed D Laing (Bannatyne Club, 1859).

429 The laterally gabled St Andrews Chapel in the east bay of the north nave aisle of Stirling Holy Rude remains in place, and St Mary's Chapel, which used to project from the west bay of the aisle, can also be seen from the surviving roof creases to have had a lateral gable.

430 The possibility of links between Scotland and the Low Countries in the use of laterally gabled aisles or chapels is briefly discussed in R Fawcett, 'Late Gothic Architecture in Scotland: Considerations on the Influence of the Low Countries', *Proc Soc Antiq Scot* 112 (1982), 477–96.

431 F van Molle, 'De Onze Lieve Vroukerk te Aarschot', *Bulletin de la Commission de Monuments et Sites* 3 (1952), 27–79.

432 L Paffendorf and M Konrad, 'Die Abteikirche Saint-Hubert in der Ardennen', in P Clemen (ed), *Belgische Kunstdenkmäler* 1 (Munich, 1923), 292–308.

433 For discussion of this tracery type see Fawcett, 'Window Tracery', 148–86, and particularly 177–80.

434 W R Macdonald, 'Notes on the Heraldry of Elgin and its Neighbourhood', *Proc Soc Antiq Scot* 34 (1899–1900), 345–6; three cushions lozenge-ways within a royal tressure.

435 Macdonald, 'Heraldry', 345–6; a lion rampant within a bordure charged with eight roses.

436 See F Bond, *The Chancel of English Churches* (London, etc, 1916), 149.

437 The Linlithgow example of this window type is in the bay of the south nave aisle immediately west of the transeptal chapel. It is of a different type from the other nave aisle windows, and its arch apex breaks the string course below the parapet, suggesting that it was a secondary insertion.

438 For discussion of the significance of the incomplete tressure in the royal arms see C Burnett, 'The Act of 1471 and its Effect on the Royal Arms of Scotland', *Proc Soc Antiq Scot* 105 (1972–4), 312–15.

439 Macdonald, 'Heraldry', 350–3; quarterly 1st and 4th a lymphiad; 2nd and 3rd a fess chequy.

440 N Pevsner and J Harris, *The Buildings of England*, Lincolnshire (Harmondsworth, 1964), 122–4.

441 S Brown, *'Our Magnificent Fabrick': York Minster, and Architectural History c 1220–1500* (English Heritage, 2003), 51–5.

442 Kirkdale Archaeology, *Historic Scotland Properties in Care: Minor Archaeological Works, 1999, Elgin Cathedral* (no date).

443 *Memorialls of the Trubles in Scotland and in England . . . by John Spalding*, vol i, ed John Stuart (Spalding Club, 1850), 376–7.

444 M R Apted and W Robertson, 'Late Fifteenth Century Paintings from Guthrie and Foulis Easter', *Proc Soc Antiq Scot* 95 (1961–2), 262–79. A similar arrangement, with depictions of the last judgement, is known to have existed at a number of English churches, as at Wenhaston in Suffolk (F Bond, *Screens and Galleries in English Churches* (London, 1908), 124, 127) and Penn in Buckinghamshire (R Marks and P Williamson (eds), *Gothic, Art for England* (Victoria and Albert Museum exhibition catalogue, 2003), 386).

445 Keith, *Bishops*; Andrew de Moravia, 138; Simon, Archibald, 139; David de Moravia, 140; Alexander Bur, William de Spynie, 142; Andrew Stewart, 146.

446 Keith, *Bishops*, 139.

447 N Saul, 'The Medieval Monuments of Rochester Cathedral', in T Ayers and T Tatton-Brown (eds), *Medieval Art, Architecture and Archaeology at Rochester*, British Archaeological Association Conference Transactions 28 (Leeds, 2006), 164–80 at 168–70.

448 F Bond, *Chancel of English Churches*, 220–41; V Sekules, 'The Tomb of Christ at Lincoln and the Development of the Sacrament Shrine: Easter Sepulchres Reconsidered', in T A Heslop and V A Sekules (eds), *Medieval Art and Architecture at Lincoln Cathedral*, British Archaeological Association Conference Transactions for the Year 1982 (Leeds, 1986), 118–31; P Sheingorn, *The Easter Sepulchre in England* (Kalamazoo, 1987), 26–32.

449 M Rubin, *Corpus Christi* (Cambridge, 1991), 294.

450 N Saul, *English Church Monuments in the Middle Ages* (Oxford, 2009), 163–4.

451 Keith, *Bishops*, 146.

452 Some caution must be applied in drawing comparisons, however, since many tombs have undergone modification. At Ely Cathedral, for example, the tomb of Bishop Richard Redman, who died in 1505, appears to be comparable to that at Elgin in being set within the north arcade immediately to the east of the choir stalls, and in having two arches over the tomb chest and a third over an entrance from the aisle. However, in that case it has been suggested that the entrance was only created in the eighteenth century, and that the tomb chest had to be truncated in order to make space for it (P Lindley, *Gothic to Renaissance* (Stamford, 1995), 91).

453 F H Crossley, *English Church Monuments* (London, 1921), 96.

454 G H Cook, *Medieval Chantries and Chantry Chapels*, revised edition (London, 1963), plate 22.

455 Keith, *Bishops*, 138.

456 'Here lies of honourable memory John Winchester lord bishop of Moray: who died the twenty-second day of the month of April the Year of the Lord 1460'.

457 A E Mahood, *Banff and Disrict* (Banff, 1919), gives the inscription as '*Hic nobiles viri Jacobus Ogilvy de Deskfvrd miles et Jacob ej filivs et haeres apparen obitvs vero dicti militis 13 Februarii a° d¹ 1505 obiit aute dicti fillii 1° Februarii a° d¹ 1505. Orate pro aiab eorum*'. Professor Geoffrey Barrow has pointed out to me that at least part of this inscription must have been misread, and that after the first 1505 it should probably be either '*obitus aute[m] dicti filii*' or '*obiit aute[m] dictus filius*'.

458 R Fawcett, *Scottish Medieval Churches, Architecture and Furnishings* (Stroud, 2002), 318–21.

459 His seal is described in H Laing, *Descriptive Catalogue of Impressions from Ancient Scottish Seals* (Bannatyne and Maitland Clubs, 1850), 156.

460 NRS file MW/1/426 (SC 22107/2B). In a letter of 5 April 1924 it was said it had been agreed to move the tomb from the site of the altar, where it had probably been since the seventeenth century.

461 'Here lies the noble and powerful Lord Alexander Gordon, first earl of Huntly, lord of Gordon and Badenoch, who died at Huntly on the fifteenth of July in the year of the Lord 1470.'

462 'Here lies William de la Hay, sometime lord of Lochloy, who died on the eighth day of the month of December in the year of the Lord 1422, for whose soul may the Lord be propitiated.'

463 For details see Macdonald, 'Heraldry', 361–5.

464 Macdonald, 'Heraldry', 367; see below 1st, etc, a fess chequy between three open crowns.

465 Macdonald, 'Heraldry', 367; quarterly 1st and 4th a fess chequy between three open crowns; 2nd and 3rd a bend between six cross crosslets.

[466] Macdonald, 'Heraldry', 369; three stars. Macdonald gives the incomplete inscription below the effigy as '[hic ja]cet nobilis vir robert innes de innmkye qui obiit'.

[467] 'Remember the end.'

[468] Macdonald, 'Heraldry', 369–70; a fess chequy between two crescents in chief and an open crown in base, impaling, a fess chequy between two open crowns in chief; the charge in base is broken away.

[469] Macdonald, 'Heraldry'; 369–70, a tree, dexter side broken away, on sinister a squirrel, on a chief three buckles.

[470] Keith, Bishops, 265.

[471] Macdonald, 'Heraldry'; 348–50, three cushions lozenge-ways.

[472] Keith, Bishops, 143, says that this aisle was the burial place of Bishop Columba de Dunbar and at least three other Dunbar burials took place here on the evidence of heraldry or inscriptions.

[473] Macdonald, 'Heraldry', 346–8.

[474] Keith, Bishops, 142.

[475] A Blunt, Art and Architecture in France 1500–1700, 3rd edition (Harmondsworth, 1973), plate 23.

[476] L Stone, Sculpture in Britain: The Middle Ages, (Harmondsworth, 1955), plate 137.

[477] E Panofsky, Tomb Sculpture (London, 1992), plates 263–4.

[478] J S Richardson, The Medieval Stone Carver in Scotland (Edinburgh, 1964), 68.

[479] J Cooper, 'Rubbing of a Medieval Brass from Elgin Cathedral', Transactions of the Scottish Ecclesiological Society 1/3 (1906), 299–300.

[480] Jedburgh is mentioned as being given to Lindisfarne c 830 in Historia Dunelmensis Ecclesiae (Symeonis Monachi Opera Omnia, vol i, ed T Arnold (London, 1882), 52–3); Eadwulf Rus is referred to in the Historia Regum (Symeonis Monachi Opera Omnia, vol ii, ed T Arnold (London, 1885), 198); I B Cowan, The Parishes of Medieval Scotland (Scottish Record Society, 1967), 91, 188.

[481] Duncan, Making of the Kingdom, 298.

[482] Oram, Domination and Lordship, 347–50.

[483] Early Scottish Charters prior to 1153, ed A C Lawrie (Glasgow, 1910), no. XXXIII.

[484] Cowan, Parishes, 11, 61, 69, 89–90.

[485] Cowan, Parishes, 205.

[486] Moray Registrum, nos 81, 251–2.

[487] Cowan, Parishes, 43, 109.

[488] RRS, vol ii, no. 477; Arbroath Liber, nos 205, 206.

[489] Arbroath Liber, no. 208; Cowan, Parishes, 1.

[490] Moray Registrum, no. 70.

[491] RRS, vol ii, no. 272.

[492] RRS, vol ii, no. 465.

[493] Cowan, Parishes, 18, 48, 56, 61, 72, 92, 158–9, 174, 206–7.

[494] Moray Registrum, nos 81, 133.

[495] Liber S Marie de Calchou, ed C Innes (Bannatyne Club, 1846), nos 371, 460; Moray Registrum, nos 41, 227.

[496] Moray Registrum, nos 94, 281; Cowan, Parishes, 158–9.

[497] Moray Registrum, no. 281; Cowan, Parishes, 159.

[498] Moray Registrum, no. 21.

[499] Moray Registrum, no. 22.

[500] Moray Registrum, no. 56.

[501] Cowan, Parishes, 206–7.

[502] RRS, vol ii, 476.

[503] Moray Registrum, no. 46.

[504] Moray Registrum, no. 69.

[505] Cowan, Parishes, 173.

[506] RRS, vol ii, no. 142 and notes.

[507] Cowan, Parishes, 87, 205.

[508] Cowan, Parishes, 59, 69.

[509] Cowan, Parishes, 46, 175, 187.

[510] Moray Registrum, no. 69.

[511] Cowan, Parishes, 4, 21, 40, 51, 61, 89, 115, 153, 171.

[512] Moray Registrum, no. 81.

[513] Moray Registrum, no. 133.

[514] Moray Registrum, no. 41.

[515] Cowan, Parishes, 18, 19–20.

[516] At Laggan the mensal land of the bishop extended to a full davoch and at Barevan no extent of the mensal lands is recorded in the 1239 deed.

[517] Moray Registrum, no. 227.

[518] Cowan, Medieval Church, 95.

[519] CPL, vol xii, 336.

[520] Moray Registrum, Introduction, xxiii; Cowan, Parishes, 43.

[521] Moray Registrum, no. 41; CPL, ii, 284.

[522] Cowan, Parishes, 110; Cowan, Medieval Church, 95.

[523] Moray Registrum, no. 474. The chaplainry had been established in the time of Bishop Brice and was initially sustained on the garbal teinds of 'Auldton', a property near Kintrae on the south of the great area of marshland which separated the castle and parish of Duffus from the high ground immediately north of Elgin (Moray Registrum, no. 211).

[524] Moray Registrum, no. 210.

[525] Moray Registrum, 268–9.

[526] Moray Registrum, 268.

[527] Kelso Liber, nos 371, 460.

[528] Moray Registrum, no. 41.

[529] Registrum de Dunfermelyn, ed C Innes (Bannatyne Club, 1842), nos 33–4, 238.

[530] Cowan, Parishes, 205.

[531] Cowan, Parishes, 16.

[532] Scottish History Society Miscellany, vi, 46.

[533] Cowan, Parishes, 43.

[534] Arbroath Liber, vol i, nos 1, 31, 203–4, 207–8, 237.

535 Cowan, *Parishes*, 89–90.

536 *RRS*, vol ii, no. 477; *Arbroath Liber*, nos 205, 206.

537 Cowan, *Parishes*, 1; *Moray Registrum*, no. 365.

538 *Moray Registrum*, no. 71.

539 Cowan, *Parishes*, 52.

540 *Moray Registrum*, nos 71–2.

541 *Moray Registrum*, no. 75.

542 *Aberdeen Registrum*, vol ii, 253; Cowan, *Parishes*, 52, 109.

543 *The Charters of the Priory of Beauly*, ed E C Batten (Grampian Club, 1877), 33, 38, 236–7; Cowan, *Parishes*, 4.

544 *Moray Registrum*, 365.

545 Cowan, *Parishes*, 4.

546 *Moray Registrum*, nos 21, 51.

547 *Scottish History Society Miscellany*, vol vi, 46, 76.

548 S R Macphail, *History of the Religious House of Pluscardyn* (Edinburgh, 1886), 201, 205, 207–9.

549 Macphail, *Pluscardyn*, 201–3; *Spalding Miscellany*, vol ii, 403.

550 Cowan, *Parishes*, 47.

551 *Moray Registrum*, nos 31, 61, 67, 69; Cowan, *Parishes*, 3.

552 *Moray Registrum*, nos 69, 81; Cowan, *Parishes*, 8, 44.

553 Cowan, *Parishes*, 21.

554 *Moray Registrum*, no. 61; Cowan, *Parishes*, 22.

555 Cowan, *Parishes*, 48, 72.

556 *Moray Registrum*, nos 23, 31, 41, 281; Cowan, *Parishes*, 8–9.

557 *Moray Registrum*, no. 41; Cowan, *Parishes*, 22.

558 Cowan, *Parishes*, 6.

559 Cowan, *Parishes*, 35, 47.

560 Cowan, *Parishes*, 19.

561 *Moray Registrum*, 365.

562 *Registrum Secreti Sigili Regum Scotorum*, ed M Livingstone *et al* (Edinburgh, 1908–), vol i, no. 2416; *RMS*, vol v, no. 2280.

563 *Moray Registrum*, no. 41; Cowan, *Parishes*, 19–20.

564 Cowan, *Parishes*, 53.

565 *Moray Registrum*, no. 30.

566 Cowan, *Parishes*, 62.

567 *Moray Registrum*, no. 30.

568 *Moray Registrum*, nos 111–13; *Liber Cartarum Prioratus Sancti Andree in Scotia*, ed T Thomson (Bannatyne Club, 1841), 326–7.

569 Cowan, *Parishes*, 173.

570 *Moray Registrum*, no. 36.

571 For example, *ER*, vol vi, 29, 219, 317, 374, 464, 479, 517, 652, recording annual payments from 1455 to 1460.

572 *RMS*, vol ii, no. 984.

573 *Moray Registrum*, nos 215, 216, 217.

574 *Moray Registrum*, no. 236.

575 *Moray Registrum*, no. 221.

576 *Moray Registrum*, no. 250.

577 Keith, *Bishops*, 143; Mackintosh and Richardson, *Elgin Cathedral*, 14; Fawcett, *Elgin Cathedral*, 6, 74–5.

578 'in cimiterio ejusdem ecclesie ex parte australi'.

579 For an example of such structures, see Corpus of Scottish Medieval Parish Churches, Forgandenny.

580 *Moray Registrum*, no. 224.

581 See, for example, *ER*, vol vi, 219, 374, 464, 479, 516, 652.

582 *Moray Registrum*, no. 227.

583 *Moray Registrum*, nos 225, 227.

584 *Moray Registrum*, no. 225.

585 *Moray Registrum*, nos 230, 231, 233. Payment to the chaplain of the Holy Rude was made from the receipts of the sheriffdom of Elgin and Forres in 1456 following the annexation of the Murray lands as part of the forfeited estates of the earl of Douglas: see *ER*, vol vi, 220.

586 *Moray Registrum*, no. 232.

587 Cowan, *Parishes*, 1.

588 *Moray Registrum*, no. 228.

589 See, for example, *ER*, vol vi, 220, 375, 464, 479, 517, 652.

590 *Moray Registrum*, no. 239.

591 *Moray Registrum*, no. 243.

592 *RMS*, vol iv, no. 366.

593 *RMS*, vol ii, no. 984.

594 *RMS*, vol ii, no. 2625. The will established that the *pro anima* masses offered by the chaplain were not just for Bishop Stewart, but also for his half-royal brothers the earls of Atholl and Buchan and their families, and for various of his clerical associates. The royal association of the chaplainry expedited the mortification confirmation.

595 *RMS*, vol iii, nos 818, 835.

596 *RPS*, vol iv, no. 1375.

597 *RMS*, vol iv, no. 1109.

598 *ER*, vol vi, 219, 483.

599 *RPS*, vol viii, no. 246.

600 *RPS*, vol viii, nos 659, 1319.

601 *RPS*, vol viii, nos 623, 1180, 2750.

602 *RPS*, vol viii, nos 798, 1103.

603 *RPS*, vol viii, nos 998, 1812.

604 *RPS*, vol viii, no. 1966.

605 *Moray Registrum*, nos 53, 54.

606 *Moray Registrum*, no. 59.

607 Cowan, *Parishes*, 45.

608 *Moray Registrum*, no. 65; Cowan, *Parishes*, 43.

609 *Moray Registrum*, nos 66, 283.

610 *Moray Registrum*, no. 160.

611 Inventories for Aberdeen are reprinted in *Aberdeen Registrum*, vol ii, 127–99. Inventories for Tain are in E McGill (ed), *Old Ross-shire and Scotland as seen in the Tain and Balnagown Documents*, vol i (Inverness, 1909), no. 8.

612 *Moray Registrum*, no. 205.

613 *Moray Registrum*, 271.

614 Edinburgh University Library MS 50.

615 Cowan and Easson, *Religious Houses*, 118, 131.

616 Cowan and Easson, *Religious Houses*, 179.

617 *Moray Registrum*, no. 114.

618 *Moray Registrum*, no. 39.

619 *Moray Registrum*, 381.

620 *Moray Registrum*, no. 115.

621 *Moray Registrum*, no. 116.

622 *Moray Registrum*, no. 117; Watt, *Scottish Graduates*, 317.

623 Watt, *Scottish Graduates*, 578–9.

624 Watt, *Scottish Graduates*, 79–80.

625 *A Genealogical Deduction of the Family of Rose of Kilravock*, ed C Innes (Spalding Club, 1848), 117; D E R Watt, *Fasti Ecclesiae Scoticanae Medii Aevi*, 2nd draft (Scottish Record Society, 1969), 231.

626 *Moray Registrum*, no. 117.

627 *Moray Registrum*, no. 118.

628 *CPL* Benedict XIII, 5.

629 *Calendar of Scottish Supplications to Rome, 1428–1432*, ed A I Dunlop and I B Cowan (Scottish History Society, 1970), 205.

630 Cowan and Easson, *Medieval Religious Houses*, 179.

631 Cowan, *Medieval Church*, 153.

632 *Moray Registrum*, no. 117.

633 *Moray Registrum*, no. 236.

634 *Moray Registrum*, 263.

635 Cowan, *Medieval Church*, 181.

636 *Moray Registrum*, 270.

637 Aspinall, Bogdan and Dransart, 'Kinneddar'.

638 *Moray Registrum*, nos 130, 131.

639 *Moray Registrum*, no. 127.

640 *Moray Registrum*, no. 134.

641 *Moray Registrum*, 151.

642 *Moray Registrum*, no. 289.

643 *RMS*, vol iv, no. 1886.

644 *Moray Registrum*, no. 288.

645 J Lewis and D Pringle, *Spynie Palace and the Bishops of Moray* (Society of Antiquaries of Scotland, 2002).

646 *Moray Registrum*, no. 236.

647 Mackintosh and Richardson, *Elgin Cathedral*, 35.

648 *Moray Registrum*, 268.

649 *Moray Registrum*, 269.

650 *RMS*, vol iv, no. 2681.

651 *Moray Registrum*, no. 132.

652 *Moray Registrum*, no. 284.

653 McGladdery, *James II*, 104.

654 *ER*, vol vi, 483–5.

655 *Moray Registrum*, 265.

656 *Moray Registrum*, 270.

657 *Moray Registrum*, no. 236.

658 *RMS*, vol iv, nos 2510, 2656.

659 *RMS*, vol iv, no. 2681.

660 *RMS*, vol iv, no. 3014.

661 *RPS*, 1592/4/152. Date accessed: 1 February 2012.

662 One aspect of lordship which the bishops of Moray seem to have sought to retain was control over a servile population living on their estates who were legally 'unfree' and treated as part of the property on which they were born and where they worked. They were *nativus* (native-born) and unable to leave their 'native' land without their lord's permission. The last recorded legal action pursued in medieval Scotland by a lord seeking the return of runaways or *fugitivi* was brought before the sheriff-court of Banff in April 1364 by Bishop Alexander Bur in respect of three men – Robert Curry, Nevin Achres and Donald Rogerson – whom the bishop claimed were his runaway *natives*. *Moray Registrum*, no. 143.

663 *Moray Registrum*, no. 193.

664 S Maxwell, 'Discoveries Made in 1934 on King Fergus' Isle and Elsewhere in Loch Laggan, Invernessshire', *Proc Soc Antiq Scot* 85 (1950–51), 160–5.

665 *Moray Registrum*, nos 285, 286, 287, 288.

666 *Moray Registrum*, no. 163.

667 *RRS*, vol ii, no. 362.

668 *RRS*, vol ii, no. 362.

669 *Moray Registrum*, no. 134.

670 *Moray Registrum*, no. 135. Before c 1400 Middle Haugh was held by one John Murray. On his death, Bishop William Spynie gave possession of the land to John's daughter Margaret and her husband, John of Dallas More, for an annual rent of five shillings, military service pertaining to the half-davoch of land, and obligations to the mill of Malathy: *Moray Registrum*, no. 185.

671 *Moray Registrum*, no. 136.

672 *Moray Registrum*, no. 174.

673 *Moray Registrum*, no. 181.

674 *Moray Registrum*, no. 188.

675 *Moray Registrum*, no. 162.

676 *Moray Registrum*, no. 167.

677 *Moray Registrum*, no. 161.

678 *Moray Registrum*, no. 138.

679 *Moray Registrum*, no. 168.

680 *RRS*, vol ii, no. 362.

681 *ER*, vol vi, 222; *RMS*, vol ii, no. 1074.

682 *Moray Registrum*, no. 135.

683 *Moray Registrum*, no. 136.

684 *RRS*, vol ii, no. 362.

685 *Moray Registrum*, no. 181.

686 *Moray Registrum*, no. 163.

687 *Moray Registrum*, no. 193.

688 *ER*, vol vi, 222.

689 *RMS*, vol iv, no. 2679

690   *Moray Registrum*, no. 211 (*salinas australes*).

691   Keith, *Bishops*, 151.

692   *RPS*, 1581/10/87. Date accessed: 1 February 2012.

693   Keith, *Bishops*, 151.

694   Keith, *Bishops*, 152.

695   Keith, *Bishops*, 152.

696   Keith, *Bishops*, 153.

697   Keith, *Bishops*, 154.

698   Keith, *Bishops*, 154.

699   Keith, *Bishops*, 155.

700   Keith, *Bishops*, 155.

701   D McRoberts, 'Material Destruction caused by the Scottish Reformation', *Innes Review* 10.1 (1959), 155.

702   RPC, vol i, 608–10.

703   *Aberdeen Registrum* vol i, lxvi.

704   *Aberdeen Registrum* vol i, 677–8.

705   J C Stone, *The Pont Manuscript Maps of Scotland: Sixteenth Century Origins of a Blaeu Atlas* (Tring, 1989), 202–3.

706   P H Brown, *Early Travellers in Scotland* (Edinburgh, 1891), 124.

707   *The Records of Elgin*, ed W Cramond (New Spalding Club, 1903 and 1908), vol ii, 141.

708   *Elgin Recs*, vol ii, 144.

709   Shaw, *Moray*, vol viii, 285.

710   Shaw, *Moray*, vol iii, 290.

711   *Spalding Memorialls*, vol i, 376–7.

712   *Elgin Recs*, vol i, 337.

713   Oxford University Bodleian Library, Gough maps 38, f24r. It was identified by John Dunbar (see note 417).

714   H B Mackintosh, *Elgin Past and Present* (Elgin, 1914), 67.

715   Shaw, *Moray*, vol iii, 289.

716   In the collections of Historic Scotland.

717   A reproduction of this view is held in the Scottish National Monuments Record.

718   R Young, *Annals of the Parish and Burgh of Elgin* (Elgin, 1879), 162–3.

719   S Johnson, *A Journey to the Western Isles of Scotland* (Edinburgh, 1996), 19.

720   National Galleries of Scotland, Topographic Collection, D67.

721   National Library of Scotland, Adv MS. 30.5.22 39d.

722   Mackintosh, *Elgin*, 68.

723   National Library of Scotland, Adv MS. 30.5.22 39e.

724   *An Account of the Improvements Effected by John Shanks, Keeper of Elgin Cathedral* (Elgin, 1830), 3.

725   H Colvin, *A Biographical Dictionary of British Architects 1600–1840*, 4th edition (New Haven and London, 2008), 440.

726   NRS file MW/1/428/1 (SC 22107/3A pt1), minute of 23 August 1824.

727   *The History of the King's Works*, vi, 1782–1851, ed J M Crook and M H Port, (London, 1973), 251–4; R Fawcett, 'Robert Reid and the Early Involvement of the State in the Care of Scottish Ecclesiastical Buildings and Sites', *Antiquaries Journal* 82 (2002), 269–84.

728   The legal situation was usefully summarised in an opinion on St Andrews Cathedral by James Reid, issued from the Exchequer Chambers in Edinburgh on 25 January 1838 (NRS file MW/1/395 (SC 22032/3L)): '... now that the whole Hereditary Revenues [of the Crown], including the *Bishops* rents, which more especially fall to be burdened with the expense of preserving Old Ecclesiastical Buildings are received by the Commissioners [of Woods, Forests, Land Revenues, Works and Public Buildings] I apprehend the expense ought to be defrayed by them and pass through their accounts'.

729   W Clark, *A Series of Views of the Ruins of Elgin Cathedral* (Elgin, 1826).

730   *Shanks' Improvements*, 2–3.

731   NRS file on Arbroath Abbey, MW/1/464 (SC 22234/2C), minute of 16 August 1834.

732   NRS file MW/1/428/1 (SC 22107/3A pt.1), minute of 16 January 1827.

733   Mackintosh, *Elgin*, 289.

734   Clark, *Views*.

735   *Shanks' Improvements*.

736   R W Billings, *The Baronial and Ecclesiastical Antiquities of Scotland*, vol ii (Edinburgh and London, 1845–52).

737   *Elgin: and a Guide to Elgin Cathedral once Denominated the Lantern of the North ... by the Old Cicerone of Elgin Cathedral* (London, 1866).

738   Mackintosh, *Elgin*, 69.

739   In NRS file MW/1/426 (SC 22107/2B) there are references to lowering ground levels in minutes of 5 April and 14 October 1924 and 2 February 1925.

740   NRS file on Arbroath Abbey, MW/1/464 (SC 22234/2C), minute of 26 July 1834.

741   NRS file MW/1/428/1 (SC 22107/3A pt 1), minutes of 31 March 1847 and 23 December 1848.

742   NRS files MW/1/426 (SC 22107/2A and 2B).

743   Information on these incised dates was provided by John Knight.

744   *Ancient Monuments and Historic Buildings, Report of the Inspector of Ancient Monuments for the Year ending 31st March 1913* (London, 1913), 13–15.

745   NRS file MW/1/427 (SC 22107/2E pt 1), minute of 6 May 1921 referring to finds in Autumn 1913.

746   NRS file MW/1/426 (SC 22107/2B), minute of 5 April 1924.

747   NRS file MW/1/927 (SC 22107/2C), minutes of 25 October and 13 December 1935 and 11 July 1939.

[748]   NRS file MW/1/927 (SC 22107/2C), minute of 9
        December 1936; Richardson, *Medieval Stone Carver,* 67.

[749]   Reconstruction studies of the window of 17 September
        1936, 459/142/135–6, in Historic Scotland collections;
        NRS file MW/1/927 (SC 22107/2C), minute of 10
        June 1938. The design of the window has since been
        authoritatively discussed in Harrison, 'The Western
        Rose Window'.

[750]   NRS file MW/1/927 (SC 22107/2C), minute of 11
        July 1939, and working drawings 459/142/119–20 in
        Historic Scotland collections.

[751]   Unless otherwise stated, these dates are based on
        a combination of the evidence of file records and
        of drawings and photographs in Historic Scotland
        collections.

[752]   Stewart Cruden, 'Monuments in Guardianship',
        Discovery and Excavation in Scotland 1957, 39.

[753]   NRS file DD 27/3719 (AML/GE/8/1/4).

BIBLIOGRAPHY

Unpublished Primary Sources

National Records of Scotland
GD124 Papers of the Erskine Family, Earls of Mar and Kellie
NAS GD124/1/136
GD198 Papers of the Haldane Family of Gleneagles
NAS GD198/11

Published Primary Sources
(The) Anglo-Saxon Chronicle, trans G N Garmonsway, new edition (London, 1972).

Annals of Ulster, ed B MacCarthy (Dublin, 1887).

'(The) Auchinleck Chronicle', in W A Craigie, ed, The Asloan Manuscript vol i (Scottish Text Society, 1923).

(The) Black Book of Taymouth, ed C Innes (Bannatyne Club, 1855).

Calendar of Documents relating to Scotland, ed J Bain et al (Edinburgh, 1881–).

Calendar of Entries in the Papal Registers relating to Great Britain and Ireland: Petitions to the Pope, ed W H Bliss (London, 1896–).

Calendar of Entries in the Papal Registers relating to Great Britain and Ireland. Papal Letters, ed W H Bliss et al (London, 1893–).

Calendar of Papal Letters to Scotland of Benedict XIII of Avignon, 1394–1419, ed F McGurk (Scottish History Society, 1976).

Calendar of Scottish Supplications to Rome, 1418–1422, ed E R Lindsay and A I Cameron (Scottish History Society, 1934).

Calendar of Scottish Supplications to Rome, 1423–1428, ed A I Dunlop (Scottish History Society, 1956).

Calendar of Scottish Supplications to Rome, 1428–1432, ed A I Dunlop and I B Cowan (Scottish History Society, 1970).

(The) Charters of the Priory of Beauly, ed E C Batten (Grampian Club, 1877).

Chronica de Mailros, ed J Stevenson (Bannatyne Club, 1835).

Early Scottish Charters prior to 1153, ed A C Lawrie (Glasgow, 1910).

Exchequer Rolls of Scotland, ed J Stewart et al (Edinburgh, 1878–1908).

Ferguson, P C, Medieval Papal Representatives in Scotland (Stair Society, 1997).

Ferrerii Historia Abbatum de Kynlos, ed W D Wilson (Bannatyne Club, 1839).

Foedera, Conventiones, Litterae et Cuiuscunque Generis Acta Publica, ed T Rymer (London, 1816–69).

(A) Genealogical Deduction of the Family of Rose of Kilravock, ed C Innes (Spalding Club, 1848)

Hectoris Boetii Murthlacensium et Aberdonensium Episcoporum Vitae, ed J Moir (New Spalding Club, 1894).

Historia Dunelmensis Ecclesiae, in Symeonis Monachi Opera Omnia vol i, ed T Arnold (London, 1882).

Historia Regum, in Symeonis Monachi Opera Omnia vol ii, ed T Arnold (London, 1885).

(An) Historical Catalogue of the Bishops of Scotland down to the Year 1668 by the Right Rev Robert Keith, ed M Russel (Edinburgh and London, 1824).

Johannis de Fordun, Chronica Gentis Scotorum, ed W F Skene (Edinburgh, 1872).

Knox's History of the Reformation in Scotland, ed W C Dickinson (Edinburgh, 1949).

(The) Letters of James the Fourth 1505–1513, ed R K Hannay (Scottish History Society, 1953).

(The) Letters of James V, ed R K Hannay and D Hay (Edinburgh, 1954).

Liber Cartarum Prioratus Sancti Andree in Scotia, ed T Thomson (Bannatyne Club, 1841).

Liber Ecclesie de Scon (Bannatyne and Matland Clubs, 1843).

Liber S Marie de Calchou, ed C Innes, (Bannatyne Club, 1846).

Liber S Thome de Aberbrothoc, ed C Innes and P Chalmers (Bannatyne Club, 1848–56).

Memorialls of the Trubles in Scotland and in England. A.D. 1624–A.D. 1645. By John Spalding, vol i, ed John Stuart (Spalding Club, 1850)

Monteith, R, MA, An Theater of Mortality (London, 1704).

Francis Palgrave (ed), Documents and Records Illustrating the History of Scotland (London, 1837).

(The) Original Chronicle of Andrew of Wyntoun, ed F J Amours (Scottish Text Society, 1903–14).

(The) Records of Elgin, ed W Cramond (New Spalding Club, 1903 and 1908)

Records of the Parliaments of Scotland (web resource, www.rps.ac.uk).

Regesta Regum Scottorum, vol i: The Acts of Malcom IV, ed G W S Barrow (Edinburgh, 1960).

Regesta Regum Scottorum, vol ii: The Acts of William I, ed G W S Barrow (Edinburgh, 1971).

(The) Register of the Privy Council of Scotland, ed J H Burton (Edinburgh, 1877).

Registrum Cartarum Ecclesie Sancti Egidii de Edinburgh, ed D Laing (Bannatyne Club, 1859).

Registrum de Dunfermelyn, ed C Innes (Bannatyne Club, 1842).

Registrum Episcopatus Aberdonensis, ed C Innes (Maitland Club, 1845).

Registrum Episcopatus Glasguensis, ed C Innes (Bannatyne and Maitland Clubs, 1843).

Registrum Episcopatus Moraviensis, ed C Innes (Bannatyne Club, 1837).

Registrum Magni Sigilii Regum Scotorum, ed J M Thomson et al (Edinburgh, 1882–1914).

Registrum Secreti Sigili Regum Scotorum, ed M Livingstone et al (Edinburgh, 1908–).

Scotichronicon by Walter Bower, ed D E R Watt et al (Aberdeen or Edinburgh, 1987–98).

(A) Scottish Chronicle known as the Chronicle of Holyrood, ed M O Anderson (Scottish History Society, 1938).

Vetera Monumenta Hibernorum et Scotorum Illustrantia, ed A Theiner (Rome, 1864).

Vitae Dunkeldensis Ecclesiae Episcoporum, a Prima Sedis Fundatione, ad Annum MDXV. Ab Alexandro Myln, Eiusdem Ecclesiae Canonico, Conscriptae, ed T Thomson (Bannatyne Club, 1823).

(The) Warrender Papers, ed A I Cameron (Scottish History Society, 1931–2).

Secondary Works

(An) Account of the Improvements Effected by John Shanks, Keeper of Elgin Cathedral (Elgin, 1830).

Ancient Monuments and Historic Buildings, Report of the Inspector of Ancient Monuments for the Year ending 31st March 1913 (London, 1913).

Apted, M R and Robertson, W, 'Late Fifteenth Century Paintings from Guthrie and Foulis Easter', Proceedings of the Society of Antiquaries of Scotland 95 (1961–2).

Aspinall, A, Bogdan, N Q and Dransart, P Z, 'Kinneddar', *Discovery and Excavation Scotland* (1995).

Barrow, G W S, *Robert Bruce and the Community of the Realm of Scotland*, 3rd edition (Edinburgh, 1988).

Barrow, G W S (ed), *Charters of David I* (Woodbridge, 1999).

Billings, R W, *The Baronial and Ecclesiastical Antiquities of Scotland* (Edinburgh and London, 1845–52).

Bilson, J, 'The Architecture of the Cistercians, with Special Reference to some of their Earlier Churches in England', *Archaeological Journal* 66 (1909).

Binski, P, *Westminster Abbey and the Plantagenets* (New Haven and London, 1995).

Blunt, A, *Art and Architecture in France 1500–1700*, 3rd edition (Harmondsworth, 1973).

Boardman, S, 'The Man who would be King: The Lieutenancy and Death of David, Duke of Rothesay, 1378–1402', in R Mason and N MacDougall (eds), *People and Power in Scotland* (Edinburgh, 1992).

Boardman, S, *The Early Stewart Kings: Robert II and Robert III, 1371–1406* (East Linton, 1996).

Bond, F, *Screens and Galleries in English Churches* (London, 1908).

Bond, F, *The Chancel of English Churches* (London, 1916).

Bony, J, *French Gothic Architecture of the 12th and 13th Centuries* (Berkeley, 1983).

Branner, R, *St Louis and the Court Style* (London, 1965).

Brieger, P, *English Art 1216–1307* (Oxford, 1957).

Brown, M, *James I* (Edinburgh, 1994).

Brown, M, *The Black Douglases* (East Linton, 1998).

Brown, P H, *Early Travellers in Scotland* (Edinburgh, 1891).

Brown, S, 'Our Magnificent Fabrick': York Minster, and Architectural History c 1220–1500 (English Heritage, 2003).

Burnett, C, 'The Act of 1471 and its Effect on the Royal Arms of Scotland', *Proceedings of the Society of Antiquaries of Scotland* 105 (1972–4).

Clark, W, *A Series of Views of the Ruins of Elgin Cathedral* (Elgin, 1826).

Colchester, L S, *Wells Cathedral* (London, 1987).

Colvin, H, *A Biographical Dictionary of British Architects 1600–1840*, 4th edition (New Haven and London, 2008).

Cook, G H, *Medieval Chantries and Chantry Chapels*, revised edition (London, 1963).

Cooper, J, 'Rubbing of a Medieval Brass from Elgin Cathedral', *Transactions of the Scottish Ecclesiological Society* 1.3 (1906).

Cowan, I B, *The Parishes of Medieval Scotland* (Scottish Record Society, 1967).

Cowan, I B, 'The Medieval Church in the Diocese of Aberdeen', *Northern Scotland* 1.1 (1972).

Cowan, I B and Easson, D E, *Medieval Religious Houses, Scotland*, 2nd edition (London and New York, 1976).

Crook, J M and Port, M H (eds), *The History of the King's Works*, vol vi: *1782–1851* (London, 1973).

Crossley, F H, *English Church Monuments* (London, 1921).

Dawson, J E, *Scotland Reformed, 1488–1587* (Edinburgh, 2007).

Dimier, A, *Recueil de Plans d'Eglises Cisterciennes* (Paris, 1949).

Donaldson, G, 'The Scottish Episcopate at the Reformation', *English Historical Review* 60 (1945).

Donaldson, G, *Scotland: James V to James VII* (Edinburgh, 1971).

Dowden, J, *The Medieval Church in Scotland* (Glasgow, 1910).

Dowden, J, *The Bishops of Scotland* (Glasgow, 1912).

Dransart, P, 'Two Shrine Fragments from Kinneddar, Moray', in M Redknap, N Edwards, S Youngs, A Lane and J Knight (eds), *Patterns and Purpose in Insular Art* (Oxford, 2001).

Dransart, P, 'Saints, Stones and Shrines: The Cults of Sts Moluag and Gerardine in Pictland', in J Cartwright (ed), *Celtic Hagiography and Saints' Cults* (Cardiff, 2003).

Dunbar, J, 'Two Drawings for John Slezer's *Theatrum Scotiae*? Elgin and Fortrose Cathedrals', *Review of Scottish Culture* 20 (2008).

Duncan, A A M, *Scotland: The Making of the Kingdom*, revised paperback edition (Edinburgh, 1978).

Elgin: and a Guide to Elgin Cathedral once Denominated the Lantern of the North: Together with some Pious and Religious Reflections within the Old Walls, Evoked by the Resident Spirit of the Ruins by the Old Cicerone of Elgin Cathedral (London, 1866).

Engel, U, 'Two-storeyed Elevations: The Choir of Southwell Minster and the West Country', in J S Alexander (ed), *Southwell and Nottinghamshire, Medieval Art, Architecture and Industry*, British Archaeological Association Conference Transactions 21 (Leeds, 1998).

Eyre-Todd, G (ed), *The Book of Glasgow Cathedral* (Glasgow, 1898).

Fawcett, R, 'Dunblane Cathedral: Evidence for a Change in the Design of the Nave', *Proceedings of the Society of Antiquaries of Scotland* 112 (1982).

Fawcett, R, 'Late Gothic Architecture in Scotland: Considerations on the Influence of the Low Countries', *Proceedings of the Society of Antiquaries of Scotland* 112 (1982).

Fawcett, R, 'Scottish Medieval Window Tracery', in D Breeze (ed), *Studies in Scottish Antiquity* (Edinburgh, 1984).

Fawcett, R, 'The Blackadder Aisle at Glasgow Cathedral: A Reconsideration of the Architectural Evidence for its Date', *Proceedings of the Society of Antiquaries of Scotland* 115 (1985).

Fawcett, R, *Beauly Priory and Fortrose Cathedral* (Edinburgh, 1987).

Fawcett, R, 'The Priory Church', in F McCormick *et al*, 'Excavations at Pluscarden Priory, Moray', *Proceedings of the Society of Antiquaries of Scotland* 124 (1994).

Fawcett, R, 'The Architectural Development of the Abbey Church', in J Lewis and G Ewart (eds), *Jedburgh Abbey the Archaeology and Architecture* (Society of Antiquaries of Scotland, 1995).

Fawcett, R, *Scottish Cathedrals* (London, 1997).

Fawcett, R, 'Introduction', in R Fawcett (ed), *Medieval Art and Architecture in the Diocese of Glasgow*, British Archaeological Association Transactions 23 (Leeds, 1998).

Fawcett, R, 'Paisley Abbey: The Medieval Architecture', in J Malden (ed), *The Monastery and Abbey of Paisley* (Paisley, 2000).

Fawcett, R, *Elgin Cathedral* (Edinburgh, 2001).

Fawcett, R, 'Robert Reid and the Early Involvement of the State in the Care of Scottish Ecclesiastical Buildings and Sites', *Antiquaries Journal* 82 (2002).

Fawcett, R, *Scottish Medieval Churches, Architecture and Furnishings* (Stroud, 2002).

Fawcett, R, 'Arbroath Abbey: A Note on its Architecture and Early Conservation History', in G Barrow (ed), *The Declaration of Arbroath* (Society of Antiquaries of Scotland, 2003).

Fawcett, R, 'Reliving Bygone Glories? The Revival of Earlier Architectural Forms in Scottish Late Medieval Church Architecture', *Journal of the British Archaeological Association* 156 (2003).

Fawcett, R, 'Dunfermline Abbey Church', in R Fawcett, *Royal Dunfermline* (Society of Antiquaries of Scotland, 2005).

Fawcett, R, *The Architecture of the Scottish Medieval Church, 1100–1560* (New Haven and London, 2011).

Fawcett, R and Oram, R, *Melrose Abbey* (Stroud, 2004).

Fawcett, R and Oram, R, *Dryburgh Abbey* (Stroud, 2005).

Ferguson, P C, *Medieval Papal Representatives in Scotland* (Stair Society, 1997).

Frankl, P, *Gothic Architecture*, 2nd edition, revised Paul Crossley (New Haven and London, 2000).

Gordon, J F S and White, A D (eds), *Ecclesiastical Chronicle for Scotland* (London, 1875).

Grant, A, *Independence and Nationhood, Scotland 1306–1469* (London, 1984).

Grant, A, 'The Wolf of Badenoch', in W D H Sellar (ed), *Moray, Province and People* (Edinburgh, 1993).

Grant, L, *Architecture and Society in Normandy 1120–1270* (New Haven and London, 2005).

Harrison, S, 'Elgin Cathedral: The Western Rose Window Reconstructed', *Journal of the British Archaeological Association* 156 (2003).

Harrison, S and Barker, P, 'Byland Abbey, North Yorkshire: The West Front and Rose Window Reconstructed', *Journal of the British Archaeological Association* 140 (1987).

Héliot, P, 'La Suppression du Triforium au Début de la Période Gothique', *Révue Archéologique* 1 (1964).

Hoey, L, 'Pier Design in Early Gothic Architecture in East-Central Scotland, c 1170–1250', in J Higgitt (ed), *Medieval Art and Architecture in the Diocese of St Andrews*, British Archaeological Association Transactions for the Year 1986 (Leeds, 1994).

Jansen, V, 'Dying Mouldings, Unarticulated Springing Blocks, and Hollow Chamfers in Thirteenth-Century Architecture', *Journal of the British Archaeological Association* 135 (1982).

Johnson, S, *A Journey to the Western Isles of Scotland* (Edinburgh, 1996).

Kirkdale Archaeology, *Historic Scotland Properties in Care, Minor Archaeological Works, 1999, Elgin Cathedral* (no date).

Kirk, J, 'Hepburn, Patrick (c. 1487–1573)', *Oxford Dictionary of National Biography* (Oxford, 2004).

Laing, H, *Descriptive Catalogue of Impressions from Ancient Scottish Seals* (Bannatyne and Maitland Clubs, 1850).

Lefèvre-Pontalis, E, 'L'origine des gables', *Bulletin Monumental* 71 (1907).

Lewis, J and Pringle, D, *Spynie Palace and the Bishops of Moray* (Society of Antiquaries of Scotland, 2002).

Lindley, P, *Gothic to Renaissance* (Stamford, 1995).

Lynch, M, *Scotland: A New History* (London, 1991).

Macdonald, W R, 'Notes on the Heraldry of Elgin and its Neighbourhood', *Proceedings of the Society of Antiquaries of Scotland* 34 (1899–1900).

MacDougall, N, *James III: A Political Study* (Edinburgh, 1982).
MacDougall, N, *James IV* (Edinburgh, 1989).

Macfarlane, L J, 'The Primacy of the Scottish Church, 1472–1521', *Innes Review* 20 (1969).

MacGibbon, D and Ross, T, *The Ecclesiastical Architecture of Scotland* (Edinburgh, 1896–7).

Mackintosh, H B, *Elgin Past and Present* (Elgin, 1914).

Mackintosh, H B and Richardson, J S, *Elgin Cathedral: The Cathedral Kirk of Moray*, new edition (Edinburgh, 1980).

Macphail, S R, *History of the Religious House of Pluscardyn* (Edinburgh, 1886).

Mahood, A E, *Banff and District* (Banff, 1919).

Marks, R and Williamson, P (eds), *Gothic: Art for England 1400–1547* (Victoria and Albert Museum exhibition catalogue, 2003).

Maxwell, S, 'Discoveries Made in 1934 on King Fergus' Isle and Elsewhere in Loch Laggan, Invernessshire', *Proceedings of the Society of Antiquaries of Scotland* 85 (1950–51), 160–5.

McAleer, J P, 'A Unique Façade in Great Britain: The West Front of Holyrood Abbey', *Proceedings of the Society of Antiquaries of Scotland* 115 (1985).

McAleer, J P, 'Towards an Architectural History of Kilwinning Abbey', *Proceedings of the Society of Antiquaries of Scotland* 125 (1995).

McBrien, H, *An Interim Report on Excavations at the West Front of Glasgow Cathedral* (Scottish Urban Archaeological Trust, 1989).

McGill, E (ed), *Old Ross-shire and Scotland as Seen in the Tain and Balnagown Documents*, vol i (Inverness, 1909), no. 8.

McGladdery, C A, *James II* (Edinburgh, 1990).

McMillan, A A, *Quarries of Scotland* (Historic Scotland, Technical Conservation, Research and Education Division, Technical Advice Note 12, 1997).

McMillan, A, Gillanders, R J and Fairhurst, J A, *Building Stones of Edinburgh*, 2nd edition (Edinburgh, 1999).

McNeill, J, 'The Chronology of the Choir of Southwell Minster', in J S Alexander (ed), *Southwell and Nottinghamshire, Medieval Art, Architecture and Industry*, British Archaeological Association Conference Transactions 21 (Leeds, 1998).

McRoberts, D, 'The Material Destruction Caused by the Scottish Reformation', *Innes Review* 10.1 (1959).

McRoberts, D, 'Dunblane Cathedral under the Chisholms', *Journal of the Society of Friends of Dunblane Cathedral* 11 (1971).

Milburn, C, 'Pershore Abbey: The Thirteenth-Century Choir', *Journal of the British Archaeological Association* 137 (1984).

Molle, F Van, 'De Onze Lieve Vroukerk te Aarschot', *Bulletin de la Commission de Monuments et Sites* 3 (1952).

Nairn, I and Pevsner, N, *The Buildings of England, Sussex* (Harmondsworth, 1965).

National Art Survey of Scotland, vol iv, J Begg and G P H Watson (eds), *Examples of Scottish Architecture from the 12th to the 17th Century* (Edinburgh, 1933).

Nicholson, R, *Scotland: The Later Middle Ages* (Edinburgh, 1974).

Oram, R, *Moray and Badenoch: A Historical Guide* (Edinburgh, 1996).

Oram, R D, *Domination and Lordship: Scotland 1070–1230* (Edinburgh, 2011).

Oram, R D, 'Alexander Bur, Bishop of Moray (1362–1397)', in B E Crawford (ed), *Church, Chronicle and Learning in Medieval and Early Renaissance Scotland* (Edinburgh, 1999).

Oram, R D, 'The Buildings', in C Lowe (ed), *'Clothing for the Soul Divine': Burials at the Tomb of St Ninian* (Edinburgh, 2009).

Oram, R and Adderley, P, 'Lordship and Environmental Change in Central Highland and Scotland, c 1300–c 1400', *Journal of the North Atlantic* 1 (2008).

Paffendorf, L and Konrad, M, 'Die Abteikirche Saint-Hubert in der Ardennen', in P Clemen (ed), *Belgische Kunstdenkmäler* 1 (Munich, 1923).

Panofsky, E, *Tomb Sculpture* (London, 1992).

Parsons, D, 'Review and Prospect: The Stone Industry in Roman, Anglo-Saxon and Medieval England', in D Parsons (ed), *Stone Quarrying and Building in England AD 43–1525* (Chichester, 1990).

Pevsner, N and Harris, J, *The Buildings of England, Lincolnshire* (Harmondsworth, 1964).

Richardson, J S, *The Medieval Stone Carver in Scotland* (Edinburgh, 1964).

Royal Commission on Historical Monuments (England), *Inventory of the Historical Monuments of London*, vol i: *Westminster Abbey* (London, 1924).

Royal Commission on the Ancient and Historical Monuments of Scotland, *Inventory for Berwickshire* (Edinburgh, 1915).

Royal Commission on the Ancient and Historical Monuments of Scotland, *Inventory for Fife* (Edinburgh, 1933).

Royal Commission on the Ancient and Historical Monuments of Scotland, *Inventory for the City of Edinburgh* (Edinburgh, 1951).

Rubin, M, *Corpus Christi* (Cambridge, 1991).

Salzman, L F, *Building in England down to 1540*, revised edition (Oxford, 1967).

Saul, N, 'The Medieval Monuments of Rochester Cathedral', in T Ayers and T Tatton-Brown (eds), *Medieval Art, Architecture and Archaeology at Rochester*, British Archaeological Association Conference Transactions 28 (Leeds, 2006).

Saul, N, *English Church Monuments in the Middle Ages* (Oxford, 2009).

Sekules, V, 'The Tomb of Christ at Lincoln and the Development of the Sacrament Shrine: Easter Sepulchres Reconsidered', in T A Heslop and V A Sekules (eds), *Medieval Art and Architecture at Lincoln Cathedral*, British Archaeological Association Conference Transactions for the Year 1982 (Leeds, 1986).

Sharpe, E, *Supplement to Architectural Parallels* (London, 1848).

Shaw, L, *The History of the Province of Moray*, 2nd edition, enlarged by J F S Gordon (Glasgow, 1882).

Sheingorn, P, *The Easter Sepulchre in England* (Kalamazoo, 1987).

Simpson, W D, 'The Architectural History of the Cathedral', in C D Bentinck, *Dornoch Cathedral and Parish* (Inverness, 1926).

Stone, J C, *The Pont Manuscript Maps of Scotland, Sixteenth Century Origins of a Blaeu Atlas* (Tring, 1989).

Stone, L, *Sculpture in Britain: The Middle Ages*, (Harmondsworth, 1955).

Stratford, N, 'Notes on the Norman Chapter House at Worcester', *Medieval Art and Architecture at Worcester Cathedral*, British Archaeological Association Conference Transactions for the Year 1975 (Leeds, 1978).

Thurlby, M, 'St Andrews Cathedral-Priory and the Beginnings of Gothic Architecture in Northern Britain', in J Higgitt (ed), *Medieval Art and Architecture in the Diocese of St Andrews*, British Archaeological Association Transactions for the Year 1986 (Leeds, 1994).

Thurlby, M, 'Jedburgh Abbey Church: The Romanesque Fabric', *Proceedings of the Society of Antiquaries of Scotland* 125 (1995).

Thurlby, M, 'Glasgow Cathedral and the Wooden Barrel Vault in Twelfth- and Thirteenth-Century Architecture in Scotland', in R Fawcett (ed), *Medieval Art and Architecture in the Diocese of Glasgow*, British Archaeological Association Transactions 23 (Leeds, 1998).

Watson, J, *British and Foreign Building Stones: A Descriptive Catalogue of the Specimens in the Sedgwick Museum, Cambridge* (Cambridge, 1911).

Watt, D E R, *Fasti Ecclesiae Scoticanae Medii Aevi*, 2nd draft (Scottish Record Society, 1969).

Watt, D E R, *A Biographical Dictionary of Scottish Graduates to AD 1410* (Oxford, 1977).

Watt, D E R, *Medieval Church Councils in Scotland* (Edinburgh, 2000)

Watt, D E R and Shead, N F (eds), *The Heads of Religious Houses in Scotland from the Twelfth to the Sixteenth Centuries* (Scottish Record Society, 2001).

Webb, G, *Architecture in Britain: The Middle Ages* (Harmondsworth, 1956).

Wickham, W A, 'Some Notes on Chapter Houses', *Transactions of the Historical Society of Lancashire and Cheshire* 64 (1912).

Willis, R, *The Architectural History of Chichester Cathedral* (Chichester, 1861).

Woolf, A, *From Pictland to Alba 789–1070* (Edinburgh, 2007).

Young, R, *Annals of the Parish and Burgh of Elgin* (Elgin, 1879).

INDEX